Alice in Wonderland

Alice nel Paese delle Meraviglie

Originally written by Lewis Carroll. Translation by T. Pietrocola-Rosetti.

Edited by MostUsedWords
Dictionary by MostUsedWords

First Printing, November 2018

MostUsedWords.com
10685-B Hazelhurst Dr. # 22933
HOUSTON, TX 77043
United States

www.MostUsedWords.com

Table of Contents

Contents

Preface

Hello. Thank you for your purchase! We at MostUsedWords value each and every customer.

You probably already know the value of reading when it comes to expanding your vocabulary in a language you're learning. If not, we'll give you some short pointers in the next chapter.

We made this book to help you improve your Italian. This is Lewis Carroll's original version of the story, aligned with its official translation by T. Pietrocola-Rosetti.

It's a great book for beginner to intermediate students. But ultimately, everyone can enjoy this wonderful story.

As you can see from the numbers below, this book only contains 2270 different lemmas. A lemma is the dictionary form of a word.

Lexical Information (Italian version)

Number of characters (including spaces) :	149156
Number of characters (without spaces) :	112576
Number of words :	27607
Number of lemmas:	2270
Lexical density :	20.0025
Number of sentences :	1632
Number of syllables :	43848

We hope this book brings you much value and helps you on your journey of learning Italian.

If you have read this book, please let us know your feedback by leaving us a review on Amazon or any other online retailer, our website store.mostusedwords.com or by sending an e-mail to info@mostusedwords.com.

Customer feedback helps us to improve our products. With your help, we can find out about our strengths and discover where we can do better.

Thank you in advance,

Edmond @ MostUsedWords.com

On Bilingual Books

A tried and tested method, bilingual books, also known as parallel text books or dual language books, have been used to assist language learning for hundreds of years.

There are several benefits to be gained by reading bilingual books.

You will naturally broaden your vocabulary.

The best-known benefit of reading is that you broaden your vocabulary quickly. We know that a single exposure to a word does not let you learn that piece of vocabulary. Experts in language learning believe that you need to encounter a word or phrase in different contexts between 15 and 20 times to have a high possibility of remembering the word or phrase.

You will become a better reader

The more language students read, the better readers they become. A big part of this is learning new vocabulary. But several studies have shown that reading also significantly helps to increase other crucial language skills.

You will improve your writing skills

If you spend a lot of time reading Italian texts, your proficiency in written Italian will improve. (Elley and Mangubhai 1981, and Hafiz and Tudor 1989). This is probably because as you encounter more language, more frequently, through extensive reading, your language acquisition mechanism is ready to reproduce what you learned by reading in writing.

You will become better at listening and speaking

Research shows that if you read a lot, you improve your listening and speaking skills. For example, Cho and Krashen (1994) reported that their four adult ESL learners increased competence in both listening and speaking abilities through reading extensively. Extensive reading benefits all language skills, not only reading and writing.

You will be more motivated to read.

The one-to-one sentence correspondence will save you from reaching for the dictionary to look up the meaning of a word. You can read a more complex text without feeling lost in translation.

You can also discover how the grammar rules of your target language compare with your own, thanks to this layout. You'll be able to take advantage of the similarities, and be aware of the differences between English and Italian.

Learn anytime, anywhere, on your own schedule.

Language students can read anywhere and at any time. Reading helps them become more independent learners. You should decide what, when, where and how often you read. By sitting down and reading, you're going to get yourself farther, faster. Invest in yourself now, and get this book.

How To Use This Dictionary

abbreviation	*abr*
adjective	*adj*
adverb	*adv*
article	*art*
auxiliary verb	*av*
conjunction	*con*
interjection	*int*
noun	*gli, i, il, le, la, lo*
numeral	*num*
particle	*part*
phrase	*phr*
prefix	*pfx*
preposition	*prp*
pronoun	*prn*
suffix	*sfx*
verb	*vb*
singular	*sg*
plural	*pl*

Word Order

The most common translations are generally given first. This resets by every new respective part of speech. Different parts of speech are divided by ";".

Translations

We made the decision to give the most common translation(s) of a word, and respectively the most common part(s) of speech. It does, however, not mean that this is the only possible translations or the only part of speech the word can be used for. This is a learners dictionary, meaning that we give you only the most common translation(s) of Italian lemma´s.

Lemmatization

Italian words in this book have been lemmatized. All inflections of a words have been grouped together, and linked back to their lemma, or dictionary form.

International Phonetic Alphabet (IPA)

The pronunciation of foreign vocabulary can be tricky. To help you get it right, we added IPA entries for each entry. If you already have a base understanding of the pronunciation, you will find the IPA pronunciation straightforward. For more information, please visit www.internationalphoneticalphabet.org

1. Down the Rabbit Hole

Alice was beginning to get very tired of sitting by her sister on the bank, and of having nothing to do: once or twice she had peeped into the book her sister was reading, but it had no pictures or conversations in it:
'and what is the use of a book,' thought Alice 'without pictures or conversation?'
So she was considering in her own mind (as well as she could, for the hot day made her feel very sleepy and stupid), whether the pleasure of making a daisy-chain would be worth the trouble of getting up and picking the daisies, when suddenly a White Rabbit with pink eyes ran close by her.
There was nothing so very remarkable in that; nor did Alice think it so very much out of the way to hear the Rabbit say to itself,
Oh dear! Oh dear! I shall be late!'

(when she thought it over afterwards, it occurred to her that she ought to have wondered at this, but at the time it all seemed quite natural);
but when the Rabbit actually took a watch out of its waistcoat-pocket, and looked at it, and then hurried on, Alice started to her feet, for it flashed across her mind that she had never before seen a rabbit with either a waistcoat-pocket, or a watch to take out of it, and burning with curiosity, she ran across the field after it, and fortunately was just in time to see it pop down a large rabbit-hole under the hedge.
In another moment down went Alice after it, never once considering how in the world she was to get out again.
The rabbit-hole went straight on like a tunnel for some way, and then dipped suddenly down, so suddenly that Alice had not a moment to think about stopping herself before she found herself falling down a very deep well.

Either the well was very deep, or she fell very slowly, for she had plenty of time as she went down to look about her and to wonder what was going to happen next.

First, she tried to look down and make out what she was coming to, but it was too dark to see anything; then she looked at the sides of the well, and noticed that they were filled with cupboards and book-shelves; here and there she saw maps and pictures hung upon pegs.
She took down a jar from one of the shelves as she passed; it was labelled 'ORANGE MARMALADE', but to her great disappointment it was empty:
she did not like to drop the jar for fear of killing somebody, so managed to put it into one of the cupboards as she fell past it.
Well!' thought Alice to herself: 'after such a fall as this, I shall think nothing of tumbling down stairs! How brave they'll all think me at home! Why, I wouldn't say anything about it, even if I fell off the top of the house!' (Which was very likely true.)
Down, down, down. Would the fall never come to an end! 'I wonder how many miles I've fallen by this time?' she said

1. I Nella Conigliera

Alice cominciava a sentirsi assai stanca di sedere sul poggetto accanto a sua sorella, senza far niente: aveva una o due volte data un'occhiata al libro che la sorella stava leggendo, ma non v'erano nè dialoghi nè figure,
— e a che serve un libro, pensò Alice, — senza dialoghi nè figure?
E si domandava alla meglio, (perchè la canicola l'aveva mezza assonnata e istupidita), se per il piacere di fare una ghirlanda di margherite mettesse conto di levarsi a raccogliere i fiori, quand'ecco un coniglio bianco dagli occhi rosei passarle accanto, quasi sfiorandola.
Non c'era troppo da meravigliarsene, nè Alice pensò che fosse troppo strano sentir parlare il Coniglio, il quale diceva fra se:
"Oimè! oimè! ho fatto tardi!"

(quando in seguito ella se ne ricordò, s'accorse che avrebbe dovuto meravigliarsene, ma allora le sembrò una cosa naturalissima):
ma quando il Coniglio trasse un orologio dal taschino della sottoveste e lo consultò, e si mise a scappare, Alice saltò in piedi pensando di non aver mai visto un coniglio con la sottoveste e il taschino, nè con un orologio da cavar fuori, e, ardente di curiosità, traversò il campo correndogli appresso e arrivò appena in tempo per vederlo entrare in una spaziosa conigliera sotto la siepe.
Un istante dopo, Alice scivolava giù correndogli appresso, senza pensare a come avrebbe fatto poi per uscirne.
La buca della conigliera filava dritta come una galleria, e poi si sprofondava così improvvisamente che Alice non ebbe un solo istante l'idea di fermarsi: si sentì cader giù rotoloni in una specie di precipizio che rassomigliava a un pozzo profondissimo.
Una delle due: o il pozzo era straordinariamente profondo o ella ruzzolava giù con grande lentezza, perchè ebbe tempo, cadendo, di guardarsi intorno e di pensar meravigliata alle conseguenze.
Aguzzò gli occhi, e cercò di fissare il fondo, per scoprire qualche cosa; ma in fondo era buio pesto e non si scopriva nulla. Guardò le pareti del pozzo e s'accorse che erano rivestite di scaffali di biblioteche; e sparse qua e là di mappe e quadri, sospesi a chiodi.
Mentre continuava a scivolare, afferrò un barattolo con un'etichetta, lesse l'etichetta: "Marmellata d'Arance" ma, oimè! con sua gran delusione, era vuoto;
non volle lasciar cadere il barattolo per non ammazzare chi si fosse trovato in fondo, e quando arrivò più giù, lo depose su un altro scaffale.
"Bene, — pensava Alice, — dopo una caduta come questa, se mai mi avviene di ruzzolare per le scale, mi sembrerà meno che nulla; a casa poi come mi crederanno coraggiosa! Anche a cader dal tetto non mi farebbe nessun effetto!" (E probabilmente diceva la verità).
E giù, e giù, e giù! Non finiva mai quella caduta? — Chi sa quante miglia ho fatte a quest'ora? — esclamò Alice. —

aloud. 'I must be getting somewhere near the centre of the earth. Let me see: that would be four thousand miles down, I think—'
(for, you see, Alice had learnt several things of this sort in her lessons in the schoolroom, and though this was not a very good opportunity for showing off her knowledge, as there was no one to listen to her, still it was good practice to say it over)
'—yes, that's about the right distance—but then I wonder what Latitude or Longitude I've got to?' (Alice had no idea what Latitude was, or Longitude either, but thought they were nice grand words to say.)

Presently she began again. 'I wonder if I shall fall right through the earth! How funny it'll seem to come out among the people that walk with their heads downward! The Antipathies, I think—'
(she was rather glad there was no one listening, this time, as it didn't sound at all the right word)
'—but I shall have to ask them what the name of the country is, you know. Please, Ma'am, is this New Zealand or Australia?'
(and she tried to curtsey as she spoke—fancy curtseying as you're falling through the air! Do you think you could manage it?)
'And what an ignorant little girl she'll think me for asking! No, it'll never do to ask: perhaps I shall see it written up somewhere.'
Down, down, down. There was nothing else to do, so Alice soon began talking again. 'Dinah'll miss me very much to-night, I should think!' (Dinah was the cat.)
'I hope they'll remember her saucer of milk at tea-time. Dinah my dear! I wish you were down here with me! There are no mice in the air, I'm afraid, but you might catch a bat, and that's very like a mouse, you know.
But do cats eat bats, I wonder?' And here Alice began to get rather sleepy, and went on saying to herself, in a dreamy sort of way,
'Do cats eat bats? Do cats eat bats?' and sometimes: 'Do bats eat cats?' for, you see, as she couldn't answer either question, it didn't much matter which way she put it.

She felt that she was dozing off, and had just begun to dream that she was walking hand in hand with Dinah, and saying to her very earnestly,
'Now, Dinah, tell me the truth: did you ever eat a bat?' when suddenly, thump! thump! down she came upon a heap of sticks and dry leaves, and the fall was over.
Alice was not a bit hurt, and she jumped up on to her feet in a moment: she looked up, but it was all dark overhead; before her was another long passage, and the White Rabbit was still in sight, hurrying down it.
There was not a moment to be lost: away went Alice like the wind, and was just in time to hear it say, as it turned a corner: 'Oh my ears and whiskers, how late it's getting!'
She was close behind it when she turned the corner, but the Rabbit was no longer to be seen: she found herself in a long, low hall, which was lit up by a row of lamps hanging from the roof.

Forse sto per toccare il centro della terra. Già saranno più di quattrocento miglia di profondità.

— (Alice aveva apprese molte cose di questa specie a scuola, ma quello non era il momento propizio per sfoggiare la sua erudizione, perchè nessuno l'ascoltava; ma ad ogni modo non era inutile riandarle mentalmente.)

— Sì, sarà questa la vera distanza, o press'a poco,... ma vorrei sapere a qual grado di latitudine o di longitudine sono arrivata. (Alice veramente, non sapeva che fosse la latitudine o la longitudine, ma le piaceva molto pronunziare quelle parole altisonanti!)
Passò qualche minuto e poi ricominciò: — Forse traverso la terra! E se dovessi uscire fra quelli che camminano a capo in giù! Credo che si chiamino gli Antitodi. —

Fu lieta che in quel momento non la sentisse nessuno, perchè quella parola non le sonava bene...
— Domanderei subito come si chiama il loro paese... Per piacere, signore, è questa la Nova Zelanda? o l'Australia? —

e cercò di fare un inchino mentre parlava (figurarsi, fare un inchino, mentre si casca giù a rotta di collo! Dite, potreste voi fare un inchino?).
— Ma se farò una domanda simile mi prenderanno per una sciocca. No, non la farò: forse troverò il nome scritto in qualche parte.
E sempre giù, e sempre giù, e sempre giù! Non avendo nulla da fare, Alice ricominciò a parlare: — Stanotte Dina mi cercherà. (Dina era la gatta).
Spero che penseranno a darle il latte quando sarà l'ora del tè. Cara la mia Dina! Vorrei che tu fossi qui con me! In aria non vi son topi, ma ti potresti beccare un pipistrello: i pipistrelli somigliano ai topi.
Ma i gatti, poi, mangiano i pipistrelli? — E Alice cominciò a sonnecchiare, e fra sonno e veglia continuò a dire fra i denti:

— I gatti, poi, mangiano i pipistrelli? I gatti, poi, mangiano i pipistrelli? — E a volte: — I pipistrelli mangiano i gatti? — perchè non potendo rispondere nè all'una nè all'altra domanda, non le importava di dirla in un modo o nell'altro. Sonnecchiava di già e sognava di andare a braccetto con Dina dicendole con faccia grave:

"Dina, dimmi la verità, hai mangiato mai un pipistrello?" quando, patapunfete! si trovò a un tratto su un mucchio di frasche e la caduta cessò.
Non s'era fatta male e saltò in piedi, svelta. Guardo in alto: era buio: ma davanti vide un lungo corridoio, nel quale camminava il Coniglio bianco frettolosamente.

Non c'era tempo da perdere: Alice, come se avesse le ali, gli corse dietro, e lo sentì esclamare, svoltando al gomito: — Perdinci! veramente ho fatto tardi! —
Stava per raggiungerlo, ma al gomito del corridoio non vide più il coniglio; ed essa si trovò in una sala lunga e bassa, illuminata da una fila di lampade pendenti dalla volta.

There were doors all round the hall, but they were all locked; and when Alice had been all the way down one side and up the other, trying every door, she walked sadly down the middle, wondering how she was ever to get out again.

Suddenly she came upon a little three-legged table, all made of solid glass; there was nothing on it except a tiny golden key, and Alice's first thought was that it might belong to one of the doors of the hall; but, alas! either the locks were too large, or the key was too small, but at any rate it would not open any of them.
However, on the second time round, she came upon a low curtain she had not noticed before, and behind it was a little door about fifteen inches high: she tried the little golden key in the lock, and to her great delight it fitted!

Alice opened the door and found that it led into a small passage, not much larger than a rat-hole: she knelt down and looked along the passage into the loveliest garden you ever saw.
How she longed to get out of that dark hall, and wander about among those beds of bright flowers and those cool fountains, but she could not even get her head though the doorway;
and even if my head would go through,' thought poor Alice: 'it would be of very little use without my shoulders. Oh, how I wish I could shut up like a telescope! I think I could, if I only know how to begin.' For, you see, so many out-of-the-way things had happened lately, that Alice had begun to think that very few things indeed were really impossible.
There seemed to be no use in waiting by the little door, so she went back to the table, half hoping she might find another key on it, or at any rate a book of rules for shutting people up like telescopes: this time she found a little bottle on it, ('which certainly was not here before,' said Alice,) and round the neck of the bottle was a paper label, with the words 'DRINK ME' beautifully printed on it in large letters.
It was all very well to say 'Drink me,' but the wise little Alice was not going to do that in a hurry.
'No, I'll look first,' she said: 'and see whether it's marked "poison" or not'; for she had read several nice little histories about children who had got burnt, and eaten up by wild beasts and other unpleasant things, all because they would not remember the simple rules their friends had taught them: such as, that a red-hot poker will burn you if you hold it too long; and that if you cut your finger very deeply with a knife, it usually bleeds; and she had never forgotten that, if you drink much from a bottle marked 'poison,' it is almost certain to disagree with you, sooner or later.
However, this bottle was not marked 'poison,' so Alice ventured to taste it, and finding it very nice,
(it had, in fact, a sort of mixed flavour of cherry-tart, custard, pine-apple, roast turkey, toffee, and hot buttered toast,) she very soon finished it off.
'What a curious feeling!' said Alice; 'I must be shutting up like a telescope.'
And so it was indeed: she was now only ten inches high, and her face brightened up at the thought that she was now the

Intorno intorno alla sala c'erano delle porte ma tutte chiuse. Alice andò su e giù, picchiando a tutte, cercando di farsene aprire qualcuna, ma invano, e malinconicamente si mise a passeggiare in mezzo alla sala, pensando a come venirne fuori.
A un tratto si trovò accanto a un tavolinetto, tutto di solido cristallo, a tre piedi: sul tavolinetto c'era una chiavetta d'oro. Subito Alice pensò che la chiavetta appartenesse a una di quelle porte; ma oimè! o le toppe erano troppo grandi, o la chiavetta era troppo piccola.

Il fatto sta che non potè aprirne alcuna. Fatto un secondo giro nella sala, capitò innanzi a una cortina bassa non ancora osservata: e dietro v'era un usciolo alto una trentina di centimetri: provò nella toppa la chiavettina d'oro, e con molta gioia vide che entrava a puntino!
Aprì l'uscio e guardò in un piccolo corridoio, largo quanto una tana da topi: s'inginocchiò e scorse di là dal corridoio il più bel giardino del mondo.

Oh! quanto desiderò di uscire da quella sala buia per correre su quei prati di fulgidi fiori, e lungo le fresche acque delle fontane; ma non c'era modo di cacciare neppure il capo nella buca.
"Se almeno potessi cacciarvi la testa! — pensava la povera Alice. — Ma a che servirebbe poi, se non posso farci passare le spalle! Oh, se potessi chiudermi come un telescopio! Come mi piacerebbe! Ma come si fa?" E quasi andava cercando il modo. Le erano accadute tante cose straordinarie, che Alice aveva cominciato a credere che poche fossero le cose impossibili. Ma che serviva star lì piantata innanzi all'uscio? Alice tornò verso il tavolinetto quasi con la speranza di poter trovare un'altra chiave, o almeno un libro che indicasse la maniera di contrarsi come fa un cannocchiale: vi trovò invece un'ampolla, (e certo prima non c'era, — disse Alice), con un cartello sul quale era stampato a lettere di scatola: "Bevi."
— È una parola, bevi! — Alice che era una bambina prudente, non volle bere.
— Voglio vedere se c'è scritto: "Veleno" — disse, perchè aveva letto molti raccontini intorno a fanciulli ch'erano stati arsi, e mangiati vivi da bestie feroci, e cose simili, e tutto perchè non erano stati prudenti, e non s'erano ricordati degl'insegnamenti ricevuti in casa e a scuola;
come per esempio, di non maneggiare le molle infocate perchè scottano; di non maneggiare il coltello perchè taglia e dalla ferita esce il sangue; e non aveva dimenticato quell'altro avvertimento: "Se tu bevi da una bottiglia che porta la scritta "Veleno", prima o poi ti sentirai male."
Ma quell'ampolla non aveva l'iscrizione "Veleno". Quindi Alice si arrischiò a berne un sorso. Era una bevanda deliziosa (aveva un sapore misto di torta di ciliegie, di crema, d'ananasso, di gallinaccio arrosto, di torrone, e di crostini imburrati) e la tracannò d'un fiato.
— Che curiosa impressione! — disse Alice, — mi sembra di contrarmi come un cannocchiale!
Proprio così. Ella non era più che d'una ventina di centimetri d'altezza, e il suo grazioso visino s'irradiò tutto pensando che

right size for going through the little door into that lovely garden.

First, however, she waited for a few minutes to see if she was going to shrink any further: she felt a little nervous about this; 'for it might end, you know,' said Alice to herself: 'in my going out altogether, like a candle. I wonder what I should be like then?'

And she tried to fancy what the flame of a candle is like after the candle is blown out, for she could not remember ever having seen such a thing.

After a while, finding that nothing more happened, she decided on going into the garden at once;

but, alas for poor Alice, when she got to the door, she found she had forgotten the little golden key, and when she went back to the table for it, she found she could not possibly reach it:

she could see it quite plainly through the glass, and she tried her best to climb up one of the legs of the table, but it was too slippery; and when she had tired herself out with trying, the poor little thing sat down and cried.

Come, there's no use in crying like that!' said Alice to herself, rather sharply; 'I advise you to leave off this minute!'

She generally gave herself very good advice, (though she very seldom followed it), and sometimes she scolded herself so severely as to bring tears into her eyes;

and once she remembered trying to box her own ears for having cheated herself in a game of croquet she was playing against herself, for this curious child was very fond of pretending to be two people.

'But it's no use now,' thought poor Alice: 'to pretend to be two people! Why, there's hardly enough of me left to make one respectable person!'

Soon her eye fell on a little glass box that was lying under the table: she opened it, and found in it a very small cake, on which the words 'EAT ME' were beautifully marked in currants.

Well, I'll eat it,' said Alice: 'and if it makes me grow larger, I can reach the key; and if it makes me grow smaller, I can creep under the door; so either way I'll get into the garden, and I don't care which happens!'

She ate a little bit, and said anxiously to herself: 'Which way? Which way?', holding her hand on the top of her head to feel which way it was growing, and she was quite surprised to find that she remained the same size:

to be sure, this generally happens when one eats cake, but Alice had got so much into the way of expecting nothing but out-of-the-way things to happen, that it seemed quite dull and stupid for life to go on in the common way.

So she set to work, and very soon finished off the cake.

finalmente ella era ridotta alla giusta statura per passar per quell'uscio, ed uscire in giardino.

Prima attese qualche minuto per vedere se mai diventasse più piccola ancora. È vero che provò un certo sgomento di quella riduzione: — perchè, chi sa, potrei rimpicciolire tanto da sparire come una candela, — si disse Alice. — E allora a chi somiglierei? —

E cercò di farsi un'idea dell'apparenza della fiamma d'una candela spenta, perchè non poteva nemmeno ricordarsi di non aver mai veduto niente di simile!

Passò qualche momento, e poi vedendo che non le avveniva nient'altro, si preparò ad uscire in giardino.

Ma, povera Alice, quando di fronte alla porticina si accorse di aver dimenticata la chiavetta d'oro, e quando corse al tavolo dove l'aveva lasciata, rilevò che non poteva più giungervi:

vedeva chiaramente la chiave attraverso il cristallo, e si sforzò di arrampicarsi ad una delle gambe del tavolo, e di salirvi, ma era troppo sdrucciolevole. Dopo essersi chi sa quanto affaticata per vincere quella difficoltà, la poverina si sedette in terra e pianse.

— Sì, ma che vale abbandonarsi al pianto! — si disse Alice.

— Ti consiglio invece, cara mia, di finirla con quel piagnucolio!

Di solito ella si dava dei buoni consigli (benchè raramente poi li seguisse), e a volte poi si rimproverava con tanta severità che ne piangeva.

Si rammentò che una volta stava lì lì per schiaffeggiarsi, per aver rubato dei punti in una partita di croquet giocata contro sè stessa; perchè quella strana fanciulla si divertiva a credere di essere in due.

"Ma ora è inutile voler credermi in due — pensò la povera Alice, — mi resta appena tanto da formare un'unica bambina."

Ecco che vide sotto il tavolo una cassettina di cristallo. L'aprì e vi trovò un piccolo pasticcino, sul quale con uva di Corinto era scritto in bei caratteri "Mangia".

— Bene! mangerò, — si disse Alice, — e se mi farà crescere molto, giungerò ad afferrare la chiavetta, e se mi farà rimpicciolire mi insinuerò sotto l'uscio: in un modo o nell'altro arriverò nel giardino, e poi sarà quel che sarà!

Ne mangiò un pezzetto, e, mettendosi la mano in testa, esclamò ansiosa: "Ecco, ecco!" per avvertire il suo cambiamento; ma restò sorpresa nel vedersi della stessa statura.

Certo avviene sempre così a quanti mangiano pasticcini; ma Alice s'era tanto abituata ad assistere a cose straordinarie, che le sembrava stupido che la vita si svolgesse in modo naturale.

E tornò alla carica e in pochi istanti aveva mangiato tutto il pasticcino.

2. The Pool of Tears

Curiouser and curiouser!' cried Alice (she was so much surprised, that for the moment she quite forgot how to speak good English);

'now I'm opening out like the largest telescope that ever was! Good-bye, feet!' (for when she looked down at her feet, they seemed to be almost out of sight, they were getting so far off).

'Oh, my poor little feet, I wonder who will put on your shoes and stockings for you now, dears? I'm sure I shan't be able! I shall be a great deal too far off to trouble myself about you: you must manage the best way you can;

—but I must be kind to them,' thought Alice: 'or perhaps they won't walk the way I want to go! Let me see: I'll give them a new pair of boots every Christmas.'

And she went on planning to herself how she would manage it. 'They must go by the carrier,' she thought; 'and how funny it'll seem, sending presents to one's own feet! And how odd the directions will look!

ALICE'S RIGHT FOOT, ESQ.

HEARTHRUG,

NEAR THE FENDER,

(WITH ALICE'S LOVE).

Oh dear, what nonsense I'm talking!'

Just then her head struck against the roof of the hall: in fact she was now more than nine feet high, and she at once took up the little golden key and hurried off to the garden door. Poor Alice! It was as much as she could do, lying down on one side, to look through into the garden with one eye; but to get through was more hopeless than ever: she sat down and began to cry again.

You ought to be ashamed of yourself,' said Alice: 'a great girl like you,' (she might well say this): 'to go on crying in this way! Stop this moment, I tell you!'

But she went on all the same, shedding gallons of tears, until there was a large pool all round her, about four inches deep and reaching half down the hall.

After a time she heard a little pattering of feet in the distance, and she hastily dried her eyes to see what was coming.

It was the White Rabbit returning, splendidly dressed, with a pair of white kid gloves in one hand and a large fan in the other: he came trotting along in a great hurry, muttering to himself as he came,

'Oh! the Duchess, the Duchess! Oh! won't she be savage if I've kept her waiting!' Alice felt so desperate that she was ready to ask help of any one; so, when the Rabbit came near her, she began, in a low, timid voice,

'If you please, sir—' The Rabbit started violently, dropped the white kid gloves and the fan, and skurried away into the darkness as hard as he could go.

2. Lo Stagno di Lacrime

— Stranissimo, e sempre più stranissimo! esclamò Alice (era tanta la sua meraviglia che non sapeva più parlare correttamente)

— mi allungo come un cannocchiale, come il più grande cannocchiale del mondo! Addio piedi! (perchè appena si guardò i piedi le sembrò di perderli di vista, tanto s'allontanavano.)

— Oh i miei poveri piedi! chi mai v'infilerà più le calze e vi metterà le scarpe? Io non potrò più farlo! Sarò tanto lontana che non potrò più pensare a voi: bisogna che vi adattiate.

Eppure bisognerebbe che io li trattassi bene, — pensò Alice, — se no, non vorranno andare dove voglio andare io! Vediamo un po'... ogni anno a Natale regalerò loro un bel paio di stivaletti!

E andava nel cervello mulinando come dovesse fare. "Li manderò per mezzo del procaccia, — ella pensava, — ma sarà curioso mandar a regalar le scarpe ai propri piedi! E che strano indirizzo!

Al signor Piedestro d'Alice

Tappeto

Accanto al parafuoco

(con i saluti di Alice)

"Poveretta me! quante sciocchezze dico!"

In quel momento la testa le urtò contro la volta della sala: aveva più di due metri e settanta di altezza! Subito afferrò la chiavettina d'oro e via verso la porta del giardino. Povera Alice! Non potè far altro che sedersi in terra, poggiandosi di fianco per guardare il giardino con la coda dell'occhio; ma entrarvi era più difficile che mai: si sedè di nuovo dunque e si rimise a piangere.

— Ti dovresti vergognare, — si disse Alice, — figurarsi, una ragazzona come te (e davvero lo poteva dire allora) mettersi a piangere. Smetti, ti dico! —

Pure continuò a versar lacrime a fiotti, tanto che riuscì a formare uno stagno intorno a sè di più d'un decimetro di altezza, e largo più di metà della sala.

Qualche minuto dopo sentì in lontananza come uno scalpiccio; e si asciugò in fretta gli occhi, per vedere chi fosse.

Era il Coniglio bianco di ritorno, splendidamente vestito, con un paio di guanti bianchi in una mano, e un gran ventaglio nell'altra: trotterellava frettolosamente e mormorava:

"Oh! la Duchessa, la Duchessa! Monterà certamente in bestia. L'ho fatta tanto attendere!" Alice era così disperata, che avrebbe chiesto aiuto a chiunque le fosse capitato: così quando il Coniglio le passò accanto, gli disse con voce tremula e sommessa:

— "Di grazia, signore..." Il Coniglio sussultò, lasciò cadere a terra i guanti e il ventaglio, e in mezzo a quel buio si mise a correre di sghembo precipitosamente.

Alice took up the fan and gloves, and, as the hall was very hot, she kept fanning herself all the time she went on talking:

'Dear, dear! How queer everything is to-day! And yesterday things went on just as usual. I wonder if I've been changed in the night? Let me think: was I the same when I got up this morning? I almost think I can remember feeling a little different. But if I'm not the same, the next question is, Who in the world am I? Ah, that's the great puzzle!' And she began thinking over all the children she knew that were of the same age as herself, to see if she could have been changed for any of them.
I'm sure I'm not Ada,' she said: 'for her hair goes in such long ringlets, and mine doesn't go in ringlets at all; and I'm sure I can't be Mabel, for I know all sorts of things, and she, oh! she knows such a very little!
Besides, she's she, and I'm I, and—oh dear, how puzzling it all is! I'll try if I know all the things I used to know. Let me see: four times five is twelve, and four times six is thirteen, and four times seven is—oh dear! I shall never get to twenty at that rate!
However, the Multiplication Table doesn't signify: let's try Geography. London is the capital of Paris, and Paris is the capital of Rome, and Rome—no, that's all wrong, I'm certain! I must have been changed for Mabel!
I'll try and say "How doth the little—"' and she crossed her hands on her lap as if she were saying lessons, and began to repeat it, but her voice sounded hoarse and strange, and the words did not come the same as they used to do:—
'How doth the little crocodile

Improve his shining tail,

And pour the waters of the Nile

On every golden scale!

'How cheerfully he seems to grin,

How neatly spread his claws,

And welcome little fishes in

With gently smiling jaws!'

I'm sure those are not the right words,' said poor Alice, and her eyes filled with tears again as she went on,
'I must be Mabel after all, and I shall have to go and live in that poky little house, and have next to no toys to play with, and oh! ever so many lessons to learn!
No, I've made up my mind about it; if I'm Mabel, I'll stay down here! It'll be no use their putting their heads down and saying "Come up again, dear!"
I shall only look up and say "Who am I then? Tell me that first, and then, if I like being that person, I'll come up: if not, I'll stay down here till I'm somebody else"
—but, oh dear!' cried Alice, with a sudden burst of tears: 'I do wish they would put their heads down! I am so very tired of being all alone here!'
As she said this she looked down at her hands, and was surprised to see that she had put on one of the Rabbit's little white kid gloves while she was talking.
How can I have done that?' she thought. 'I must be growing small again.' She got up and went to the table to measure herself by it, and found that, as nearly as she could guess, she

Alice raccolse il ventaglio e i guanti, e perchè la sala sembrava una serra si rinfrescò facendosi vento e parlando fra sè:
— Povera me! Come ogni cosa è strana oggi! Pure ieri le cose andavano secondo il loro solito. Non mi meraviglierei se stanotte fossi stata cambiata! Vediamo: non son stata io, io in persona a levarmi questa mattina? Mi pare di ricordarmi che mi son trovata un po' diversa. Ma se non sono la stessa dovrò domandarmi: Chi sono dunque? Questo è il problema.
— E ripensò a tutte le bambine che conosceva, della sua stessa età, per veder se non fosse per caso una di loro.

— Certo non sono Ada, — disse, — perchè i suoi capelli sono ricci e i miei no. Non sono Isabella, perchè io so tante belle cose e quella poverina è tanto ignorante!

e poi Isabella è Isabella e io sono io. Povera me! in che imbroglio sono! Proviamo se mi ricordo tutte le cose che sapevo una volta: quattro volte cinque fanno dodici, e quattro volte sei fanno tredici, e quattro volte sette fanno... Oimè! Se vado di questo passo non giungerò mai a venti! Del resto la tavola pitagorica non significa niente: proviamo la geografia: Londra è la capitale di Parigi, e Parigi è la capitale di Roma, e Roma... no, sbaglio tutto! Davvero che debbo essere Isabella!
Proverò a recitare "La vispa Teresa"; incrociò le mani sul petto, come se stesse per ripetere una lezione, e cominciò a recitare quella poesiola, ma la sua voce sonava strana e roca, e le parole non le uscivano dalle labbra come una volta:
La vispa Teresa avea su una fetta

di pane sorpresa

gentile cornetta;

e tutta giuliva

a chiunque l'udiva

gridava a distesa:

— L'ho intesa, l'ho intesa! —

— Mi pare che le vere parole della poesia non siano queste, — disse la povera Alice, e le tornarono i lacrimoni.
— Insomma, — continuò a dire, — forse sono Isabella, dovrò andare ad abitare in quella stamberga, e non aver più balocchi, e tante lezioni da imparare!
Ma se sono Isabella, caschi il mondo, resterò qui!
Inutilmente, cari miei, caccerete il capo dal soffitto per dirmi: "Carina, vieni su!"
Leverò soltanto gli occhi e dirò: "Chi sono io? Ditemi prima chi sono. Se sarò quella che voi cercate, verrò su; se no, resterò qui inchiodata finchè non sarò qualche altra."
"Ma oimè! — esclamò Alice con un torrente di lacrime: — Vorrei che qualcuno s'affacciasse lassù! Son tanto stanca di esser qui sola!"
E si guardò le mani, e si stupì vedendo che s'era infilato uno dei guanti lasciati cadere dal Coniglio.

— Come mai, — disse, — sono ridiventata piccina? Si levò, s'avvicinò al tavolo per misurarvisi; e osservò che s'era ridotta a circa sessanta centimetri di altezza e che andava

was now about two feet high, and was going on shrinking rapidly:

she soon found out that the cause of this was the fan she was holding, and she dropped it hastily, just in time to avoid shrinking away altogether.

That was a narrow escape!' said Alice, a good deal frightened at the sudden change, but very glad to find herself still in existence;

'and now for the garden!' and she ran with all speed back to the little door: but, alas! the little door was shut again, and the little golden key was lying on the glass table as before, and things are worse than ever,' thought the poor child: 'for I never was so small as this before, never! And I declare it's too bad, that it is!'

As she said these words her foot slipped, and in another moment, splash! she was up to her chin in salt water. Her first idea was that she had somehow fallen into the sea: 'and in that case I can go back by railway,' she said to herself. (Alice had been to the seaside once in her life, and had come to the general conclusion, that wherever you go to on the English coast you find a number of bathing machines in the sea, some children digging in the sand with wooden spades, then a row of lodging houses, and behind them a railway station.)

However, she soon made out that she was in the pool of tears which she had wept when she was nine feet high.

I wish I hadn't cried so much!' said Alice, as she swam about, trying to find her way out.

'I shall be punished for it now, I suppose, by being drowned in my own tears! That will be a queer thing, to be sure! However, everything is queer to-day.'

Just then she heard something splashing about in the pool a little way off, and she swam nearer to make out what it was: at first she thought it must be a walrus or hippopotamus, but then she remembered how small she was now, and she soon made out that it was only a mouse that had slipped in like herself.

Would it be of any use, now,' thought Alice: 'to speak to this mouse? Everything is so out-of-the-way down here, that I should think very likely it can talk: at any rate, there's no harm in trying.'

So she began: 'O Mouse, do you know the way out of this pool? I am very tired of swimming about here, O Mouse!'

(Alice thought this must be the right way of speaking to a mouse: she had never done such a thing before, but she remembered having seen in her brother's Latin Grammar: 'A mouse—of a mouse—to a mouse—a mouse—O mouse!') The Mouse looked at her rather inquisitively, and seemed to her to wink with one of its little eyes, but it said nothing.

Perhaps it doesn't understand English,' thought Alice; 'I daresay it's a French mouse, come over with William the Conqueror.'

(For, with all her knowledge of history, Alice had no very clear notion how long ago anything had happened.)

rapidamente rimpicciolendosi: indovinò che la cagione di quella nuova trasformazione era il ventaglio che aveva in mano.

Lo buttò subito a terra. Era tempo; se no, si sarebbe assottigliata tanto che sarebbe interamente scomparsa.

— L'ho scampata bella! — disse Alice tutta sgomenta di quell'improvviso cambiamento, ma lieta di esistere ancora.

— E ora andiamo in giardino! — Si diresse subito verso l'usciolino; ma ahi! l'usciolino era chiuso, e la chiavettina d'oro era sul tavolo come prima. "Si va male, — pensò la bambina disperata, — non sono stata mai così piccina! E dichiaro che tutto questo non mi piace, non mi piace, non mi piace!" Mentre diceva così, sdrucciolò e punfete! affondò fino al mento nell'acqua salsa. Sulle prime credè di essere caduta in mare e: "In tal caso, potrò tornare a casa in ferrovia" — disse fra sè. (Alice era stata ai bagni e d'allora immaginava che dovunque s'andasse verso la spiaggia si trovassero capanni sulla sabbia, ragazzi che scavassero l'arena, e una fila di villini, e di dietro una stazione di strada ferrata).

Ma subito si avvide che era caduta nello stagno delle lacrime versate da lei quando aveva due e settanta di altezza.

Peccato ch'io abbia pianto tanto! — disse Alice, nuotando e cercando di giungere a riva.

— Ora sì che sarò punita, naufragando nelle mie stesse lacrime! Sarà proprio una cosa straordinaria! Ma tutto è straordinario oggi!

E sentendo qualche cosa sguazzare nello stagno, si volse e

le parve vedere un vitello marino o un ippopotamo, ma si ricordò d'essere in quel momento assai piccina, e s'accorse che l'ippopotamo non era altro che un topo, cascato come lei nello stagno.

Pensava Alice: "Sarebbe bene, forse, parlare a questo topo. Ogni cosa è strana quaggiù che non mi stupirei se mi rispondesse. A ogni modo, proviamo."

— E cominciò: — O topo, sai la via per uscire da questo stagno? O topo, io mi sento veramente stanca di nuotare qui. —

Alice pensava che quello fosse il modo migliore di parlare a un topo: non aveva parlato a un topo prima, ma ricordava di aver letto nella grammatica latina di suo fratello: "Un topo — di un topo — a un topo — un topo. —" Il topo la guardò, la squadrò ben bene co' suoi occhiettini ma non rispose. — Forse non capisce la mia lingua, — disse Alice;

— forse è un francese, ed è venuto qui con l'esercito napoleonico:

— Con tutte le sue nozioni storiche, Alice non sapeva esattamente quel che si dicesse.

So she began again: 'Ou est ma chatte?' which was the first sentence in her French lesson-book. The Mouse gave a sudden leap out of the water, and seemed to quiver all over with fright.

Oh, I beg your pardon!' cried Alice hastily, afraid that she had hurt the poor animal's feelings. 'I quite forgot you didn't like cats.'

'Not like cats!' cried the Mouse, in a shrill, passionate voice. 'Would you like cats if you were me?'

Well, perhaps not,' said Alice in a soothing tone: 'don't be angry about it. And yet I wish I could show you our cat Dinah: I think you'd take a fancy to cats if you could only see her. She is such a dear quiet thing,'

Alice went on, half to herself, as she swam lazily about in the pool: 'and she sits purring so nicely by the fire, licking her paws and washing her face—and she is such a nice soft thing to nurse—and she's such a capital one for catching mice— oh, I beg your pardon!'

cried Alice again, for this time the Mouse was bristling all over, and she felt certain it must be really offended. 'We won't talk about her any more if you'd rather not.'

We indeed!' cried the Mouse, who was trembling down to the end of his tail. 'As if I would talk on such a subject!

Our family always hated cats: nasty, low, vulgar things! Don't let me hear the name again!'

I won't indeed!' said Alice, in a great hurry to change the subject of conversation. 'Are you—are you fond—of—of dogs?'

The Mouse did not answer, so Alice went on eagerly: 'There is such a nice little dog near our house I should like to show you!

A little bright-eyed terrier, you know, with oh, such long curly brown hair! And it'll fetch things when you throw them, and it'll sit up and beg for its dinner, and all sorts of things—I can't remember half of them—and it belongs to a farmer, you know, and he says it's so useful, it's worth a hundred pounds!

He says it kills all the rats and—oh dear!' cried Alice in a sorrowful tone: 'I'm afraid I've offended it again!' For the Mouse was swimming away from her as hard as it could go, and making quite a commotion in the pool as it went.

So she called softly after it: 'Mouse dear! Do come back again, and we won't talk about cats or dogs either, if you don't like them!'

When the Mouse heard this, it turned round and swam slowly back to her: its face was quite pale (with passion, Alice thought), and it said in a low trembling voice,

'Let us get to the shore, and then I'll tell you my history, and you'll understand why it is I hate cats and dogs.'

It was high time to go, for the pool was getting quite crowded with the birds and animals that had fallen into it: there were a Duck and a Dodo, a Lory and an Eaglet, and several other curious creatures. Alice led the way, and the whole party swam to the shore.

E riprese: "Où est ma chatte?" che era la prima frase del suo libriccino di francese. Il topo fece un salto nell'acqua e tremò come una canna al vento.

— Scusami, — soggiunse Alice, avvedendosi di aver scossi i nervi delicati della bestiola. — Non ho pensato che a te non piacciono i gatti.

— Come mi possono piacere i gatti? — domandò il topo con voce stridula e sdegnata — Piacerebbero a te i gatti, se fossi in me?

— Forse no, — rispose Alice carezzevolmente, — ma non ti adirare, sai! E pure, se ti facessi veder Dina, la mia gatta, te ne innamoreresti. È una bestia così tranquilla e bella. —

E nuotando di mala voglia e parlando a volte a sè stessa, Alice continuava: — E fa così bene le fusa quando si accovaccia accanto al fuoco, leccandosi le zampe e lavandosi il muso, ed è così soffice e soave quando l'accarezzo, ed è così svelta ad acchiappare i topi... Oh! scusa! — esclamò di nuovo Alice, perchè il topo aveva il pelo tutto arruffato e pareva straordinariamente offeso. — No, non ne parleremo più, se ti dispiace.

— Già, non ne parleremo, — gridò il Topo, che aveva la tremarella fino alla punta dei baffi. — Come se stessi io a parlar di gatti!

La nostra famiglia ha odiato sempre i gatti; bestie sozze, volgari e basse! non me li nominare più.

— No, no! — rispose volonterosa Alice, e cambiando discorso, aggiunse: — Di', ti piacciono forse... ti piacciono... i cani? —

Il topo non rispose, e Alice continuò: — vicino a casa mia abita un bellissimo cagnolino, se lo vedessi!

Ha certi begli occhi luccicanti, il pelo cenere, riccio e lungo! Raccoglie gli oggetti che gli si gettano e siede sulle gambe di dietro per chiedere lo zucchero, e fa tante altre belle cosettine... non ne ricordo neppure la metà... appartiene a un fattore, il quale dice che la sua bestiolina vale un tesoro, perchè gli è molto utile,

e uccide tutti i topi... oimè! — esclamò Alice tutta sconsolata: — Temo di averti offeso di nuovo! — E veramente l'aveva offeso, perchè il Topo si allontanò, nuotando in furia e agitando le acque dello stagno.

Alice lo richiamò con tono soave: — Topo caro, vieni qua; ti prometto di non parlar più di gatti e di cani! —

Il Topo si voltò nuotando lentamente: aveva il muso pallido (d'ira, pensava Alice) e disse con voce tremante:

— Approdiamo, e ti racconterò la mia storia. Comprenderai perchè io detesti tanto i gatti e i cani.

Era tempo d'uscire, perchè lo stagno si popolava di uccelli e d'altri animali cadutivisi dentro:

un'anitra, un Dronte, un Lori, un Aquilotto, ed altre bestie curiose. Alice si mise alla loro testa e tutti la seguirono alla riva.

3. A Caucas Race and a Long Tail

They were indeed a queer-looking party that assembled on the bank—the birds with draggled feathers, the animals with their fur clinging close to them, and all dripping wet, cross, and uncomfortable.

The first question of course was, how to get dry again: they had a consultation about this, and after a few minutes it seemed quite natural to Alice to find herself talking familiarly with them, as if she had known them all her life.

Indeed, she had quite a long argument with the Lory, who at last turned sulky, and would only say: 'I am older than you, and must know better';

and this Alice would not allow without knowing how old it was, and, as the Lory positively refused to tell its age, there was no more to be said.

At last the Mouse, who seemed to be a person of authority among them, called out: 'Sit down, all of you, and listen to me! I'll soon make you dry enough!'

They all sat down at once, in a large ring, with the Mouse in the middle. Alice kept her eyes anxiously fixed on it, for she felt sure she would catch a bad cold if she did not get dry very soon.

Ahem!' said the Mouse with an important air: 'are you all ready? This is the driest thing I know. Silence all round, if you please!

William the Conqueror, whose cause was favoured by the pope, was soon submitted to by the English, who wanted leaders, and had been of late much accustomed to usurpation and conquest. Edwin and Morcar, the earls of Mercia and Northumbria—'

'Ugh!' said the Lory, with a shiver.

'I beg your pardon!' said the Mouse, frowning, but very politely: 'Did you speak?'

'Not I!' said the Lory hastily.

I thought you did,' said the Mouse. '—I proceed. "Edwin and Morcar, the earls of Mercia and Northumbria, declared for him: and even Stigand, the patriotic archbishop of Canterbury, found it advisable—""Found what?' said the Duck.

'Found it,' the Mouse replied rather crossly: 'of course you know what "it" means.'

'I know what "it" means well enough, when I find a thing,' said the Duck: 'it's generally a frog or a worm. The question is, what did the archbishop find?'

The Mouse did not notice this question, but hurriedly went on,

"—found it advisable to go with Edgar Atheling to meet William and offer him the crown. William's conduct at first was moderate. But the insolence of his Normans—

How are you getting on now, my dear?' it continued, turning to Alice as it spoke.

3. Corsa Scompigliata Racconto con la Coda

L'assemblea che si raccolse sulla riva era molto bizzarra. Figurarsi, gli uccelli avevano le penne inzuppate, e gli altri animali, col pelo incollato ai corpi, grondavano tutti acqua tristi e melanconici.

La prima questione, messa sul tappeto, fu naturalmente il mezzo per asciugarsi: si consultarono tutti, e Alice dopo poco si mise a parlar familiarmente con loro, come se li conoscesse da un secolo uno per uno.

Discusse lungamente col Lori, ma tosto costui le mostrò un viso accigliato, dicendo perentoriamente: — Son più vecchio di te, perciò ne so più di te; —

ma Alice non volle convenirne se prima non le avesse detto quanti anni aveva. Il Lori non volle dirglielo, e la loro conversazione fu troncata.

Il Topo, che sembrava persona d'una certa autorità fra loro, gridò: — Si seggano, signori, e mi ascoltino! In pochi momenti seccherò tutti! —

Tutti sedettero in giro al Topo. Alice si mise a guardare con una certa ansia, convinta che se non si fosse rasciugata presto, si sarebbe beccato un catarro coi fiocchi.

— Ehm! — disse il Topo, con accento autorevole, — siete tutti all'ordine? Questa domanda è bastantemente secca, mi pare! Silenzio tutti, per piacere!

Guglielmo il Conquistatore, la cui causa era favorita dal papa, fu subito sottomesso dagli inglesi...

— Uuff! — fece il Lori con un brivido.

— Scusa! — disse il Topo con cipiglio, ma con molta cortesia: — Dicevi qualche cosa?

— Niente affatto! — rispose in fretta il Lori.

— M'era parso di sì — soggiunse il Topo. — Continuo: Edwin e Morcar, i conti di Mercia e Northumbria, si dichiararono per lui; e anche, Stigand, il patriottico arcivescovo di Canterbury, trovò che...

— Che cosa? — disse l'anitra.

Trovo che — replicò vivamente il Topo — tu sai che significa "che?"

Significa una cosa, quando trovo qualche cosa? — rispose l'Anitra; — un ranocchio o un verme. Si tratta di sapere che cosa trovò l'arcivescovo di Canterbury.

Il Topo non le badò e continuò:

— Trovò che era opportuno andare con Edgar Antheling incontro a Guglielmo per offrirgli la corona. In principio Guglielmo usò moderazione; ma l'insolenza dei Normanni... Ebbene, cara, come stai ora? — disse rivolto ad Alice.

'As wet as ever,' said Alice in a melancholy tone: 'it doesn't seem to dry me at all.'

In that case,' said the Dodo solemnly, rising to its feet: 'I move that the meeting adjourn, for the immediate adoption of more energetic remedies—'

Speak English!' said the Eaglet. 'I don't know the meaning of half those long words, and, what's more, I don't believe you do either!'

And the Eaglet bent down its head to hide a smile: some of the other birds tittered audibly.

What I was going to say,' said the Dodo in an offended tone: 'was, that the best thing to get us dry would be a Caucus-race.'

'What is a Caucus-race?' said Alice; not that she wanted much to know, but the Dodo had paused as if it thought that somebody ought to speak, and no one else seemed inclined to say anything.

Why,' said the Dodo: 'the best way to explain it is to do it.' (And, as you might like to try the thing yourself, some winter day, I will tell you how the Dodo managed it.)

First it marked out a race-course, in a sort of circle, ('the exact shape doesn't matter,' it said,) and then all the party were placed along the course, here and there.

There was no 'One, two, three, and away,' but they began running when they liked, and left off when they liked, so that it was not easy to know when the race was over. However, when they had been running half an hour or so, and were quite dry again, the Dodo suddenly called out 'The race is over!' and they all crowded round it, panting, and asking: 'But who has won?'

This question the Dodo could not answer without a great deal of thought, and it sat for a long time with one finger pressed upon its forehead (the position in which you usually see Shakespeare, in the pictures of him), while the rest waited in silence.

At last the Dodo said: 'everybody has won, and all must have prizes.'

But who is to give the prizes?' quite a chorus of voices asked.

'Why, she, of course,' said the Dodo, pointing to Alice with one finger; and the whole party at once crowded round her, calling out in a confused way: 'Prizes! Prizes!'

Alice had no idea what to do, and in despair she put her hand in her pocket, and pulled out a box of comfits, (luckily the salt water had not got into it), and handed them round as prizes.

There was exactly one a-piece all round. 'But she must have a prize herself, you know,' said the Mouse.

'Of course,' the Dodo replied very gravely. 'What else have you got in your pocket?' he went on, turning to Alice.

'Only a thimble,' said Alice sadly.

'Hand it over here,' said the Dodo.

Then they all crowded round her once more, while the Dodo solemnly presented the thimble, saying:

'We beg your acceptance of this elegant thimble'; and, when it had finished this short speech, they all cheered.

Alice thought the whole thing very absurd, but they all looked so grave that she did not dare to laugh; and, as she

— Bagnata come un pulcino, — rispose Alice afflitta, — mi sembra che il tuo racconto secchi, ma non asciughi affatto.

— In questo caso, — disse il Dronte in tono solenne, levandosi in piedi, — propongo che l'assemblea si aggiorni per l'adozione di rimedi più energici...

Ma parla italiano! — esclamò l'Aquilotto. — Non capisco neppur la metà di quei tuoi paroloni, e forse tu stesso non ne capisci un'acca. —

L'Aquilotto chinò la testa per nascondere un sorriso, ma alcuni degli uccelli si misero a sghignazzare sinceramente.

— Volevo dire, — continuò il Dronte, offeso, — che il miglior modo di asciugarsi sarebbe di fare una corsa scompigliata.

— Che è la corsa scompigliata? — domandò Alice. Non le premeva molto di saperlo, ma il Dronte taceva come se qualcheduno dovesse parlare, mentre nessuno sembrava disposto ad aprire bocca o becco.

— Ecco, — disse il Dronte, — il miglior modo di spiegarla è farla. — (E siccome vi potrebbe venire in mente di provare questa corsa in qualche giorno d'inverno, vi dirò come la diresse il Dronte.)

Prima tracciò la linea dello steccato, una specie di circolo, (— che la forma sia esatta o no, non importa, — disse) e poi tutta la brigata entrò nello steccato disponendosi in questo o in quel punto.

Non si udì: — Uno, due tre... via! 'ma tutti cominciarono a correre a piacere; e si fermarono quando vollero, di modo che non si seppe quando la corsa fosse terminata. A ogni modo, dopo che ebbero corso una mezz'ora o quasi, e si sentirono tutti bene asciugati, il Dronte esclamò: — La corsa è finita! — e tutti lo circondarono anelanti domandando: — Ma chi ha vinto?

Per il Dronte non era facile rispondere, perciò sedette e restò a lungo con un dito appoggiato alla fronte (tale e quale si rappresenta Shakespeare nei ritratti), mentre gli altri tacevano.

Finalmente il Dronte disse: — Tutti hanno vinto e tutti debbono essere premiati.

—. Ma chi distribuirà i premi? — replicò un coro di voci. — Lei, s'intende! — disse il Dronte, indicando con un dito Alice. E tutti le si affollarono intorno; gridando confusamente: — I premi! i premi!

Alice non sapeva che fare, e nella disperazione si cacciò le mani in tasca, e ne cavò una scatola di confetti (per buona sorte non v'era entrata l'acqua,) e li distribuì in giro.

Ce n'era appunto uno per ciascuno. — Ma dovrebbe esser premiata anche lei, — disse il Topo.

Naturalmente, — soggiunse gravemente il Dronte; — Che altro hai in tasca? — chiese ad Alice.

— Un ditale, rispose mestamente la fanciulla.

Dài qui, — replicò il Dronte.

E tutti l'accerchiarono di nuovo, mentre il Dronte con molta gravità le offriva il ditale, dicendo:

— La preghiamo di accettare quest'elegante ditale; — e tutti applaudirono a quel breve discorso.

(text left out in original translation)

could not think of anything to say, she simply bowed, and took the thimble, looking as solemn as she could.

The next thing was to eat the comfits: this caused some noise and confusion, as the large birds complained that they could not taste theirs, and the small ones choked and had to be patted on the back.

However, it was over at last, and they sat down again in a ring, and begged the Mouse to tell them something more. 'You promised to tell me your history, you know,' said Alice: 'and why it is you hate—C and D,' she added in a whisper, half afraid that it would be offended again.

'Mine is a long and a sad tale!' said the Mouse, turning to Alice, and sighing.

'It is a long tail, certainly,' said Alice, looking down with wonder at the Mouse's tail; 'but why do you call it sad?' And she kept on puzzling about it while the Mouse was speaking, so that her idea of the tale was something like this:

— 'Fury said to a mouse, that he met in the house, "Let us both go to law: I will prosecute you. —Come, I'll take no denial; We must have a trial: For really this morning I've nothing to do." Said the mouse to the cur, "Such a trial, dear Sir, With no jury or judge, would be wasting our breath." "I'll be judge, I'll be jury," said cunning old Fury: "I'll try the whole cause, and condemn you to death."'

'You are not attending!' said the Mouse to Alice severely. 'What are you thinking of?'

'I beg your pardon,' said Alice very humbly: 'you had got to the fifth bend, I think?'

'I had not!' cried the Mouse, sharply and very angrily.

'A knot!' said Alice, always ready to make herself useful, and looking anxiously about her. 'Oh, do let me help to undo it!'

'I shall do nothing of the sort,' said the Mouse, getting up and walking away. 'You insult me by talking such nonsense!' 'I didn't mean it!' pleaded poor Alice. 'But you're so easily offended, you know!' The Mouse only growled in reply. 'Please come back and finish your story!' Alice called after it; and the others all joined in chorus: 'Yes, please do!' but the Mouse only shook its head impatiently, and walked a little quicker.

'What a pity it wouldn't stay!' sighed the Lory, as soon as it was quite out of sight; and an old Crab took the opportunity of saying to her daughter 'Ah, my dear! Let this be a lesson to you never to lose your temper!' 'Hold your tongue, Ma!' said the young Crab, a little snappishly. 'You're enough to try the patience of an oyster!' 'I wish I had our Dinah here, I know I do!' said Alice aloud, addressing nobody in particular. 'She'd soon fetch it back!'

'And who is Dinah, if I might venture to ask the question?' said the Lory.

Alice replied eagerly, for she was always ready to talk about her pet:

'Dinah's our cat. And she's such a capital one for catching mice you can't think! And oh, I wish you could see her after the birds! Why, she'll eat a little bird as soon as look at it!'

Bisognava ora mangiare i confetti; cosa che cagionò un po' di rumore e di confusione, perchè gli uccelli grandi si lagnavano che non avevano potuto assaporarli, e i piccoli, avendoli inghiottiti d'un colpo, corsero il rischio di strozzarsi e si dovè picchiarli sulla schiena.

Ma anche questo finì, e sedettero in circolo pregando il Topo di dire qualche altra cosa.

— Ricordati che mi hai promesso di narrarmi la tua storia, — disse Alice, — e la ragione per cui tu odii i G. e i C., — soggiunse sommessamente, temendo di offenderlo di nuovo.

— La mia storia è lunga e triste e con la coda! — rispose il Topo, sospirando.

— Certo è una coda lunga, — disse Alice, guardando con meraviglia la coda del topo, — ma perchè la chiami trista? — E continuò a pensarci impacciata, mentre il Topo parlava. Così l'idea che ella si fece di quella storia con la coda fu press'a poco questa:

Furietta disse al Topo che avea sorpreso in casa: Andiamo in tribunale; per farti processare; Non voglio le tue scuse, o Topo scellerato. Quest'oggi non ho niente nel mio villin da fare. — Disse a Furietta il Topo: Ma come andare in Corte? Senza giurati e giudici Sarebbe una vendetta! Sarò giurato e giudice, rispose; Furietta, E passerò soffiando la tua sentenza a morte.

Tu non stai attenta! — disse il Topo ad Alice severamente. — A che cosa pensi?

— Scusami, — rispose umilmente Alice: — sei giunto alla quinta vertebra della coda, non è vero?

— No, do...po, — riprese il Topo irato, scandendo le sillabe.

— C'è un nodo? — esclamò Alice sempre pronta e servizievole, e guardandosi intorno. — Ti aiuterò a scioglierlo!

— Niente affatto! — rispose il Topo, levandosi e facendo l'atto di andarsene. Tu m'insulti dicendo tali sciocchezze!

— Ma, no! — disse Alice con umiltà. — Tu t'offendi con facilità! Per tutta risposta il Topo si mise a borbottare.

— Per piacere, ritorna e finisci il tuo racconto! — gridò Alice; e tutti gli altri s'unirono in coro: — Via finisci il racconto! — Ma il Topo crollò il capo con un moto d'impazienza, e affrettò il passo.

— Peccato che non sia rimasto! — disse sospirando il Lori; appena il Topo si fu dileguato. Un vecchio granchio colse quell'occasione per dire alla sua piccina: — Amor mio, ti serva di lezione, e bada di non adirarti mai!

— Papà, — disse la piccina sdegnosa, — tu stancheresti anche la pazienza d'un'ostrica!

— Ah, se Dina fosse qui! — disse Alice parlando ad alta voce, ma senza rivolgersi particolarmente a nessuno. — Lo riporterebbe indietro subito!

— Scusa la domanda, chi è Dina? — domandò il Lori.

Alice rispose sollecitamente sempre pronta a parlare del suo animale prediletto:

— La mia gatta. Fa prodigi, quando caccia i topi! E se la vedessi correr dietro gli uccelli! Un uccellino lo fa sparire in un boccone.

This speech caused a remarkable sensation among the party. Some of the birds hurried off at once:

one old Magpie began wrapping itself up very carefully, remarking: 'I really must be getting home; the night-air doesn't suit my throat!' and a Canary called out in a trembling voice to its children:
Come away, my dears! It's high time you were all in bed!' On various pretexts they all moved off, and Alice was soon left alone.
I wish I hadn't mentioned Dinah!' she said to herself in a melancholy tone.
'Nobody seems to like her, down here, and I'm sure she's the best cat in the world! Oh, my dear Dinah! I wonder if I shall ever see you any more!'
And here poor Alice began to cry again, for she felt very lonely and low-spirited.
In a little while, however, she again heard a little pattering of footsteps in the distance, and she looked up eagerly, half hoping that the Mouse had changed his mind, and was coming back to finish his story.

Questo discorso produsse una grande impressione nell'assemblea. Alcuni uccelli spiccarono immediatamente il volo:
una vecchia gazza si avviluppò ben bene dicendo: — è tempo di tornare a casa; l'aria notturna mi fa male alla gola!

— Un canarino chiamò con voce tremula tutti i suoi piccini.
— Via, via cari miei! È tempo di andare a letto! — Ciascuno trovò un pretesto per andarsene, e Alice rimase sola.
"Non dovevo nominare Dina! — disse malinconicamente tra sè.
— Pare che quaggiù nessuno le voglia bene; ed è la migliore gatta del mondo! Oh, cara Dina, chi sa se ti rivedrò mai più!"

E la povera Alice ricominciò a piangere, perchè si sentiva soletta e sconsolata.
Ma alcuni momenti dopo avvertì di nuovo uno scalpiccio in lontananza, e guardò fissamente nella speranza che il Topo, dopo averci ripensato, tornasse per finire il suo racconto.

4. The Rabbit Sends in a Little Bill

It was the White Rabbit, trotting slowly back again, and looking anxiously about as it went, as if it had lost something; and she heard it muttering to itself 'The Duchess! The Duchess! Oh my dear paws! Oh my fur and whiskers! She'll get me executed, as sure as ferrets are ferrets! Where can I have dropped them, I wonder?'

Alice guessed in a moment that it was looking for the fan and the pair of white kid gloves, and she very good-naturedly began hunting about for them, but they were nowhere to be seen.
Everything seemed to have changed since her swim in the pool, and the great hall, with the glass table and the little door, had vanished completely.
Very soon the Rabbit noticed Alice, as she went hunting about, and called out to her in an angry tone:
'Why, Mary Ann, what are you doing out here? Run home this moment, and fetch me a pair of gloves and a fan! Quick, now!'
And Alice was so much frightened that she ran off at once in the direction it pointed to, without trying to explain the mistake it had made.
He took me for his housemaid,' she said to herself as she ran. 'How surprised he'll be when he finds out who I am! But I'd better take him his fan and gloves—that is, if I can find them.'
As she said this, she came upon a neat little house, on the door of which was a bright brass plate with the name 'W. RABBIT' engraved upon it.
She went in without knocking, and hurried upstairs, in great fear lest she should meet the real Mary Ann, and be turned out of the house before she had found the fan and gloves.
How queer it seems,' Alice said to herself: 'to be going messages for a rabbit! I suppose Dinah'll be sending me on messages next!'
And she began fancying the sort of thing that would happen: '"Miss Alice! Come here directly, and get ready for your walk!"
Coming in a minute, nurse! But I've got to see that the mouse doesn't get out. Only I don't think,' Alice went on: 'that they'd let Dinah stop in the house if it began ordering people about like that!'

By this time she had found her way into a tidy little room with a table in the window, and on it (as she had hoped) a fan and two or three pairs of tiny white kid gloves:

she took up the fan and a pair of the gloves, and was just going to leave the room, when her eye fell upon a little bottle that stood near the looking-glass.
There was no label this time with the words 'DRINK ME,' but nevertheless she uncorked it and put it to her lips. 'I

4. La Casettina del Coniglio

Era il Coniglio bianco che tornava trotterellando bel bello e guardandosi ansiosamente intorno, come avesse smarrito qualche cosa, e mormorando tra sè:
"Oh la duchessa! la duchessa! Oh zampe care! pelle e baffi miei, siete accomodati per le feste ora! Ella mi farà ghigliottinare, quant'è vero che le donnole sono donnole! Ma dove li ho perduti?"
Alice indovinò subito ch'egli andava in traccia del ventaglio e del paio di guanti bianchi, e, buona e servizievole com'era, si diede un gran da fare per ritrovarli. Ma invano.

Tutto sembrava trasformato dal momento che era caduta nello stagno; e la gran sala col tavolino di cristallo, e la porticina erano interamente svanite.
Non appena il Coniglio si accorse di Alice affannata alla ricerca, gridò in tono d'ira:
— Marianna, che fai qui? Corri subito a casa e portami un paio di guanti e un ventaglio! Presto, presto! —

Alice fu così impaurita da quella voce, che, senz'altro, corse velocemente verso il luogo indicato, senza dir nulla sull'equivoco del Coniglio.
"Mi ha presa per la sua cameriera, — disse fra sè, mentre continuava a correre. — E si sorprenderà molto quando saprà chi sono! Ma è meglio portargli il ventaglio e i guanti, se pure potrò trovarli".
E così dicendo, giunse innanzi a una bella casettina che aveva sull'uscio una lastra di ottone lucente, con questo nome: G. Coniglio.
Entrò senza picchiare, e in fretta fece tutta la scala, temendo d'incontrare la vera Marianna, ed essere da lei espulsa di lì prima di trovare il ventaglio e i guanti.
"Strano, — pensava Alice, — essere mandata da un Coniglio a far dei servizi! Non mi meraviglierò, se una volta o l'altra, Dina mi manderà a sbrigare delle commissioni per lei!"
E cominciò a fantasticare intorno alle probabili scene:
"Signorina Alice! Venga qui subito, e si prepari per la passeggiata!"
"Eccomi qui, zia! Ma dovrei far la guardia a questo buco fino al ritorno di Dina, perchè non ne scappi il topo..." "Ma non posso credere, — continuò Alice, — che si permetterebbe a Dina di rimanere in casa nostra, se cominciasse a comandare la gente a questo modo."
In quell'atto era entrata in una graziosa cameretta, con un tavolo nel vano della finestra. Sul tavolo c'era, come Alice aveva sperato, un ventaglio e due o tre paia di guanti bianchi e freschi;
prese il ventaglio e un paio di guanti, e si preparò ad uscire, quando accanto allo specchio scorse una boccettina.

Questa volta non v'era alcuna etichetta con la parola "Bevi". Pur nondimeno la stappò e se la portò alle labbra. "Qualche

know something interesting is sure to happen,' she said to herself:

'whenever I eat or drink anything; so I'll just see what this bottle does. I do hope it'll make me grow large again, for really I'm quite tired of being such a tiny little thing!'

It did so indeed, and much sooner than she had expected: before she had drunk half the bottle, she found her head pressing against the ceiling, and had to stoop to save her neck from being broken.

She hastily put down the bottle, saying to herself "That's quite enough—I hope I shan't grow any more—As it is, I can't get out at the door—I do wish I hadn't drunk quite so much!'

Alas! it was too late to wish that! She went on growing, and growing, and very soon had to kneel down on the floor: in another minute there was not even room for this, and she tried the effect of lying down with one elbow against the door, and the other arm curled round her head.

Still she went on growing, and, as a last resource, she put one arm out of the window, and one foot up the chimney, and said to herself 'Now I can do no more, whatever happens. What will become of me?'

Luckily for Alice, the little magic bottle had now had its full effect, and she grew no larger:

still it was very uncomfortable, and, as there seemed to be no sort of chance of her ever getting out of the room again, no wonder she felt unhappy.

It was much pleasanter at home,' thought poor Alice: 'when one wasn't always growing larger and smaller, and being ordered about by mice and rabbits.

I almost wish I hadn't gone down that rabbit-hole—and yet—and yet—it's rather curious, you know, this sort of life! I do wonder what can have happened to me!

When I used to read fairy-tales, I fancied that kind of thing never happened, and now here I am in the middle of one! There ought to be a book written about me, that there ought!

And when I grow up, I'll write one—but I'm grown up now,' she added in a sorrowful tone; 'at least there's no room to grow up any more here."But then,' thought Alice: 'shall I never get any older than I am now?

That'll be a comfort, one way—never to be an old woman— but then—always to have lessons to learn! Oh, I shouldn't like that!"Oh, you foolish Alice!' she answered herself.

'How can you learn lessons in here? Why, there's hardly room for you, and no room at all for any lesson-books!'

And so she went on, taking first one side and then the other, and making quite a conversation of it altogether; but after a few minutes she heard a voice outside, and stopped to listen.

Mary Ann! Mary Ann!' said the voice. 'Fetch me my gloves this moment!' Then came a little pattering of feet on the stairs.

Alice knew it was the Rabbit coming to look for her, and she trembled till she shook the house, quite forgetting that she was now about a thousand times as large as the Rabbit, and had no reason to be afraid of it.

Presently the Rabbit came up to the door, and tried to open it; but, as the door opened inwards, and Alice's elbow was pressed hard against it, that attempt proved a failure.

cosa di straordinario mi accade tutte le volte che bevo o mangio, — disse fra sè;

vediamo dunque che mi farà questa bottiglia. Spero che mi farà crescere di nuovo, perchè son proprio stanca di essere così piccina!"

E così avvenne, prima di quando s'aspettasse: non aveva ancor bevuto metà della boccettina che urtò con la testa contro la volta, di modo che dovette abbassarsi subito, per non rischiare di rompersi l'osso del collo.

Subito depose la fiala dicendo: — Basta per ora, spero di non crescere di più; ma intanto come farò ad uscire! Se avessi bevuto un po' meno!

Oimè! troppo tardi! Continuò a crescere, a crescere, e presto dovette inginocchiarsi, perchè non poteva più star in piedi; e dopo un altro minuto non c'era più spazio neanche per stare inginocchiata. Dovette sdraiarsi con un gomito contro l'uscio, e con un braccio intorno al capo.

E cresceva ancora. Con un estremo sforzo, cacciò una mano fuori della finestra, ficcò un piede nel caminetto, e si disse: Qualunque cosa accada non posso far di più. Che sarà di me?

Fortunatamente, la virtù della boccettina magica aveva prodotto il suo massimo effetto, ed Alice non crebbe più: ma avvertiva un certo malessere, e, giacchè non era probabile uscire da quella gabbia, non c'è da stupire se si giudicò infelicissima:

"Stavo così bene a casa! — pensò la povera Alice, — senza diventar grande o piccola e sentirmi comandare dai sorci e dai conigli.

Ah; se non fossi discesa nella conigliera!... e pure... e pure... questo genere di vita è curioso! Ma che cosa mi è avvenuto?

Quando leggevo i racconti delle fate, credevo che queste cose non accadessero mai, ed ora eccomi un perfetto racconto di fate. Si dovrebbe scrivere un libro sulle mie avventure, si dovrebbe!

Quando sarò grande lo scriverò io... Ma sono già grande, — soggiunse afflitta, — e qui non c'è spazio per crescere di più. Ma come, — pensò Alice, — non sarò mai maggiore di quanto sono adesso?

Da una parte, sarebbe un bene non diventare mai vecchia; ma da un'altra parte dovrei imparare sempre le lezioni, e mi seccherebbe! Ah sciocca che sei! — rispose Alice a sè stessa. — Come potrei imparare le lezioni qui? C'è appena posto per me! I libri non c'entrano!"

E continuò così, interrogandosi e rispondendosi, sostenendo una conversazione tra Alice e Alice; ma dopo pochi minuti sentì una voce di fuori, e si fermò per ascoltare.

— Marianna! Marianna! — diceva la voce, — portami subito i guanti! — Poi s'udì uno scalpiccio per la scala.

Alice pensò che il Coniglio venisse per sollecitarla e tremò da scuotere la casa, dimenticando d'esser diventata mille volte più grande del Coniglio, e che non aveva alcuna ragione di spaventarsi.

Il Coniglio giunse alla porta, e cercò di aprirla. Ma la porta si apriva al di dentro e il gomito d'Alice era puntellato di dietro; così che ogni sforzo fu vano.

Alice heard it say to itself 'Then I'll go round and get in at the window.'

That you won't' thought Alice, and, after waiting till she fancied she heard the Rabbit just under the window, she suddenly spread out her hand, and made a snatch in the air. She did not get hold of anything, but she heard a little shriek and a fall, and a crash of broken glass, from which she concluded that it was just possible it had fallen into a cucumber-frame, or something of the sort.

Next came an angry voice—the Rabbit's—'Pat! Pat! Where are you?' And then a voice she had never heard before: 'Sure then I'm here! Digging for apples, yer honour!'

'Digging for apples, indeed!' said the Rabbit angrily. 'Here! Come and help me out of this!' (Sounds of more broken glass.)

'Now tell me, Pat, what's that in the window?'

'Sure, it's an arm, yer honour!' (He pronounced it 'arrum.')

'An arm, you goose! Who ever saw one that size? Why, it fills the whole window!'

'Sure, it does, yer honour: but it's an arm for all that.'

'Well, it's got no business there, at any rate: go and take it away!'

There was a long silence after this, and Alice could only hear whispers now and then; such as:

Sure, I don't like it, yer honour, at all, at all!' 'Do as I tell you, you coward!' and at last she spread out her hand again, and made another snatch in the air. This time there were two little shrieks, and more sounds of broken glass.

'What a number of cucumber-frames there must be!' thought Alice. 'I wonder what they'll do next! As for pulling me out of the window, I only wish they could! I'm sure I don't want to stay in here any longer!'

She waited for some time without hearing anything more: at last came a rumbling of little cartwheels, and the sound of a good many voices all talking together: she made out the words: 'Where's the other ladder?

—Why, I hadn't to bring but one; Bill's got the other—Bill! fetch it here, lad!—Here, put 'em up at this corner—No, tie 'em together first—they don't reach half high enough yet— Oh! they'll do well enough; don't be particular…

—Here, Bill! catch hold of this rope—Will the roof bear?— Mind that loose slate—Oh, it's coming down! Heads below!' (a loud crash)—'Now, who did that?

—It was Bill, I fancy—Who's to go down the chimney?— Nay, I shan't! you do it!—That I won't, then!—Bill's to go down—Here, Bill! the master says you're to go down the chimney!'

'Oh! So Bill's got to come down the chimney, has he?' said Alice to herself. 'Shy, they seem to put everything upon Bill! I wouldn't be in Bill's place for a good deal: this fireplace is narrow, to be sure; but I think I can kick a little!'

She drew her foot as far down the chimney as she could, and waited till she heard a little animal (she couldn't guess of what sort it was) scratching and scrambling about in the chimney close above her: then, saying to herself 'This is Bill,' she gave one sharp kick, and waited to see what would happen next.

Alice udì che il Coniglio diceva tra sè: — Andrò dalla parte di dietro, ed entrerò dalla finestra.

"Non ci entrerai!" pensò Alice, e aspettò sinchè le parve che il Coniglio fosse arrivato sotto la finestra. Allora aprì d'un tratto la mano e fece un gesto in aria.

Non afferrò nulla; ma sentì delle piccole strida e il rumore d'una caduta, poi un fracasso di vetri rotti e comprese che il poverino probabilmente era cascato su qualche campana di cocomeri o qualche cosa di simile.

Poi s'udì una voce adirata, quella del Coniglio: — Pietro! Pietro! — Dove sei? — E una voce ch'essa non aveva mai sentita: — Sono qui! Stavo scavando le patate, eccellenza! Scavando le patate! — fece il Coniglio, pieno d'ira. — Vieni qua! Aiutami ad uscire di qui...! — Si sentì un secondo fracasso di vetri infranti

— Dimmi, Pietro, che c'è lassù alla finestra?

— Perbacco! è un braccio, eccellenza!

— Un braccio! Zitto, bestia! Esistono braccia così grosse? Riempie tutta la finestra!

— Certo, eccellenza: eppure è un braccio!

— Bene, ma che c'entra con la mia finestra? Va a levarlo!

Vi fu un lungo silenzio, poi Alice sentì qua e là un bisbiglio, e un dialogo come questo:

Davvero non me la sento, eccellenza, per nulla affatto! — Fa come ti dico, vigliacco! — E allora Alice di nuovo aprì la mano e fece un gesto in aria. Questa volta si udirono due strilli acuti, e un nuovo fracasso di vetri.

"Quante campane di vetro ci sono laggiù! — pensò Alice. Chi sa che faranno dopo! Magari potessero cacciarmi fuori dalla finestra. Certo non intendo di rimanere qui!"

Attese un poco senza udire più nulla; finalmente s'udì un cigolìo di ruote di carri e molte voci che parlavano insieme. Essa potè afferrare queste parole: — Dov'è l'altra scala?...

Ma io non dovevo portarne che una... Guglielmo ha l'altra. Guglielmo! portala qui. Su, appoggiala a quest'angolo... No, no, lègale insieme prima. Non vedi che non arrivano neppure a metà!... Oh! vi arriveranno! Non fare il difficile!...

Qua, Guglielmo, afferra questa fune... Ma reggerà il tetto? Bada a quella tegola che si muove.... Ehi! casca! attenti alla testa! "Punfete" Chi è stato?

Guglielmo, immagino!... Chi andrà giù per il camino?... Io no!... Vuoi andare tu?... No, neppure io!... Scenderà Guglielmo!... Ohi! Guglielmo! il padrone dice che devi scendere giù nel camino!

"Magnifico!" — disse Alice fra sè. — Così questo Guglielmo scenderà dal camino? Pare che quei signori aspettino tutto da Guglielmo! Non vorrei essere nei suoi panni. Il camino è molto stretto, ma qualche calcio, credo, glielo potrò assestare."

E ritirò il piede più che potè lungi dal camino, ed attese sinchè sentì un animaletto (senza che potesse indovinare a che specie appartenesse) che raschiava e scendeva adagino adagino per la canna del camino. — È Guglielmo! — ella disse, e tirò un gran calcio, aspettando il seguito.

The first thing she heard was a general chorus of 'There goes Bill!' then the Rabbit's voice along—'Catch him, you by the hedge!' then silence, and then another confusion of voices—

'Hold up his head—Brandy now—Don't choke him—How was it, old fellow? What happened to you? Tell us all about it!'

Last came a little feeble, squeaking voice, ('That's Bill,' thought Alice,) 'Well, I hardly know—No more, thank ye; I'm better now—but I'm a deal too flustered to tell you—all I know is, something comes at me like a Jack-in-the-box, and up I goes like a sky-rocket!'

'So you did, old fellow!' said the others.

We must burn the house down!' said the Rabbit's voice; and Alice called out as loud as she could: 'If you do. I'll set Dinah at you!'

There was a dead silence instantly, and Alice thought to herself: 'I wonder what they will do next! If they had any sense, they'd take the roof off.' After a minute or two, they began moving about again, and Alice heard the Rabbit say: 'A barrowful will do, to begin with.'

A barrowful of what?' thought Alice; but she had not long to doubt, for the next moment a shower of little pebbles came rattling in at the window, and some of them hit her in the face.

'I'll put a stop to this,' she said to herself, and shouted out: 'You'd better not do that again!' which produced another dead silence.

Alice noticed with some surprise that the pebbles were all turning into little cakes as they lay on the floor, and a bright idea came into her head.

'If I eat one of these cakes,' she thought: 'it's sure to make some change in my size; and as it can't possibly make me larger, it must make me smaller, I suppose.'

So she swallowed one of the cakes, and was delighted to find that she began shrinking directly.

As soon as she was small enough to get through the door, she ran out of the house, and found quite a crowd of little animals and birds waiting outside.

The poor little Lizard, Bill, was in the middle, being held up by two guinea-pigs, who were giving it something out of a bottle.

They all made a rush at Alice the moment she appeared; but she ran off as hard as she could, and soon found herself safe in a thick wood.

The first thing I've got to do,' said Alice to herself, as she wandered about in the wood: 'is to grow to my right size again; and the second thing is to find my way into that lovely garden. I think that will be the best plan.'

It sounded an excellent plan, no doubt, and very neatly and simply arranged; the only difficulty was, that she had not the smallest idea how to set about it;

and while she was peering about anxiously among the trees, a little sharp bark just over her head made her look up in a great hurry.

An enormous puppy was looking down at her with large round eyes, and feebly stretching out one paw, trying to touch her.

La prima cosa che sentì fu un coro di voci che diceva: — Ecco Guglielmo che vola! — e poi la voce sola del Coniglio: — Pigliatelo voi altri presso la siepe! — e poi silenzio, e poi di nuovo una gran confusione di voci...

— Sostenetegli il capo... un po' d'acquavite... Non lo strozzate... Com'è andata amico?... Che cosa ti è accaduto? Racconta!

Finalmente si sentì una vocina esile e stridula (— Guglielmo, — pensò Alice): — Veramente, non so. Basta, grazie, ora mi sento meglio... ma son troppo agitato per raccontarvelo... tutto quello che mi ricordo si è qualche cosa come un babau che m'ha fatto saltare in aria come un razzo!

— Davvero, poveretto! — dissero gli altri.

— Si deve appiccar fuoco alla casa! — esclamò la voce del Coniglio; ma Alice gridò subito con quanta forza aveva in gola: — Se lo fate, guai! Vi farò acchiappare da Dina!

Si fece immediatamente un silenzio mortale, e Alice disse fra sè: "Chi sa che faranno ora! Se avessero tanto di cervello in testa scoperchierebbero la casa." Dopo uno o due minuti cominciarono a muoversi di nuovo e sentì il Coniglio dire: — Basterà una carriola piena per cominciare. —

"Piena di che?" — pensò Alice; ma non restò molto in dubbio, perchè subito una grandine di sassolini cominciò a tintinnare contro la finestra ed alcuni la colpirono in faccia.

"Bisogna finirla!" — pensò Alice, e strillò: — Non vi provate più! — Successe di nuovo un silenzio di tomba.

Alice osservò con sorpresa che i sassolini si trasformavano in pasticcini, toccando il pavimento, e subito un'idea la fece sussultare di gioia:

— Se mangio uno di questi pasticcini, — disse, — certo avverrà un mutamento nella mia statura. Giacchè non potranno farmi più grande, mi faranno forse più piccola. E ingoiò un pasticcino, e si rallegrò di veder che cominciava a contrarsi.

Appena si sentì piccina abbastanza per uscir dalla porta, scappò da quella casa, e incontrò una folla di piccoli animali e d'uccelli che aspettavano fuori.

La povera Lucertola (era Guglielmo) stava nel mezzo, sostenuta da due Porcellini d'India, che la facevano bere da una bottiglia.

Appena comparve Alice, tutti le si scagliarono contro; ma la fanciulla si mise a correre più velocemente che le fu possibile, e riparò incolume in un folto bosco.

"La prima cosa che dovrò fare, — pensò Alice, vagando nel bosco, — è di ricrescere e giungere alla mia statura normale; la seconda, di trovare la via per entrare in quel bel giardino. Credo che non ci sia altro di meglio da fare".

Il suo progetto era eccellente, senza dubbio; ma la difficoltà stava nel fatto ch'ella non sapeva di dove cominciare a metterlo in atto.

Mentre aguzzava gli occhi, guardando fra gli alberi della foresta, un piccolo latrato acuto al di sopra di lei la fece guardare in su presto presto.

Un enorme cucciolo la squadrava con i suoi occhi tondi ed enormi, e allungando una zampa cercava di toccarla.

'Poor little thing!' said Alice, in a coaxing tone, and she tried hard to whistle to it; but she was terribly frightened all the time at the thought that it might be hungry, in which case it would be very likely to eat her up in spite of all her coaxing.

Hardly knowing what she did, she picked up a little bit of stick, and held it out to the puppy; whereupon the puppy jumped into the air off all its feet at once, with a yelp of delight, and rushed at the stick, and made believe to worry it. Then Alice dodged behind a great thistle, to keep herself from being run over; and the moment she appeared on the other side, the puppy made another rush at the stick, and tumbled head over heels in its hurry to get hold of it. Then Alice, thinking it was very like having a game of play with a cart-horse, and expecting every moment to be trampled under its feet, ran round the thistle again. Then the puppy began a series of short charges at the stick, running a very little way forwards each time and a long way back, and barking hoarsely all the while, till at last it sat down a good way off, panting, with its tongue hanging out of its mouth, and its great eyes half shut. This seemed to Alice a good opportunity for making her escape; so she set off at once, and ran till she was quite tired and out of breath, and till the puppy's bark sounded quite faint in the distance. And yet what a dear little puppy it was!' said Alice, as she leant against a buttercup to rest herself, and fanned herself with one of the leaves: 'I should have liked teaching it tricks very much, if—if I'd only been the right size to do it! Oh dear! I'd nearly forgotten that I've got to grow up again! Let me see—how is it to be managed? I suppose I ought to eat or drink something or other; but the great question is, what?'

The great question certainly was, what? Alice looked all round her at the flowers and the blades of grass, but she did not see anything that looked like the right thing to eat or drink under the circumstances.

There was a large mushroom growing near her, about the same height as herself; and when she had looked under it, and on both sides of it, and behind it, it occurred to her that she might as well look and see what was on the top of it.

She stretched herself up on tiptoe, and peeped over the edge of the mushroom, and her eyes immediately met those of a large caterpillar, that was sitting on the top with its arms folded, quietly smoking a long hookah, and taking not the smallest notice of her or of anything else.

— Poverino! — disse Alice in tono carezzevole, e per ammansirlo si provò a dirgli: — Te', te'! — ma tremava come una canna, pensando che forse era affamato. In questo caso esso l'avrebbe probabilmente divorata, nonostante tutte le sue carezze.

Per far la disinvolta, prese un ramoscello e lo presentò al cagnolino; il quale diede un balzo in aria come una palla con un latrato di gioia, e s'avventò al ramoscello come per sbranarlo.

Allora Alice si mise cautamente dietro un cardo altissimo per non esser travolta; quando si affacciò dall'altro lato, il cagnolino s'era avventato nuovamente al ramoscello, ed aveva fatto un capitombolo nella furia di afferrarlo.

Ma ad Alice sembrò che fosse come voler scherzare con un cavallo da trasporto. Temendo d'esser calpestata dalle zampe della bestia, si rifugiò di nuovo dietro al cardo.

Allora il cagnolino cominciò una serie di cariche contro il ramoscello, andando sempre più in là, e rimanendo sempre più in qua del necessario, abbaiando raucamente sinchè non s'acquattò ansante a una certa distanza con la lingua penzoloni, e i grandi occhi semichiusi.

Alice colse quell'occasione per scappare. Corse tanto da perdere il fiato, sinchè il latrato del cagnolino si perse in lontananza.

— E pure che bel cucciolo che era! — disse Alice, appoggiandosi a un ranuncolo e facendosi vento con una delle sue foglie.

— Oh, avrei voluto insegnargli dei giuochi se... se fossi stata d'una statura adatta! Poveretta me! avevo dimenticato che avevo bisogno di crescere ancora!

Vediamo, come debbo fare? Forse dovrei mangiare o bere qualche cosa; ma che cosa?

Il problema era questo: che cosa? Alice guardò intorno fra i fiori e i fili d'erba; ma non potè veder nulla che le sembrasse adatto a mangiare o a bere per l'occasione.

C'era però un grosso fungo vicino a lei, press'a poco alto quanto lei; e dopo che l'ebbe esaminato di sotto, ai lati e di dietro, le parve cosa naturale di vedere che ci fosse di sopra.

Alzandosi in punta dei piedi, si affacciò all'orlo del fungo, e gli occhi suoi s'incontrarono con quelli d'un grosso Bruco turchino che se ne stava seduto nel centro con le braccia conserte, fumando tranquillamente una lunga pipa, e non facendo la minima attenzione ne a lei, nè ad altro.

5. Advice from a Caterpillar

The Caterpillar and Alice looked at each other for some time in silence: at last the Caterpillar took the hookah out of its mouth, and addressed her in a languid, sleepy voice.
'Who are you?' said the Caterpillar.

This was not an encouraging opening for a conversation. Alice replied, rather shyly:
'I—I hardly know, sir, just at present— at least I know who I was when I got up this morning, but I think I must have been changed several times since then.'
'What do you mean by that?' said the Caterpillar sternly. 'Explain yourself!'
I can't explain myself, I'm afraid, sir' said Alice: 'because I'm not myself, you see.'
'I don't see,' said the Caterpillar.

I'm afraid I can't put it more clearly,' Alice replied very politely: 'for I can't understand it myself to begin with; and being so many different sizes in a day is very confusing.'

'It isn't,' said the Caterpillar.

Well, perhaps you haven't found it so yet,' said Alice; 'but when you have to turn into a chrysalis—you will some day, you know—and then after that into a butterfly, I should think you'll feel it a little queer, won't you?'
'Not a bit,' said the Caterpillar.

'Well, perhaps your feelings may be different,' said Alice; 'all I know is, it would feel very queer to me.'
'You!' said the Caterpillar contemptuously. 'Who are you?'

Which brought them back again to the beginning of the conversation. Alice felt a little irritated at the Caterpillar's making such very short remarks, and she drew herself up and said, very gravely: 'I think, you ought to tell me who you are, first.'
'Why?' said the Caterpillar.

Here was another puzzling question; and as Alice could not think of any good reason, and as the Caterpillar seemed to be in a very unpleasant state of mind, she turned away.
'Come back!' the Caterpillar called after her. 'I've something important to say!'
This sounded promising, certainly: Alice turned and came back again.
'Keep your temper,' said the Caterpillar.

'Is that all?' said Alice, swallowing down her anger as well as she could.
'No,' said the Caterpillar.

Alice thought she might as well wait, as she had nothing else to do, and perhaps after all it might tell her something worth hearing.
For some minutes it puffed away without speaking, but at last it unfolded its arms, took the hookah out of its mouth again, and said: 'So you think you're changed, do you?'

5. Consigli del Bruco

Il Bruco e Alice si guardarono a vicenda per qualche tempo in silenzio; finalmente il Bruco staccò la pipa di bocca, e le parlò con voce languida e sonnacchiosa:
Chi sei? — disse il Bruco.

Non era un bel principio di conversazione. Alice rispose con qualche timidezza:
— Davvero non te lo saprei dire ora. So dirti chi fossi, quando mi son levata questa mattina, ma d'allora credo di essere stata cambiata parecchie volte.
— Che cosa mi vai contando? — disse austeramente il Bruco. — Spiegati meglio.
— Temo di non potermi spiegare, — disse Alice, — perchè non sono più quella di prima, come vedi.
— Io non vedo nulla, — rispose il Bruco.

— Temo di non potermi spiegare più chiaramente, — soggiunse Alice in maniera assai gentile, — perchè dopo esser stata cambiata di statura tante volte in un giorno, non capisco più nulla.
— Non è vero! — disse il Bruco.

— Bene, non l'hai sperimentato ancora, — disse Alice, — ma quando ti trasformerai in crisalide, come ti accadrà un giorno, e poi diventerai farfalla, certo ti sembrerà un po'strano, — non è vero?
— Niente affatto, — rispose il Bruco.

— Bene, tu la pensi diversamente, — replicò Alice; — ma a me parrebbe molto strano.
— A te! — disse il Bruco con disprezzo. — Chi sei tu?

E questo li ricondusse di nuovo al principio della conversazione. Alice si sentiva un po' irritata dalle brusche osservazioni del Bruco e se ne stette sulle sue, dicendo con gravità: — Perchè non cominci tu a dirmi chi sei?

— Perchè? — disse il Bruco.

Era un'altra domanda imbarazzante. Alice non seppe trovare una buona ragione. Il Bruco pareva di cattivo umore e perciò ella fece per andarsene.
— Vieni qui! — la richiamò il Bruco. — Ho qualche cosa d'importante da dirti.
La chiamata prometteva qualche cosa: Alice si fece innanzi.

— Non arrabbiarti! — disse il Bruco.

— E questo è tutto? — rispose Alice, facendo uno sforzo per frenarsi.
— No, — disse il Bruco.

Alice pensò che poteva aspettare, perchè non aveva niente di meglio da fare, e perchè forse il Bruco avrebbe potuto dirle qualche cosa d'importante.
Per qualche istante il Bruco fumò in silenzio, finalmente sciolse le braccia, si tolse la pipa di bocca e disse: — E così, tu credi di essere cambiata?

I'm afraid I am, sir,' said Alice; 'I can't remember things as I used—and I don't keep the same size for ten minutes together!'

'Can't remember what things?' said the Caterpillar.

'Well, I've tried to say "How doth the little busy bee," but it all came different!' Alice replied in a very melancholy voice.

'Repeat, "you are old, Father William,"' said the Caterpillar.

Alice folded her hands, and began:—

'You are old, Father William,' the young man said,

'And your hair has become very white;

And yet you incessantly stand on your head — Do you think, at your age, it is right?'

'In my youth,' Father William replied to his son,

'I feared it might injure the brain;

But, now that I'm perfectly sure I have none,

Why, I do it again and again.'

You are old,' said the youth: 'as I mentioned before,

And have grown most uncommonly fat;

Yet you turned a back-somersault in at the door—

Pray, what is the reason of that?'

'In my youth,' said the sage, as he shook his grey locks,

'I kept all my limbs very supple

By the use of this ointment—one shilling the box-

Allow me to sell you a couple?'

You are old,' said the youth: 'and your jaws are too weak

For anything tougher than suet;

Yet you finished the goose, with the bones and the beak—

Pray how did you manage to do it?'

In my youth,' said his father: 'I took to the law,

And argued each case with my wife;

And the muscular strength, which it gave to my jaw,

Has lasted the rest of my life.'

You are old,' said the youth: 'one would hardly suppose

That your eye was as steady as ever;

Yet you balanced an eel on the end of your nose—

What made you so awfully clever?'

'I have answered three questions, and that is enough,' Said his father; 'don't give yourself airs! Do you think I can listen all day to such stuff?

Be off, or I'll kick you down stairs!'

'That is not said right,' said the Caterpillar.

'Not quite right, I'm afraid,' said Alice, timidly; 'some of the words have got altered.'

'It is wrong from beginning to end,' said the Caterpillar decidedly, and there was silence for some minutes.

The Caterpillar was the first to speak.

'What size do you want to be?' it asked.

— Ho paura di sì, signore, — rispose Alice. — Non posso ricordarmi le cose bene come una volta, e non rimango della stessa statura neppure per lo spazio di dieci minuti!

— Che cosa non ricordi? — disse il Bruco.

— Ecco, ho tentato di dire "La vispa Teresa" e l'ho detta tutta diversa! — soggiunse melanconicamente Alice.

— Ripetimi "Sei vecchio, caro babbo", — disse il Bruco.

Alice incrociò le mani sul petto, e cominciò:

"Sei vecchio, caro babbo" — gli disse il ragazzino —

"sulla tua chioma splende — quasi un candore alpino;

eppur costantemente — cammini sulla testa: ti sembra per un vecchio — buona maniera questa?"

"Quand'ero bambinello" — rispose il vecchio allora —

"temevo di mandare — il cerebro in malora;

ma adesso persuaso — di non averne affatto,

a testa in giù cammino — più agile d'un gatto."

"Sei vecchio, caro babbo" — gli disse il ragazzino —

e sei capace e vasto — più assai d'un grosso tino:

e pur sfondato hai l'uscio — con una capriola;

"dimmi di quali acrobati — andasti, babbo, a scuola?"

"Quand'ero bambinello." — rispose il padre saggio,

per rafforzar le membra, — io mi facea il massaggio

sempre con quest'unguento. — Un franco alla boccetta.

"chi comperarlo vuole, — fa bene se s'affretta"

"Sei vecchio, caro babbo," — gli disse il ragazzino,

"e tu non puoi mangiare — che pappa nel brodino;

pure hai mangiato un'oca — col becco e tutte l'ossa

Ma dimmi, ove la pigli, — o babbo, tanta possa?"

"Un dì apprendevo legge." — il padre allor gli disse, —

"ed ebbi con mia moglie continue liti e risse,

e tanta forza impressi — alle ganasce allora,

tanta energia, che, vedi, — mi servon bene ancora."

"Sei vecchio. caro babbo," — gli disse il ragazzino

"e certo come un tempo — non hai più l'occhio fino:

pur reggi in equilibrio — un pesciolin sul naso:

or come così desto — ti mostri in questo caso?"

"A tutte le domande — io t'ho risposto già, "e finalmente basta!" — risposegli il papà: "se tutto il giorno poi — mi vuoi così seccare.

ti faccio con un calcio — le scale ruzzolare"

— Non l'hai detta fedelmente, — disse il Bruco.

— Temo di no, — rispose timidamente Alice, — certo alcune parole sono diverse.

— L'hai detta male, dalla prima parola all'ultima, — disse il Bruco con accento risoluto. Vi fu un silenzio per qualche minuto.

Il Bruco fu il primo a parlare:

— Di che statura vuoi essere? — domandò.

'Oh, I'm not particular as to size,' Alice hastily replied; 'only one doesn't like changing so often, you know.'

'I don't know,' said the Caterpillar.

Alice said nothing: she had never been so much contradicted in her life before, and she felt that she was losing her temper. 'Are you content now?' said the Caterpillar.

'Well, I should like to be a little larger, sir, if you wouldn't mind,' said Alice: 'three inches is such a wretched height to be.'

'It is a very good height indeed!' said the Caterpillar angrily, rearing itself upright as it spoke (it was exactly three inches high).

But I'm not used to it!' pleaded poor Alice in a piteous tone. And she thought of herself: 'I wish the creatures wouldn't be so easily offended!'

'You'll get used to it in time,' said the Caterpillar; and it put the hookah into its mouth and began smoking again.

This time Alice waited patiently until it chose to speak again. In a minute or two the Caterpillar took the hookah out of its mouth and yawned once or twice, and shook itself.

Then it got down off the mushroom, and crawled away in the grass, merely remarking as it went: 'One side will make you grow taller, and the other side will make you grow shorter.'

'One side of what? The other side of what?' thought Alice to herself.

'Of the mushroom,' said the Caterpillar, just as if she had asked it aloud; and in another moment it was out of sight.

Alice remained looking thoughtfully at the mushroom for a minute, trying to make out which were the two sides of it; and as it was perfectly round, she found this a very difficult question.

However, at last she stretched her arms round it as far as they would go, and broke off a bit of the edge with each hand.

'And now which is which?' she said to herself, and nibbled a little of the right-hand bit to try the effect: the next moment she felt a violent blow underneath her chin: it had struck her foot!

She was a good deal frightened by this very sudden change, but she felt that there was no time to be lost, as she was shrinking rapidly; so she set to work at once to eat some of the other bit.

Her chin was pressed so closely against her foot, that there was hardly room to open her mouth; but she did it at last, and managed to swallow a morsel of the lefthand bit.

Come, my head's free at last!' said Alice in a tone of delight, which changed into alarm in another moment, when she found that her shoulders were nowhere to be found: all she could see, when she looked down, was an immense length of neck, which seemed to rise like a stalk out of a sea of green leaves that lay far below her.

What can all that green stuff be?' said Alice. 'And where have my shoulders got to? And oh, my poor hands, how is it I can't see you?'

— Oh, non vado tanto pel sottile in fatto di statura, — rispose in fretta Alice; — soltanto non è piacevole mutar così spesso, sai.

— Io non ne so nulla, — disse il Bruco.

Alice non disse sillaba: non era stata mai tante volte contraddetta, e non ne poteva proprio più.

— Sei contenta ora? — domandò il Bruco.

— Veramente vorrei essere un pochino più grandetta, se non ti dispiacesse, — rispose Alice, — una statura di otto centimetri è troppo meschina!

— Otto centimetri fanno una magnifica statura! — disse il Bruco collerico, rizzandosi come uno stelo, mentre parlava (egli era alto esattamente otto centimetri).

— Ma io non ci sono abituata! — si scusò Alice in tono lamentoso. E poi pensò fra sè: "Questa bestiolina s'offende per nulla!"

— Col tempo ti ci abituerai, — disse il Bruco, e rimettendosi la pipa in bocca ricominciò a fumare.

Questa volta Alice aspettò pazientemente che egli ricominciasse a parlare. Dopo due o tre minuti, il Bruco si tolse la pipa di bocca, sbadigliò due o tre volte, e si scosse tutto.

Poi discese dal fungo, e se ne andò strisciando nell'erba, dicendo soltanto queste parole: — Un lato ti farà diventare più alta e l'altro ti farà diventare più bassa.

"Un lato di che cosa? L'altro lato di che cosa?" pensò Alice fra sè.

— Del fungo, — disse il Bruco, come se Alice lo avesse interrogato ad alta voce; e subito scomparve.

Alice rimase pensosa un minuto guardando il fungo, cercando di scoprirne i due lati, ma siccome era perfettamente rotondo, trovò la cosa difficile.

A ogni modo allungò più che le fu possibile le braccia per circondare il fungo, e ne ruppe due pezzetti dell'orlo a destra e a sinistra.

— Ed ora qual è un lato e qual è l'altro? — si domandò, e si mise ad addentare, per provarne l'effetto, il pezzettino che aveva a destra; l'istante dopo si sentì un colpo violento sotto il mento. Aveva battuto sul piede!

Quel mutamento subitaneo la spaventò molto; ma non c'era tempo da perdere, perchè ella si contraeva rapidamente; così si mise subito ad addentare l'altro pezzo.

Il suo mento era talmente aderente al piede che a mala pena trovò spazio per aprir la bocca; finalmente riuscì a inghiottire una briccica del pezzettino di sinistra.

— Ecco, la mia testa è libera finalmente! — esclamò Alice gioiosa; ma la sua allegrezza si mutò in terrore, quando si accorse che non poteva più trovare le spalle: tutto ciò che poteva vedere, guardando in basso, era un collo lungo lungo che sembrava elevarsi come uno stelo in un mare di foglie verdi, che stavano a una bella distanza al di sotto.

— Che cosa è mai quel campo verde? — disse Alice. — E le mie spalle dove sono? Oh povera me! perchè non vi veggo più, o mie povere mani? —

She was moving them about as she spoke, but no result seemed to follow, except a little shaking among the distant green leaves.

As there seemed to be no chance of getting her hands up to her head, she tried to get her head down to them, and was delighted to find that her neck would bend about easily in any direction, like a serpent.

She had just succeeded in curving it down into a graceful zigzag, and was going to dive in among the leaves, which she found to be nothing but the tops of the trees under which she had been wandering, when a sharp hiss made her draw back in a hurry:

a large pigeon had flown into her face, and was beating her violently with its wings.

'Serpent!' screamed the Pigeon.

'I'm not a serpent!' said Alice indignantly. 'Let me alone!'

Serpent, I say again!' repeated the Pigeon, but in a more subdued tone, and added with a kind of sob: 'I've tried every way, and nothing seems to suit them!'

'I haven't the least idea what you're talking about,' said Alice.

'I've tried the roots of trees, and I've tried banks, and I've tried hedges,' the Pigeon went on, without attending to her; 'but those serpents! There's no pleasing them!'

Alice was more and more puzzled, but she thought there was no use in saying anything more till the Pigeon had finished.

'As if it wasn't trouble enough hatching the eggs,' said the Pigeon; 'but I must be on the look-out for serpents night and day! Why, I haven't had a wink of sleep these three weeks!'

'I'm very sorry you've been annoyed,' said Alice, who was beginning to see its meaning.

And just as I'd taken the highest tree in the wood,' continued the Pigeon, raising its voice to a shriek:

'and just as I was thinking I should be free of them at last, they must needs come wriggling down from the sky! Ugh, Serpent!'

But I'm not a serpent, I tell you!' said Alice. 'I'm a—I'm a—'

'Well! what are you?' said the Pigeon. 'I can see you're trying to invent something!'

I—I'm a little girl,' said Alice, rather doubtfully, as she remembered the number of changes she had gone through that day.

A likely story indeed!' said the Pigeon in a tone of the deepest contempt.

'I've seen a good many little girls in my time, but never one with such a neck as that! No, no! You're a serpent; and there's no use denying it. I suppose you'll be telling me next that you never tasted an egg!'

'I have tasted eggs, certainly,' said Alice, who was a very truthful child; 'but little girls eat eggs quite as much as serpents do, you know.'

'I don't believe it,' said the Pigeon; 'but if they do, why then they're a kind of serpent, that's all I can say.'

This was such a new idea to Alice, that she was quite silent for a minute or two, which gave the Pigeon the opportunity of adding:

'You're looking for eggs, I know that well enough; and what does it matter to me whether you're a little girl or a serpent?'

E andava movendole mentre parlava, ma non seguiva altro effetto che un piccolo movimento fra le foglie verdi lontane.

E siccome non sembrava possibile portar le mani alla testa, tentò di piegare la testa verso le mani, e fu contenta di rilevare che il collo si piegava e si moveva in ogni senso come il corpo d'un serpente.

Era riuscita a curvarlo in giù in forma d'un grazioso zig-zag, e stava per tuffarlo fra le foglie (le cime degli alberi sotto i quali s'era smarrita), quando sentì un sibilo acuto, che glielo fece ritrarre frettolosamente:

un grosso Colombo era volato su di lei e le sbatteva violentemente le ali contro la faccia.

— Serpente! — gridò il Colombo.

— Io non sono un serpente, — disse Alice indignata. — Vattene!

— Serpente, dico! — ripetè il Colombo, ma con tono più dimesso, e soggiunse singhiozzando: — Ho cercato tutti i rimedi, ma invano.

— Io non comprendo affatto di che parli, — disse Alice.

— Ho provato le radici degli alberi, ho provato i clivi, ho provato le siepi, — continuò il Colombo senza badarle; — ma i serpenti! Oh, non c'è modo di accontentarli!

Alice sempre più confusa, pensò che sarebbe stato inutile dir nulla, sin che il Colombo non avesse finito.

— Come se fosse poco disturbo covar le uova, — disse il Colombo. — Bisogna vegliarle giorno e notte! Sono tre settimane che non chiudo occhio!

— Mi dispiace di vederti così sconsolato! disse Alice, che cominciava a comprendere.

— E appunto quando avevo scelto l'albero più alto del bosco, — continuò il Colombo con un grido disperato,

— e mi credevo al sicuro finalmente, ecco che mi discendono dal cielo! Ih! Brutto serpente!

— Ma io non sono un serpente, ti dico! — rispose Alice. — Io sono una... Io sono una...

— Bene, chi sei? — chiese il Colombo. — È chiaro che tu cerchi dei raggiri per ingannarmi!

— Io... io sono una bambina, — rispose Alice, ma con qualche dubbio, perchè si rammentava i molti mutamenti di quel giorno.

— È una frottola! — disse il Colombo col tono del più amaro disprezzo.

— Ho veduto molte bambine in vita mia, ma con un collo come il tuo, mai. No, no! Tu sei un serpente, è inutile negarlo. Scommetto che avrai la faccia di dirmi che non hai assaggiato mai un uovo!

— Ma certo che ho mangiato delle uova, — soggiunse Alice, che era una bambina molto sincera. — Non son soli i serpenti a mangiare le uova; le mangiano anche le bambine.

— Non ci credo, — disse il Colombo, — ma se così fosse le bambine sarebbero un'altra razza di serpenti, ecco tutto.

Questa idea parve così nuova ad Alice che rimase in silenzio per uno o due minuti; il Colombo colse quell'occasione per aggiungere:

— Tu vai a caccia di uova, questo è certo, e che m'importa, che tu sia una bambina o un serpente?

'It matters a good deal to me,' said Alice hastily; 'but I'm not looking for eggs, as it happens; and if I was, I shouldn't want yours: I don't like them raw.'

Well, be off, then!' said the Pigeon in a sulky tone, as it settled down again into its nest.

Alice crouched down among the trees as well as she could, for her neck kept getting entangled among the branches, and every now and then she had to stop and untwist it.

After a while she remembered that she still held the pieces of mushroom in her hands, and she set to work very carefully, nibbling first at one and then at the other, and growing sometimes taller and sometimes shorter, until she had succeeded in bringing herself down to her usual height.

It was so long since she had been anything near the right size, that it felt quite strange at first; but she got used to it in a few minutes, and began talking to herself, as usual.

'Come, there's half my plan done now! How puzzling all these changes are! I'm never sure what I'm going to be, from one minute to another!

However, I've got back to my right size: the next thing is, to get into that beautiful garden—how is that to be done, I wonder?'

As she said this, she came suddenly upon an open place, with a little house in it about four feet high.

'Whoever lives there,' thought Alice: 'it'll never do to come upon them this size: why, I should frighten them out of their wits!'

So she began nibbling at the righthand bit again, and did not venture to go near the house till she had brought herself down to nine inches high.

— Ma importa moltissimo a me, — rispose subito Alice. — A ogni modo non vado in cerca di uova; e anche se ne cercassi, non ne vorrei delle tue; crude non mi piacciono.

— Via dunque da me! — disse brontolando il Colombo, e si accovacciò nel nido.

Alice s'appiattò come meglio potè fra gli alberi, perchè il collo le s'intralciava tra i rami, e spesso doveva fermarsi per distrigarnelo.

Dopo qualche istante, si ricordò che aveva tuttavia nelle mani i due pezzettini di fungo, e si mise all'opera con molta accortezza addentando ora l'uno ora l'altro, e così diventava ora più alta ora più bassa, finchè riuscì a riavere la sua statura giusta.

Era da tanto tempo che non aveva la sua statura giusta, che da prima le parve strano; ma vi si abituò in pochi minuti, e ricominciò a parlare fra sè secondo il solito.

— Ecco sono a metà del mio piano! Sono pure strani tutti questi mutamenti! Non so mai che diventerò da un minuto all'altro!

Ad ogni modo, sono tornata alla mia statura normale: ora bisogna pensare ad entrare in quel bel giardino... Come farò, poi?

E così dicendo, giunse senza avvedersene in un piazzale che aveva nel mezzo una casettina alta circa un metro e venti.

— Chiunque vi abiti, — pensò Alice, — non posso con questa mia statura fargli una visita; gli farei una gran paura!

E cominciò ad addentare il pezzettino che aveva nella destra, e non osò di avvicinarsi alla casa, se non quando ebbe la statura d'una ventina di centimetri.

6. Pig and Pepper

For a minute or two she stood looking at the house, and wondering what to do next, when suddenly a footman in livery came running out of the wood—
(she considered him to be a footman because he was in livery: otherwise, judging by his face only, she would have called him a fish) — and rapped loudly at the door with his knuckles.
It was opened by another footman in livery, with a round face, and large eyes like a frog; and both footmen, Alice noticed, had powdered hair that curled all over their heads.

She felt very curious to know what it was all about, and crept a little way out of the wood to listen.
The Fish-Footman began by producing from under his arm a great letter, nearly as large as himself, and this he handed over to the other, saying, in a solemn tone:
'For the Duchess. An invitation from the Queen to play croquet.' The Frog-Footman repeated, in the same solemn tone, only changing the order of the words a little: 'From the Queen. An invitation for the Duchess to play croquet.'

Then they both bowed low, and their curls got entangled together.
Alice laughed so much at this, that she had to run back into the wood for fear of their hearing her; and when she next peeped out the Fish-Footman was gone, and the other was sitting on the ground near the door, staring stupidly up into the sky.
Alice went timidly up to the door, and knocked.
There's no sort of use in knocking,' said the Footman: 'and that for two reasons. First, because I'm on the same side of the door as you are; secondly, because they're making such a noise inside, no one could possibly hear you.'
And certainly there was a most extraordinary noise going on within—a constant howling and sneezing, and every now and then a great crash, as if a dish or kettle had been broken to pieces.
Please, then,' said Alice: 'how am I to get in?'

There might be some sense in your knocking,' the Footman went on without attending to her: 'if we had the door between us. For instance, if you were inside, you might knock, and I could let you out, you know.'
He was looking up into the sky all the time he was speaking, and this Alice thought decidedly uncivil.
'But perhaps he can't help it,' she said to herself; 'his eyes are so very nearly at the top of his head. But at any rate he might answer questions.—How am I to get in?' she repeated, aloud.

I shall sit here,' the Footman remarked: 'till tomorrow—'

At this moment the door of the house opened, and a large plate came skimming out, straight at the Footman's head: it

6. Porco e Pepe

Per un po' si mise a guardare la casa, e non sapeva che fare, quando ecco un valletto in livrea uscire in corsa dalla foresta…
(lo prese per un valletto perchè era in livrea, altrimenti al viso lo avrebbe creduto un pesce), e picchiare energicamente all'uscio con le nocche delle dita.

La porta fu aperta da un altro valletto in livrea, con una faccia rotonda e degli occhi grossi, come un ranocchio; ed Alice osservò che entrambi portavano delle parrucche inanellate e incipriate.
Le venne la curiosità di sapere di che si trattasse, e uscì cautamente dal cantuccio della foresta, e si mise ad origliare.
Il pesce valletto cavò di sotto il braccio un letterone grande quasi quanto lui, e lo presentò all'altro, dicendo solennemente:
“Per la Duchessa. Un invito della Regina per giocare una partita di croquet.” Il ranocchio valletto rispose nello stesso tono di voce, ma cambiando l'ordine delle parole: “Dalla Regina. Un invito per la Duchessa per giocare una partita di croquet.”
Ed entrambi s'inchinarono sino a terra, e le ciocche de' loro capelli si confusero insieme.
Alice scoppiò in una gran risata, e si rifugiò nel bosco per non farsi sentire, e quando tornò il pesce valletto se n'era andato, e l'altro s'era seduto sulla soglia dell'uscio, fissando stupidamente il cielo.

Alice si avvicinò timidamente alla porta e picchiò.
— È inutile picchiare, — disse il valletto, — e questo per due ragioni. La prima perchè io sto dalla stessa parte della porta dove tu stai, la seconda perchè di dentro si sta facendo tanto fracasso, che non sentirebbe nessuno. —
E davvero si sentiva un gran fracasso di dentro, un guaire e uno starnutire continui, e di tempo in tempo un gran scroscio, come se un piatto o una caldaia andasse in pezzi.

— Per piacere, — domandò Alice, — che ho da fare per entrare?
— Il tuo picchiare avrebbe un significato, — continuò il valletto senza badarle, — se la porta fosse fra noi due. Per esempio se tu fossi dentro, e picchiassi, io potrei farti uscire, capisci.
E parlando continuava a guardare il cielo, il che ad Alice pareva un atto da maleducato.
“Ma forse non può farne a meno, — disse fra sè — ha gli occhi quasi sull'orlo della fronte! Potrebbe però rispondere a qualche domanda…” — Come fare per entrare? — disse Alice ad alta voce.
— Io me ne starò qui, — osservò il valletto, — fino a domani…
In quell'istante la porta si aprì, e un gran piatto volò verso la testa del valletto, gli sfiorò il naso e si ruppe in cento pezzi contro un albero più oltre.

just grazed his nose, and broke to pieces against one of the trees behind him.

—or next day, maybe,' the Footman continued in the same tone, exactly as if nothing had happened.

'How am I to get in?' asked Alice again, in a louder tone.

'Are you to get in at all?' said the Footman. 'That's the first question, you know.'

It was, no doubt: only Alice did not like to be told so. 'It's really dreadful,' she muttered to herself: 'the way all the creatures argue. It's enough to drive one crazy!'

The Footman seemed to think this a good opportunity for repeating his remark, with variations. 'I shall sit here,' he said: 'on and off, for days and days.'

'But what am I to do?' said Alice.

'Anything you like,' said the Footman, and began whistling.

'Oh, there's no use in talking to him,' said Alice desperately: 'he's perfectly idiotic!' And she opened the door and went in.

The door led right into a large kitchen, which was full of smoke from one end to the other:

the Duchess was sitting on a three-legged stool in the middle, nursing a baby; the cook was leaning over the fire, stirring a large cauldron which seemed to be full of soup.

'There's certainly too much pepper in that soup!' Alice said to herself, as well as she could for sneezing.

There was certainly too much of it in the air. Even the Duchess sneezed occasionally; and as for the baby, it was sneezing and howling alternately without a moment's pause.

The only things in the kitchen that did not sneeze, were the cook, and a large cat which was sitting on the hearth and grinning from ear to ear.

Please would you tell me,' said Alice, a little timidly, for she was not quite sure whether it was good manners for her to speak first: 'why your cat grins like that?'

It's a Cheshire cat,' said the Duchess: 'and that's why. Pig!'

She said the last word with such sudden violence that Alice quite jumped; but she saw in another moment that it was addressed to the baby, and not to her, so she took courage, and went on again:—

'I didn't know that Cheshire cats always grinned; in fact, I didn't know that cats could grin.'

'They all can,' said the Duchess; 'and most of 'em do.'

'I don't know of any that do,' Alice said very politely, feeling quite pleased to have got into a conversation.

'You don't know much,' said the Duchess; 'and that's a fact.'

Alice did not at all like the tone of this remark, and thought it would be as well to introduce some other subject of conversation.

While she was trying to fix on one, the cook took the cauldron of soup off the fire, and at once set to work throwing everything within her reach at the Duchess and the

—...forse fino a poidomani, — continuò il valletto come se nulla fosse accaduto.

— Come debbo fare per entrare? — gridò Alice più forte.

— Devi entrare? — rispose il valletto. — Si tratta di questo principalmente, sai.

Senza dubbio, ma Alice non voleva sentirlo dire. "È spaventoso, — mormorò fra sè, — il modo con cui discutono queste bestie. Mi farebbero diventar matta!"

Il valletto colse l'occasione per ripetere l'osservazione con qualche variante: — io me ne starò seduto qui per giorni e giorni.

— Ma io che debbo fare? — domandò Alice.

— Quel che ti pare e piace, — rispose il valletto, e si mise a fischiare.

— È inutile discutere con lui, — disse Alice disperata: — è un perfetto imbecille! — Aprì la porta ed entrò.

La porta conduceva di filato a una vasta cucina, da un capo all'altro invasa di fumo:

la Duchessa sedeva in mezzo su uno sgabello a tre piedi, cullando un bambino in seno; la cuoca era di fronte al fornello, rimestando in un calderone che pareva pieno di minestra.

"Certo, c'è troppo pepe in quella minestra!" — disse Alice a sè stessa, non potendo frenare uno starnuto.

Davvero c'era troppo sentor di pepe in aria. Anche la Duchessa starnutiva qualche volta; e quanto al bambino non faceva altro che starnutire e strillare senza un istante di riposo.

I soli due esseri che non starnutivano nella cucina, erano la cuoca e un grosso gatto, che se ne stava accoccolato sul focolare, ghignando con tutta la bocca, da un orecchio all'altro.

— Per piacere, — domandò Alice un po' timidamente, perchè non era certa che fosse buona creanza di cominciare lei a parlare, — perchè il suo gatto ghigna così?

— È un Ghignagatto, — rispose la Duchessa, — ecco perchè. Porco!

Ella pronunciò l'ultima parola con tanta energia, che Alice fece un balzo; ma subito comprese che quel titolo era dato al bambino, e non già a lei. Così si riprese e continuò:

— Non sapevo che i gatti ghignassero a quel modo: anzi non sapevo neppure che i gatti potessero ghignare.

— Tutti possono ghignare, — rispose la Duchessa; — e la maggior parte ghignano.

— Non ne conosco nessuno che sappia farlo, — replicò Alice con molto rispetto, e contenta finalmente di conversare.

— Tu non sai molto, — disse la Duchessa; — non c'è da dubitarne!

Il tono secco di questa conversazione non piacque ad Alice, che volle cambiar discorso.

Mentre cercava un soggetto, la cuoca tolse il calderone della minestra dal fuoco, e tosto si mise a gettare tutto ciò che le stava vicino contro la Duchessa e il bambino... Scagliò prima

baby —the fire-irons came first; then followed a shower of saucepans, plates, and dishes.

The Duchess took no notice of them even when they hit her; and the baby was howling so much already, that it was quite impossible to say whether the blows hurt it or not.

'Oh, please mind what you're doing!' cried Alice, jumping up and down in an agony of terror. 'Oh, there goes his precious nose'; as an unusually large saucepan flew close by it, and very nearly carried it off.

If everybody minded their own business,' the Duchess said in a hoarse growl: 'the world would go round a deal faster than it does.'

Which would not be an advantage,' said Alice, who felt very glad to get an opportunity of showing off a little of her knowledge.

'Just think of what work it would make with the day and night! You see the earth takes twenty-four hours to turn round on its axis—'

Talking of axes,' said the Duchess: 'chop off her head!'

Alice glanced rather anxiously at the cook, to see if she meant to take the hint; but the cook was busily stirring the soup, and seemed not to be listening, so she went on again: 'Twenty-four hours, I think; or is it twelve? I—'

'Oh, don't bother me,' said the Duchess; 'I never could abide figures!' And with that she began nursing her child again, singing a sort of lullaby to it as she did so, and giving it a violent shake at the end of every line:

'Speak roughly to your little boy,

And beat him when he sneezes:

He only does it to annoy,

Because he knows it teases.'

CHORUS

(In which the cook and the baby joined):— 'Wow! wow! wow!'

While the Duchess sang the second verse of the song, she kept tossing the baby violently up and down, and the poor little thing howled so, that Alice could hardly hear the words:—

'I speak severely to my boy,

I beat him when he sneezes;

For he can thoroughly enjoy

The pepper when he pleases!'

CHORUS

'Wow! wow! wow!'

Here! you may nurse it a bit, if you like!' the Duchess said to Alice, flinging the baby at her as she spoke.

'I must go and get ready to play croquet with the Queen,' and she hurried out of the room. The cook threw a frying-pan after her as she went out, but it just missed her.

Alice caught the baby with some difficulty, as it was a queer-shaped little creature, and held out its arms and legs in all directions: 'just like a star-fish,' thought Alice.

The poor little thing was snorting like a steam-engine when she caught it, and kept doubling itself up and straightening

le molle, la padella, e l'attizzatoio; poi un nembo di casseruole, di piatti e di tondi.

La duchessa non se ne dava per intesa, nemmeno quand'era colpita; e il bambino guaiva già tanto, che era impossibile dire se i colpi gli facessero male o no.

— Ma badi a quel che fa! — gridò Alice, saltando qua e là atterrita. — Addio naso! — continuò a dire, mentre un grosso tegame sfiorava il naso del bimbo e poco mancò non glielo portasse via.

— Se tutti badassero ai fatti loro, — esclamò la Duchessa con un rauco grido, — il mondo andrebbe molto più presto di quanto non faccia.

— Non sarebbe un bene, — disse Alice, lieta di poter sfoggiare la sua dottrina.

— Pensi che sarebbe del giorno e della notte! La terra, com'ella sa, ci mette ventiquattro ore a girare intorno al suo asse...

— A proposito di asce! — gridò la Duchessa, — tagliatele la testa!

Alice guardò ansiosamente la cuoca per vedere se ella intendesse obbedire; ma la cuoca era occupata a rimestare la minestra, e, non pareva che avesse ascoltato, perciò andò innanzi dicendo: — Ventiquattro ore, credo; o dodici? Io...

— Oh non mi seccare, — disse la Duchessa. — Ho sempre odiato i numeri! — E si rimise a cullare il bimbo, cantando una certa sua ninnananna, e dandogli una violenta scossa alla fine d'ogni strofa:

Vo col bimbo per la corte,

se starnuta dàgli forte: lui

lo sa che infastidisce

e per picca starnutisce.

Coro

(al quale si unisce la cuoca) Ahi ahi ahi!!!

Mentre la Duchessa cantava il secondo verso, scoteva il bimbo su e giù con molta violenza, e il poverino strillava tanto che Alice appena potè udire le parole della canzoncina:

Vo col bimbo per le corte,

se starnuta gli dò forte;

lui se vuole può mangiare

tutto il pepe che gli pare.

Coro

Ahi, ahi ahi!!!

— Tieni, lo potrai cullare un poco se ti piace! — disse la Duchessa ad Alice, buttandole il bimbo in braccio. — Vado a prepararmi per giocare una partita a croquet con la Regina.

— E uscì in fretta dalla stanza. La cuoca le scaraventò addosso una padella, e per un pelo non la colse.

Alice afferrò il bimbo, ma con qualche difficoltà, perchè era una creatura stranissima; springava le mani e i piedi in tutti i sensi, "proprio come una stella di mare" pensò Alice.

Il poverino quando Alice lo prese, ronfava come una macchina a vapore e continuava a contorcersi e a divincolarsi

itself out again, so that altogether, for the first minute or two, it was as much as she could do to hold it.

As soon as she had made out the proper way of nursing it, (which was to twist it up into a sort of knot, and then keep tight hold of its right ear and left foot, so as to prevent its undoing itself,) she carried it out into the open air.

'If I don't take this child away with me,' thought Alice: 'they're sure to kill it in a day or two: wouldn't it be murder to leave it behind?'

She said the last words out loud, and the little thing grunted in reply (it had left off sneezing by this time). 'Don't grunt,' said Alice; 'that's not at all a proper way of expressing yourself.'

The baby grunted again, and Alice looked very anxiously into its face to see what was the matter with it.

There could be no doubt that it had a very turn-up nose, much more like a snout than a real nose; also its eyes were getting extremely small for a baby:

altogether Alice did not like the look of the thing at all. 'But perhaps it was only sobbing,' she thought, and looked into its eyes again, to see if there were any tears.

No, there were no tears. 'If you're going to turn into a pig, my dear,' said Alice, seriously: 'I'll have nothing more to do with you. Mind now!'

The poor little thing sobbed again (or grunted, it was impossible to say which), and they went on for some while in silence.

Alice was just beginning to think to herself: 'Now, what am I to do with this creature when I get it home?' when it grunted again, so violently, that she looked down into its face in some alarm.

This time there could be no mistake about it: it was neither more nor less than a pig, and she felt that it would be quite absurd for her to carry it further.

So she set the little creature down, and felt quite relieved to see it trot away quietly into the wood.

'If it had grown up,' she said to herself: 'it would have made a dreadfully ugly child: but it makes rather a handsome pig, I think.'

And she began thinking over other children she knew, who might do very well as pigs, and was just saying to herself:

'if one only knew the right way to change them—' when she was a little startled by seeing the Cheshire Cat sitting on a bough of a tree a few yards off.

The Cat only grinned when it saw Alice. It looked good-natured, she thought: still it had very long claws and a great many teeth, so she felt that it ought to be treated with respect.

Cheshire Puss,' she began, rather timidly, as she did not at all know whether it would like the name:

however, it only grinned a little wider. 'Come, it's pleased so far,' thought Alice, and she went on. 'Would you tell me, please, which way I ought to go from here?'

'That depends a good deal on where you want to get to,' said the Cat.

I don't much care where—' said Alice.

così che, per qualche istante, ella dubitò di non poterlo neanche reggere.

Appena la fanciulla ebbe trovato la maniera di cullarlo a modo, (e questo consistè nel ridurlo a una specie di nodo, e nell'afferrarlo al piede sinistro e all'orecchio destro, per impedirgli di sciogliersi) lo portò all'aria aperta.

— Se non mi porto via questo bambino, — osservò Alice, — è certo che fra qualche giorno lo ammazzeranno; non sarebbe un assassinio l'abbandonarlo? —

Disse le ultime parole a voce alta, e il poverino si mise a grugnire per risponderle (non starnutiva più allora). — Non grugnire, — disse Alice, — non è educazione esprimersi a codesto modo.

Il bambino grugnì di nuovo, e Alice lo guardò ansiosamente in faccia per vedere che avesse.

Aveva un naso troppo all'insù, e non c'era dubbio che rassomigliava più a un grugno che a un naso vero e proprio; e poi gli occhi gli stavano diventando così piccoli che non parevano di un bambino:

in complesso quell'aspetto non piaceva ad Alice. "Forse singhiozzava", pensò, e lo guardò di nuovo negli occhi per vedere se ci fossero lacrime.

Ma non ce n'erano. — Carino mio, se tu ti trasformi in un porcellino, — disse Alice seriamente, — non voglio aver più nulla a che fare con te. Bada dunque! —

Il poverino si rimise a singhiozzare (o a grugnire, chi sa, era difficile dire) e si andò innanzi in silenzio per qualche tempo.

Alice, intanto, cominciava a riflettere: "Che cosa ho da fare di questa creatura quando arrivo a casa?" allorchè quella creatura grugnì di nuovo e con tanta energia, che ella lo guardò in faccia sgomenta.

Questa volta non c'era dubbio: era un porcellino vero e proprio, ed ella si convinse che era assurdo portarlo oltre.

Così depose la bestiolina in terra, e si sentì sollevata quando la vide trottar via tranquillamente verso il bosco.

— Se fosse cresciuto, sarebbe stato un ragazzo troppo brutto; ma diventerà un magnifico porco, credo. —

E si ricordò di certi fanciulli che conosceva, i quali avrebbero potuto essere degli ottimi porcellini, e stava per dire:

— Se si sapesse il vero modo di trasformarli... — quando sussultò di paura, scorgendo il Ghignagatto, seduto su un ramo d'albero a pochi passi di distanza.

Il Ghignagatto si mise soltanto a ghignare quando vide Alice. "Sembra di buon umore, — essa pensò; — ma ha le unghie troppo lunghe, ed ha tanti denti," perciò si dispose a trattarlo con molto rispetto.

— Ghignagatto, — cominciò a parlargli con un poco di timidezza, perchè non sapeva se quel nome gli piacesse; comunque egli fece un ghigno più grande. "Ecco, ci ha piacere," pensò Alice e continuò: — Vorresti dirmi per dove debbo andare?

— Dipende molto dal luogo dove vuoi andare, — rispose il Gatto.

— Poco m'importa dove... — disse Alice.

'Then it doesn't matter which way you go,' said the Cat.

—so long as I get somewhere,' Alice added as an explanation.
Oh, you're sure to do that,' said the Cat: 'if you only walk long enough.'
Alice felt that this could not be denied, so she tried another question. 'What sort of people live about here?'
In that direction,' the Cat said, waving its right paw round: 'lives a Hatter: and in that direction,' waving the other paw: 'lives a March Hare. Visit either you like: they're both mad.'

'But I don't want to go among mad people,' Alice remarked.

'Oh, you can't help that,' said the Cat: 'we're all mad here. I'm mad. You're mad.'
'How do you know I'm mad?' said Alice.

You must be,' said the Cat: 'or you wouldn't have come here.'

Alice didn't think that proved it at all; however, she went on 'And how do you know that you're mad?'
To begin with,' said the Cat: 'a dog's not mad. You grant that?'
'I suppose so,' said Alice.

Well, then,' the Cat went on: 'you see, a dog growls when it's angry, and wags its tail when it's pleased. Now I growl when I'm pleased, and wag my tail when I'm angry. Therefore I'm mad.'
'I call it purring, not growling,' said Alice.

'Call it what you like,' said the Cat. 'Do you play croquet with the Queen to-day?'
I should like it very much,' said Alice: 'but I haven't been invited yet.'
'You'll see me there,' said the Cat, and vanished.

Alice was not much surprised at this, she was getting so used to queer things happening. While she was looking at the place where it had been, it suddenly appeared again.
'By-the-bye, what became of the baby?' said the Cat. 'I'd nearly forgotten to ask.'
'It turned into a pig,' Alice quietly said, just as if it had come back in a natural way.

'I thought it would,' said the Cat, and vanished again.

Alice waited a little, half expecting to see it again, but it did not appear, and after a minute or two she walked on in the direction in which the March Hare was said to live.
I've seen hatters before,' she said to herself; 'the March Hare will be much the most interesting, and perhaps as this is May it won't be raving mad—at least not so mad as it was in March.'
As she said this, she looked up, and there was the Cat again, sitting on a branch of a tree.
'Did you say pig, or fig?' said the Cat.

'I said pig,' replied Alice; 'and I wish you wouldn't keep appearing and vanishing so suddenly: you make one quite giddy.'
'All right,' said the Cat; and this time it vanished quite slowly, beginning with the end of the tail, and ending with the grin, which remained some time after the rest of it had gone.

— Allora importa poco sapere per dove devi andare, — soggiunse il Gatto.
—...purchè giunga in qualche parte, — riprese Alice come per spiegarsi meglio.
— Oh certo vi giungerai! — disse il Gatto, non hai che da camminare.
Alice sentì che quegli aveva ragione e tentò un'altra domanda. — Che razza di gente c'è in questi dintorni?
— Da questa parte, — rispose il Gatto, facendo un cenno con la zampa destra, — abita un Cappellaio; e da questa parte, — indicando con l'altra zampa, — abita una Lepre di Marzo. Visita l'uno o l'altra, sono tutt'e due matti.
— Ma io non voglio andare fra i matti, — osservò Alice.

— Oh non ne puoi fare a meno, — disse il Gatto, — qui siamo tutti matti. Io sono matto, tu sei matta.
— Come sai che io sia matta? — domandò Alice.

— Tu sei matta, — disse il Gatto, — altrimenti non saresti venuta qui.
Non parve una ragione sufficiente ad Alice, ma pure continuò: — E come sai che tu sei matto?
— Intanto, — disse il Gatto, — un cane non è matto. Lo ammetti?
— Ammettiamolo, — rispose Alice.

— Bene, — continuò il Gatto, — un cane brontola quando è in collera, e agita la coda quando è contento. Ora io brontolo quando sono contento ed agito la coda quando sono triste. Dunque sono matto.
— Io direi far le fusa e non già brontolare, — disse Alice.

— Di' come ti pare, — rispose il Gatto. — Vai oggi dalla Regina a giocare a croquet?
— Sì, che ci andrei, — disse Alice, — ma non sono stata ancora invitata.
— Mi rivedrai da lei, — disse il Gatto, e scomparve.

Alice non se ne sorprese; si stava abituando a veder cose strane. Mentre guardava ancora il posto occupato dal Gatto, eccolo ricomparire di nuovo.
— A proposito, che n'è successo del bambino? — disse il Gatto. —.Avevo dimenticato di domandartelo.
— S'è trasformato in porcellino, — rispose Alice tranquillamente, come se la ricomparsa del Gatto fosse più che naturale.
— Me l'ero figurato, — disse il Gatto, e svanì di nuovo.

Alice aspettò un poco con la speranza di rivederlo, ma non ricomparve più, ed ella pochi istanti dopo prese la via dell'abitazione della Lepre di Marzo.
"Di cappellai ne ho veduti tanti, — disse fra sè: — sarà più interessante la Lepre di Marzo. Ma siccome siamo nel mese di maggio, non sarà poi tanto matta... almeno sarà meno matta che in marzo".
Mentre diceva così guardò in su, e vide di nuovo il Gatto, seduto sul ramo d'un albero.
— Hai detto porcellino o porcellana? — domandò il Gatto.

— Ho detto porcellino, — rispose Alice; — ma ti prego di non apparire e scomparire con tanta rapidità: mi fai girare il capo!
— Hai ragione, — disse il Gatto; e questa volta svanì adagio adagio; cominciando con la fine della coda e finendo col

'Well! I've often seen a cat without a grin,' thought Alice; 'but a grin without a cat! It's the most curious thing I ever saw in my life!'

She had not gone much farther before she came in sight of the house of the March Hare: she thought it must be the right house, because the chimneys were shaped like ears and the roof was thatched with fur.

It was so large a house, that she did not like to go nearer till she had nibbled some more of the lefthand bit of mushroom, and raised herself to about two feet high: even then she walked up towards it rather timidly, saying to herself 'Suppose it should be raving mad after all! I almost wish I'd gone to see the Hatter instead!'

ghigno, il quale rimase per qualche tempo sul ramo, dopo che tutto s'era dileguato.

— Curioso! ho veduto spesso un gatto senza ghigno; — osservò Alice, — mai un ghigno senza Gatto. È la cosa più strana che mi sia capitata!

Non s'era allontanata di molto, quando arrivò di fronte alla dimora della Lepre di Marzo: pensò che fosse proprio quella, perchè i comignoli avevano la forma di orecchie, e il tetto era coperto di pelo.

La casa era così grande che ella non osò avvicinarsi se non dopo aver sbocconcellato un po' del fungo che aveva nella sinistra, e esser cresciuta quasi sessanta centimetri di altezza: ma questo non la rendeva più coraggiosa. Mentre si avvicinava, diceva fra sè: "E se poi fosse pazza furiosa? Sarebbe meglio che fossi andata dal Cappellaio."

7. A Mad Tea Party

There was a table set out under a tree in front of the house, and the March Hare and the Hatter were having tea at it.

A Dormouse was sitting between them, fast asleep, and the other two were using it as a cushion, resting their elbows on it, and talking over its head. 'Very uncomfortable for the Dormouse,' thought Alice; 'only, as it's asleep, I suppose it doesn't mind.'

The table was a large one, but the three were all crowded together at one corner of it: 'No room! No room!' they cried out when they saw Alice coming. 'There's plenty of room!' said Alice indignantly, and she sat down in a large arm-chair at one end of the table. 'Have some wine,' the March Hare said in an encouraging tone.

Alice looked all round the table, but there was nothing on it but tea. 'I don't see any wine,' she remarked. 'There isn't any,' said the March Hare.

'Then it wasn't very civil of you to offer it,' said Alice angrily.

'It wasn't very civil of you to sit down without being invited,' said the March Hare. 'I didn't know it was your table,' said Alice; 'it's laid for a great many more than three.' 'Your hair wants cutting,' said the Hatter. He had been looking at Alice for some time with great curiosity, and this was his first speech. 'You should learn not to make personal remarks,' Alice said with some severity; 'it's very rude.' The Hatter opened his eyes very wide on hearing this; but all he said was: 'Why is a raven like a writing-desk?' Come, we shall have some fun now!' thought Alice. 'I'm glad they've begun asking riddles.—I believe I can guess that,' she added aloud. 'Do you mean that you think you can find out the answer to it?' said the March Hare. 'Exactly so,' said Alice.

'Then you should say what you mean,' the March Hare went on. I do,' Alice hastily replied; 'at least—at least I mean what I say—that's the same thing, you know.' 'Not the same thing a bit!' said the Hatter. 'You might just as well say that "I see what I eat" is the same thing as "I eat what I see"!' You might just as well say,' added the March Hare: 'that "I like what I get" is the same thing as "I get what I like"!'

You might just as well say,' added the Dormouse, who seemed to be talking in his sleep: 'that "I breathe when I sleep" is the same thing as "I sleep when I breathe"!' 'It is the same thing with you,' said the Hatter, and here the conversation dropped, and the party sat silent for a minute,

7. Un Tè di Matti

Sotto un albero di rimpetto alla casa c'era una tavola apparecchiata. Vi prendevano il tè la Lepre di Marzo e il Cappellaio.
Un Ghiro profondamente addormentato stava fra di loro, ed essi se ne servivano come se fosse stato un guanciale, poggiando su di lui i gomiti, e discorrendogli sulla testa.
"Un gran disturbo per il Ghiro, — pensò Alice, — ma siccome dorme, immagino che non se ne importi nè punto, nè poco."
La tavola era vasta, ma i tre stavano stretti tutti in un angolo:
— Non c'è posto! Non c'è posto! — gridarono, vedendo Alice avvicinarsi.
— C'è tanto posto! — disse Alice sdegnata, e si sdraiò in una gran poltrona, a un'estremità della tavola.
— Vuoi un po' di vino? — disse la Lepre di Marzo affabilmente.
Alice osservò la mensa, e vide che non c'era altro che tè. —
Non vedo il vino, — ella osservò.
— Non ce n'è, replicò la Lepre di Marzo.
— Ma non è creanza invitare a bere quel che non c'è, — disse Alice in collera.
— Neppure è stata creanza da parte tua sederti qui senza essere invitata, — osservò la Lepre di Marzo.
— Non sapevo che la tavola ti appartenesse, — rispose Alice; — è apparecchiata per più di tre.
— Dovresti farti tagliare i capelli, — disse il Cappellaio. Egli aveva osservato Alice per qualche istante con molta curiosità, e quelle furono le sue prime parole.
—Tu non dovresti fare osservazioni personali, — disse Alice un po' severa; — è sconveniente.
Il Cappellaio spalancò gli occhi; ma quel che rispose fu questo: — Perchè un corvo somiglia a uno scrittoio?
— Ecco, ora staremo allegri! — pensò Alice. —Sono contenta che hanno cominciato a proporre degli indovinelli... credo di poterlo indovinare, — soggiunse ad alta voce.
— Intendi dire che credi che troverai la risposta? — domandò la Lepre di Marzo.
— Appunto, — rispose Alice.

— Ebbene, dicci ciò che intendi, — disse la Lepre di Marzo.

— Ecco, — riprese Alice in fretta; — almeno intendo ciò che dico... è lo stesso, capisci.
— Ma che lo stesso! — disse il Cappellaio. — Sarebbe come dire che "veggo ciò che mangio" sia lo stesso di "mangio quel che veggo."
— Sarebbe come dire, — soggiunse la Lepre di Marzo, — che "mi piace ciò che prendo", sia lo stesso che "prendo ciò che mi piace?"
— Sarebbe come dire, — aggiunse il Ghiro che pareva parlasse nel sonno, — che "respiro quando dormo", sia lo stesso che "dormo quando respiro?"
— È lo stesso per te, — disse il Cappellaio. E qui la conversazione cadde, e tutti stettero muti per un poco,

while Alice thought over all she could remember about ravens and writing-desks, which wasn't much.

The Hatter was the first to break the silence. 'What day of the month is it?' he said, turning to Alice: he had taken his watch out of his pocket, and was looking at it uneasily, shaking it every now and then, and holding it to his ear.

Alice considered a little, and then said 'The fourth.' 'Two days wrong!' sighed the Hatter. 'I told you butter wouldn't suit the works!' he added looking angrily at the March Hare.

'It was the best butter,' the March Hare meekly replied.

'Yes, but some crumbs must have got in as well,' the Hatter grumbled: 'you shouldn't have put it in with the bread-knife.'

The March Hare took the watch and looked at it gloomily: then he dipped it into his cup of tea, and looked at it again:

but he could think of nothing better to say than his first remark: 'It was the best butter, you know.'

Alice had been looking over his shoulder with some curiosity. 'What a funny watch!' she remarked. 'It tells the day of the month, and doesn't tell what o'clock it is!'

'Why should it?' muttered the Hatter. 'Does your watch tell you what year it is?'

'Of course not,' Alice replied very readily: 'but that's because it stays the same year for such a long time together.'

'Which is just the case with mine,' said the Hatter.

Alice felt dreadfully puzzled. The Hatter's remark seemed to have no sort of meaning in it, and yet it was certainly English.

'I don't quite understand you,' she said, as politely as she could.

'The Dormouse is asleep again,' said the Hatter, and he poured a little hot tea upon its nose.

The Dormouse shook its head impatiently, and said, without opening its eyes: 'Of course, of course; just what I was going to remark myself.'

'Have you guessed the riddle yet?' the Hatter said, turning to Alice again.

'No, I give it up,' Alice replied: 'what's the answer?'

'I haven't the slightest idea,' said the Hatter.

'Nor I,' said the March Hare.

Alice sighed wearily. 'I think you might do something better with the time,' she said: 'than waste it in asking riddles that have no answers.'

If you knew Time as well as I do,' said the Hatter: 'you wouldn't talk about wasting it. It's him.'

'I don't know what you mean,' said Alice.

'Of course you don't!' the Hatter said, tossing his head contemptuously. 'I dare say you never even spoke to Time!'

'Perhaps not,' Alice cautiously replied: 'but I know I have to beat time when I learn music.'

mentre Alice cercava di ricordarsi tutto ciò che sapeva sui corvi e sugli scrittoi, il che non era molto.

Il Cappellaio fu il primo a rompere il silenzio. — Che giorno del mese abbiamo? — disse, volgendosi ad Alice. Aveva cavato l'orologio dal taschino e lo guardava con un certo timore, scuotendolo di tanto in tanto, e portandoselo all'orecchio.

Alice meditò un po' e rispose: — Oggi ne abbiamo quattro.

— Sbaglia di due giorni! — osservò sospirando il Cappellaio.

— Te lo avevo detto che il burro avrebbe guastato il congegno! — soggiunse guardando con disgusto la Lepre di Marzo.

— Il burro era ottimo, — rispose umilmente la Lepre di Marzo.

— — Sì ma devono esserci entrate anche delle molliche di pane, — borbottò il Cappellaio, — non dovevi metterlo dentro col coltello del pane.

La Lepre di Marzo prese l'orologio e lo guardò malinconicamente: poi lo tuffò nella sua tazza di tè, e l'osservò di nuovo:

ma non seppe far altro che ripetere l'osservazione di dianzi: — Il burro era ottimo, sai.

Alice, che l'aveva guardato curiosamente, con la coda dell'occhio, disse: — Che strano orologio! segna i giorni e non dice le ore.

— Perchè? — esclamò il Cappellaio. — Che forse il tuo orologio segna in che anno siamo?

— No, — si affrettò a rispondere Alice — ma l'orologio segna lo stesso anno per molto tempo.

— Quello che fa il mio, — rispose il Cappellaio.

Alice ebbe un istante di grande confusione. Le pareva che l'osservazione del Cappellaio non avesse alcun senso; e pure egli parlava correttamente.

— Non ti comprendo bene! — disse con la maggiore delicatezza possibile.

— Il Ghiro s'è di nuovo addormentato, — disse il Cappellaio, e gli versò sul naso un poco di tè bollente.

Il Ghiro scosse la testa con atto d'impazienza, e senza aprire gli occhi disse: — Già! Già! stavo per dirlo io.

— Credi ancora di aver sciolto l'indovinello? — disse il Cappellaio, volgendosi di nuovo ad Alice.

— No, ci rinunzio, — rispose Alice. — Qual'è la risposta?

— Non la so, — rispose il Cappellaio.

— Neppure io, — rispose la Lepre di Marzo.

Alice sospirò seccata, e disse: — Ma credo potresti fare qualche cosa di meglio che perdere il tempo, proponendo indovinelli senza senso.

— Se tu conoscessi il tempo come lo conosco io, — rispose il Cappellaio, — non diresti che lo perdiamo. Domandaglielo.

— Non comprendo che vuoi dire, — osservò Alice.

— Certo che non lo comprendi! — disse il Cappellaio, scotendo il capo con aria di disprezzo — Scommetto che tu non hai mai parlato col tempo.

— Forse no, — rispose prudentemente Alice; — ma so che debbo battere il tempo quando studio la musica.

Ah! that accounts for it,' said the Hatter. 'He won't stand beating. Now, if you only kept on good terms with him, he'd do almost anything you liked with the clock.

For instance, suppose it were nine o'clock in the morning, just time to begin lessons: you'd only have to whisper a hint to Time, and round goes the clock in a twinkling!

Half-past one, time for dinner!' ('I only wish it was,' the March Hare said to itself in a whisper.)

That would be grand, certainly,' said Alice thoughtfully: 'but then—I shouldn't be hungry for it, you know.'

'Not at first, perhaps,' said the Hatter: 'but you could keep it to half-past one as long as you liked.'

'Is that the way you manage?' Alice asked.

The Hatter shook his head mournfully. 'Not I!' he replied. 'We quarrelled last March—just before he went mad, you know—' (pointing with his tea spoon at the March Hare,) '—it was at the great concert given by the Queen of Hearts, and I had to sing

"Twinkle, twinkle, little bat!

How I wonder what you're at!"

You know the song, perhaps?'

'I've heard something like it,' said Alice.

It goes on, you know,' the Hatter continued: 'in this way:—

"Up above the world you fly,

Like a tea-tray in the sky.

Twinkle, twinkle—"'

Here the Dormouse shook itself, and began singing in its sleep 'Twinkle, twinkle, twinkle, twinkle—' and went on so long that they had to pinch it to make it stop.

Well, I'd hardly finished the first verse,' said the Hatter: 'when the Queen jumped up and bawled out, "He's murdering the time! Off with his head!"'

'How dreadfully savage!' exclaimed Alice.

And ever since that,' the Hatter went on in a mournful tone: 'he won't do a thing I ask! It's always six o'clock now.'

A bright idea came into Alice's head. 'Is that the reason so many tea-things are put out here?' she asked.

'Yes, that's it,' said the Hatter with a sigh: 'it's always tea-time, and we've no time to wash the things between whiles.'

'Then you keep moving round, I suppose?' said Alice.

'Exactly so,' said the Hatter: 'as the things get used up.'

'But what happens when you come to the beginning again?' Alice ventured to ask.

'Suppose we change the subject,' the March Hare interrupted, yawning. 'I'm getting tired of this. I vote the young lady tells us a story.'

'I'm afraid I don't know one,' said Alice, rather alarmed at the proposal.

'Then the Dormouse shall!' they both cried. 'Wake up, Dormouse!' And they pinched it on both sides at once.

— Ahi, adesso si spiega, — disse il Cappellaio. — Il tempo non vuol esser battuto. Se tu fossi in buone relazioni con lui, farebbe dell'orologio ciò che tu vuoi.

Per esempio, supponi che siano le nove, l'ora delle lezioni, basterebbe che gli dicessi una parolina all'orecchio, e in un lampo la lancetta andrebbe innanzi!

Mezzogiorno, l'ora del desinare! ("Vorrei che fosse mezzogiorno," bisbigliò fra sè la Lepre di Marzo).

— Sarebbe magnifico, davvero — disse Alice pensosa: — ma non avrei fame a quell'ora, capisci.

— Da principio, forse, no, — riprese il Cappellaio, — ma potresti fermarlo su le dodici fin quando ti parrebbe e piacerebbe.

— E tu fai così? — domandò Alice.

Il Cappellaio scosse mestamente la testa e rispose: — Io no. Nel marzo scorso abbiamo litigato... proprio quando diventò matta lei... (e indicò col cucchiaio la Lepre di Marzo...) Fu al gran concerto dato dalla Regina di Cuori... ivi dovetti cantare:

Splendi, splendi, pipistrello!

Su pel cielo vai bel bello!

— Conosci tu quest'aria?

— Ho sentito qualche cosa di simile, — disse Alice.

— Senti, è così, — continuò il Cappellaio:

Non t'importa d'esser solo

e sul mondo spieghi il volo.

Splendi. splendi...

A questo il Ghiro si riscosse, e cominciò a cantare nel sonno: Teco il pane; teco il pane aggiungerò.... e via via andò innanzi fino a che gli dovettero dare dei pizzicotti per farlo tacere.

— Ebbene, avevo appena finito di cantare la prima strofa, — disse il Cappellaio, — quando la Regina proruppe infuriata:

— Sta assassinando il tempo! Tagliategli la testa!

— Feroce! — esclamò Alice.

— E d'allora, — continuò melanconicamente il Cappellaio, — il tempo non fa più nulla di quel che io voglio! Segna sempre le sei!

Alice ebbe un'idea luminosa e domandò: È per questo forse che vi sono tante tazze apparecchiate?

— Per questo, — rispose il Cappellaio, — è sempre l'ora del tè, e non abbiamo mai tempo di risciacquare le tazze negl'intervalli.

— Così le fate girare a turno, immagino... disse Alice.

— Proprio così, — replicò il Cappellaio: a misura che le tazze hanno servito.

— Ma come fate per cominciare da capo? s'avventurò a chiedere Alice.

— Se cambiassimo discorso? — disse la Lepre di Marzo sbadigliando, — Questo discorso mi annoia tanto. Desidero che la signorina ci racconti una storiella.

— Temo di non saperne nessuna, — rispose Alice con un po' di timore a quella proposta.

— Allora ce la dirà il Ghiro! — gridarono entrambi. — Risvegliati Ghiro! — e gli dettero dei forti pizzicotti dai due lati.

The Dormouse slowly opened his eyes. 'I wasn't asleep,' he said in a hoarse, feeble voice: 'I heard every word you fellows were saying.'

'Tell us a story!' said the March Hare.

'Yes, please do!' pleaded Alice.

And be quick about it,' added the Hatter: 'or you'll be asleep again before it's done.'

Once upon a time there were three little sisters,' the Dormouse began in a great hurry; 'and their names were Elsie, Lacie, and Tillie; and they lived at the bottom of a well—'

'What did they live on?' said Alice, who always took a great interest in questions of eating and drinking.

'They lived on treacle,' said the Dormouse, after thinking a minute or two.

'They couldn't have done that, you know,' Alice gently remarked; 'they'd have been ill.'

'So they were,' said the Dormouse; 'very ill.'

Alice tried to fancy to herself what such an extraordinary ways of living would be like, but it puzzled her too much, so she went on: 'But why did they live at the bottom of a well?'

'Take some more tea,' the March Hare said to Alice, very earnestly.

I've had nothing yet,' Alice replied in an offended tone: 'so I can't take more.'

'You mean you can't take less,' said the Hatter: 'it's very easy to take more than nothing.'

'Nobody asked your opinion,' said Alice.

'Who's making personal remarks now?' the Hatter asked triumphantly.

Alice did not quite know what to say to this: so she helped herself to some tea and bread-and-butter, and then turned to the Dormouse, and repeated her question. 'Why did they live at the bottom of a well?'

The Dormouse again took a minute or two to think about it, and then said: 'It was a treacle-well.'

There's no such thing!' Alice was beginning very angrily, but the Hatter and the March Hare went 'Sh! sh!' and the Dormouse sulkily remarked: 'If you can't be civil, you'd better finish the story for yourself.'

'No, please go on!' Alice said very humbly; 'I won't interrupt again. I dare say there may be one.'

One, indeed!' said the Dormouse indignantly. However, he consented to go on. 'And so these three little sisters—they were learning to draw, you know—'

'What did they draw?' said Alice, quite forgetting her promise.

'Treacle,' said the Dormouse, without considering at all this time.

'I want a clean cup,' interrupted the Hatter: 'let's all move one place on.'

He moved on as he spoke, and the Dormouse followed him: the March Hare moved into the Dormouse's place, and Alice rather unwillingly took the place of the March Hare.

The Hatter was the only one who got any advantage from the change: and Alice was a good deal worse off than before, as the March Hare had just upset the milk-jug into his plate.

Il Ghiro aprì lentamente gli occhi, e disse con voce debole e roca: — Io non dormivo! Ho sentito parola per parola ciò che avete detto.

— Raccontaci una storiella! — disse la Lepre di Marzo.

— Per piacere, diccene una! — supplicò Alice.

— E sbrigati! — disse il Cappellaio, — se no ti riaddormenterai prima di finirla.

— C'erano una volta tre sorelle, — cominciò in gran fretta il Ghiro. — Si chiamavano Elsa, Lucia e Tilla; e abitavano in fondo a un pozzo...

— Che cosa mangiavano? — domandò Alice, la quale s'interessava sempre molto al mangiare e al bere.

— Mangiavano teriaca, — rispose il Ghiro dopo averci pensato un poco.

— Impossibile, — osservò gentilmente Alice. — si sarebbero ammalate.

— E infatti erano ammalate, — rispose il Ghiro, — gravemente ammalate.

Alice cercò di immaginarsi quella strana maniera di vivere, ma ne fu più che confusa e continuò: — Ma perchè se ne stavano in fondo a un pozzo?

— Prendi un po' più di tè! — disse la Lepre di Marzo con molta serietà.

— Non ne ho avuto ancora una goccia, — rispose Alice in tono offeso, — così non posso prenderne un po' di più.

— Vuoi dire che non ne puoi prendere meno. — disse il Cappellaio: — è molto più facile prenderne più di nulla che meno di nulla.

— Nessuno ha domandato il tuo parere, — soggiunse Alice.

— Chi è ora che fa delle osservazioni personali? — domandò il Cappellaio con aria di trionfo.

Alice non seppe che rispondere; ma prese una tazza di tè con pane e burro, e volgendosi al Ghiro, gli ripetè la domanda: — Perchè se ne stavano in fondo a un pozzo?

Il Ghiro si prese un minuto o due per riflettere, e rispose: — Era un pozzo di teriaca.

— Ma non s'è sentita mai una cosa simile! interruppe Alice sdegnata. Ma la Lepre di Marzo e il Cappellaio facevano: — St! st! — e il Ghiro continuò burbero: — Se non hai educazione, finisciti da te la storiella.

— No, continua pure! — disse Alice molto umilmente: — Non ti interromperò più. Forse esiste un pozzo così.

— Soltanto uno! — rispose il Ghiro indignato. A ogni modo acconsentì a continuare: — E quelle tre sorelle... imparavano a trarne...

— Che cosa traevano? — domandò Alice, dimenticando che aveva promesso di tacere.

— Teriaca, — rispose il Ghiro, questa volta senza riflettere.

— Mi occorre una tazza pulita, — interruppe il Cappellaio; — moviamoci tutti d'un posto innanzi.

E mentre parlava si mosse, e il Ghiro lo seguì: la Lepre di Marzo occupò il posto del Ghiro, e Alice si sedette di mala voglia al posto della Lepre di Marzo.

Il solo Cappellaio s'avvantaggiò dello spostamento: e Alice si trovò peggio di prima, perchè la Lepre di Marzo s'era rovesciato il vaso del latte nel piatto.

Alice did not wish to offend the Dormouse again, so she began very cautiously: 'But I don't understand. Where did they draw the treacle from?'

You can draw water out of a water-well,' said the Hatter; 'so I should think you could draw treacle out of a treacle-well—eh, stupid?'

'But they were in the well,' Alice said to the Dormouse, not choosing to notice this last remark.

'Then you shouldn't talk,' said the Hatter.

This piece of rudeness was more than Alice could bear: she got up in great disgust, and walked off; the Dormouse fell asleep instantly, and neither of the others took the least notice of her going, though she looked back once or twice, half hoping that they would call after her:

'At any rate I'll never go there again!' said Alice as she picked her way through the wood. 'It's the stupidest tea-party I ever was at in all my life!'

Just as she said this, she noticed that one of the trees had a door leading right into it. 'That's very curious!' she thought. 'But everything's curious today. I think I may as well go in at once.' And in she went.

Once more she found herself in the long hall, and close to the little glass table. 'Now, I'll manage better this time,' she said to herself, and began by taking the little golden key, and unlocking the door that led into the garden.

Then she went to work nibbling at the mushroom (she had kept a piece of it in her pocket) till she was about a foot high:

then she walked down the little passage: and then—she found herself at last in the beautiful garden, among the bright flower-beds and the cool fountains.

Alice, senza voler offender di nuovo il Ghiro disse con molta discrezione: — Non comprendo bene. Di dove traevano la teriaca?

— Tu puoi trarre l'acqua da un pozzo d'acqua? — disse il Cappellaio; — così immagina, potresti trarre teriaca da un pezzo di teriaca... eh! scioccherella!

— Ma esse erano nel pozzo, — disse Alice al Ghiro.

— Allora stai zitta, — disse il Cappellaio.

Questo saggio di sgarbatezza sdegnò grandemente Alice, la quale si levò d'un tratto e se ne uscì. Il Ghiro si addormentò immediatamente, e nessuno degli altri due si accorse che Alice se n'era andata, benchè ella si fosse voltata una o due volte, con una mezza speranza d'essere richiamata:

— Non ci tornerò mai più, — disse Alice entrando nel bosco. — È la più stupida gente che io m'abbia mai conosciuta.

Mentre parlava così osservò un albero con un uscio nel tronco. "Curioso, — pensò Alice. — Ma ogni cosa oggi è curiosa. Credo che farò bene ad entrarci subito". Ed entrò.

Si trovò di nuovo nella vasta sala, e presso il tavolino di cristallo. — Questa volta saprò far meglio, — disse, e prese la chiavetta d'oro ed aprì la porta che conduceva nel giardino.

Poi si mise a sbocconcellare il fungo (ne aveva conservato un pezzetto in tasca), finchè ebbe un trenta centimetri d'altezza o giù di lì:

percorse il piccolo corridoio: e poi si trovò finalmente nell'ameno giardino in mezzo alle aiuole fulgide di fiori, e alle freschissime fontane.

8. The Queen's Croquet Ground

A large rose-tree stood near the entrance of the garden: the roses growing on it were white, but there were three gardeners at it, busily painting them red.

Alice thought this a very curious thing, and she went nearer to watch them, and just as she came up to them she heard one of them say: 'Look out now, Five! Don't go splashing paint over me like that!'

'I couldn't help it,' said Five, in a sulky tone; 'Seven jogged my elbow.'

On which Seven looked up and said: 'That's right, Five! Always lay the blame on others!'

'You'd better not talk!' said Five. 'I heard the Queen say only yesterday you deserved to be beheaded!'

'What for?' said the one who had spoken first.

'That's none of your business, Two!' said Seven.

'Yes, it is his business!' said Five: 'and I'll tell him—it was for bringing the cook tulip-roots instead of onions.'

Seven flung down his brush, and had just begun 'Well, of all the unjust things—' when his eye chanced to fall upon Alice, as she stood watching them, and he checked himself suddenly.

The others looked round also, and all of them bowed low.

'Would you tell me,' said Alice, a little timidly: 'why you are painting those roses?'

Five and Seven said nothing, but looked at Two. Two began in a low voice:

'Why the fact is, you see, Miss, this here ought to have been a red rose-tree, and we put a white one in by mistake; and if the Queen was to find it out, we should all have our heads cut off, you know. So you see, Miss, we're doing our best, afore she comes, to—'

At this moment Five, who had been anxiously looking across the garden, called out 'The Queen! The Queen!' and the three gardeners instantly threw themselves flat upon their faces. There was a sound of many footsteps, and Alice looked round, eager to see the Queen.

First came ten soldiers carrying clubs; these were all shaped like the three gardeners, oblong and flat, with their hands and feet at the corners: next the ten courtiers; these were ornamented all over with diamonds, and walked two and two, as the soldiers did.

After these came the royal children; there were ten of them, and the little dears came jumping merrily along hand in hand, in couples: they were all ornamented with hearts.

Next came the guests, mostly Kings and Queens, and among them Alice recognised the White Rabbit: it was talking in a hurried nervous manner, smiling at everything that was said, and went by without noticing her.

Then followed the Knave of Hearts, carrying the King's crown on a crimson velvet cushion; and, last of all this grand

8. Il Croquet della Regina

Un gran cespuglio di rose stava presso all'ingresso del giardino. Le rose germogliate erano bianche, ma v'erano lì intorno tre giardinieri occupati a dipingerle rosse.

"È strano!" pensò Alice, e s'avvicinò per osservarli, e come fu loro accanto, sentì dire da uno: — Bada, Cinque! non mi schizzare la tua tinta addosso!

— E che vuoi da me? — rispose Cinque in tono burbero. — Sette mi ha urtato il braccio.

Sette lo guardò e disse: — Ma bene! Cinque dà sempre la colpa agli altri!

— Tu faresti meglio a tacere! — disse Cinque. — Proprio ieri la Regina diceva che tu meriteresti di essere decapitato!

— Perchè? — domandò il primo che aveva parlato.

— Questo non ti riguarda, Due! — rispose Sette.

Sì, che gli riguarda! — disse Cinque; — e glielo dirò io... perchè hai portato al cuoco bulbi di tulipani invece di cipolle.

Sette scagliò lontano il pennello, e stava lì lì per dire: — Di tutte le cose le più ingiuste... — quando incontrò gli occhi di Alice e si mangiò il resto della frase.

Gli altri similmente si misero a guardarla e le fecero tutti insieme una profonda riverenza.

Volete gentilmente dirmi, — domandò Alice, con molta timidezza, — perchè state dipingendo quelle rose?

Cinque e Sette non risposero, ma diedero uno sguardo a Due. Due disse allora sottovoce:

— Perchè questo qui doveva essere un rosaio di rose rosse. Per isbaglio ne abbiamo piantato uno di rose bianche. Se la Regina se ne avvedesse, ci farebbe tagliare le teste a tutti. Così, signorina, facciamo il possibile per rimediare prima ch'essa venga a...

In quell'istante Cinque che guardava attorno pieno d'ansia, gridò: — La Regina! la Regina! — e i tre giardinieri si gettarono immediatamente a faccia a terra. Si sentì un gran scalpiccìo, e Alice si volse curiosa a veder la Regina.

Prima comparvero dieci soldati armati di bastoni: erano della forma dei tre giardinieri, bislunghi e piatti, le mani e i piedi agli angoli: seguivano dieci cortigiani, tutti rilucenti di diamanti; e sfilavano a due a due come i soldati.

Venivano quindi i principi reali, divisi a coppie e saltellavano a due a due, tenendosi per mano: erano ornati di cuori.

Poi sfilavano gli invitati, la maggior parte re e regine, e fra loro Alice riconobbe il Coniglio Bianco che discorreva in fretta nervosamente, sorridendo di qualunque cosa gli si dicesse. Egli passò innanzi senza badare ad Alice.

Seguiva il fante di cuori, portando la corona reale sopra un cuscino di velluto rosso; e in fondo a tutta questa gran processione venivano IL RE E LA REGINA DI CUORI.

procession, came THE KING AND QUEEN OF HEARTS.

Alice was rather doubtful whether she ought not to lie down on her face like the three gardeners, but she could not remember ever having heard of such a rule at processions; 'and besides, what would be the use of a procession,' thought she: 'if people had all to lie down upon their faces, so that they couldn't see it?' So she stood still where she was, and waited.

When the procession came opposite to Alice, they all stopped and looked at her, and the Queen said severely 'Who is this?' She said it to the Knave of Hearts, who only bowed and smiled in reply.

Idiot!' said the Queen, tossing her head impatiently; and, turning to Alice, she went on: 'What's your name, child?'

My name is Alice, so please your Majesty,' said Alice very politely; but she added, to herself: 'Why, they're only a pack of cards, after all. I needn't be afraid of them!'

'And who are these?' said the Queen, pointing to the three gardeners who were lying round the rosetree; for, you see, as they were lying on their faces, and the pattern on their backs was the same as the rest of the pack, she could not tell whether they were gardeners, or soldiers, or courtiers, or three of her own children.

'How should I know?' said Alice, surprised at her own courage. 'It's no business of mine.'

The Queen turned crimson with fury, and, after glaring at her for a moment like a wild beast, screamed 'Off with her head! Off—'

'Nonsense!' said Alice, very loudly and decidedly, and the Queen was silent.

The King laid his hand upon her arm, and timidly said 'Consider, my dear: she is only a child!'

The Queen turned angrily away from him, and said to the Knave 'Turn them over!'

The Knave did so, very carefully, with one foot.

'Get up!' said the Queen, in a shrill, loud voice, and the three gardeners instantly jumped up, and began bowing to the King, the Queen, the royal children, and everybody else.

Leave off that!' screamed the Queen. 'You make me giddy.' And then, turning to the rose-tree, she went on: 'What have you been doing here?'

May it please your Majesty,' said Two, in a very humble tone, going down on one knee as he spoke: 'we were trying—'

'I see!' said the Queen, who had meanwhile been examining the roses. 'Off with their heads!' and the procession moved on, three of the soldiers remaining behind to execute the unfortunate gardeners, who ran to Alice for protection.

'You shan't be beheaded!' said Alice, and she put them into a large flower-pot that stood near. The three soldiers wandered about for a minute or two, looking for them, and then quietly marched off after the others.

'Are their heads off?' shouted the Queen. 'Their heads are gone, if it please your Majesty!' the soldiers shouted in reply. 'That's right!' shouted the Queen. 'Can you play croquet?'

Alice non sapeva se dovesse prosternarsi, come i tre giardinieri, ma non potè ricordarsi se ci fosse un costume simile nei cortei reali.

"E poi, a che servirebbero i cortei, — riflettè, — se tutti dovessero stare a faccia per terra e nessuno potesse vederli?" Così rimase in piedi ad aspettare.

Quando il corteo arrivò di fronte ad Alice, tutti si fermarono e la guardarono; e la Regina gridò con cipiglio severo: — Chi è costei? — e si volse al fante di cuori, il quale per tutta risposta sorrise e s'inchinò.

— Imbecille! — disse la Regina, scotendo la testa impaziente; indi volgendosi ad Alice, continuò a dire: — Come ti chiami, fanciulla?

— Maestà, mi chiamo Alice, — rispose la fanciulla con molta garbatezza, ma soggiunse fra sè: "Non è che un mazzo di carte, dopo tutto? Perchè avrei paura?"

— E quelli chi sono? — domandò la Regina indicando i tre giardinieri col viso a terra intorno al rosaio; perchè, comprendete, stando così in quella posizione, il disegno posteriore rassomigliava a quello del resto del mazzo, e la Regina non poteva distinguere se fossero giardinieri, o soldati, o cortigiani, o tre dei suoi stessi figliuoli.

— Come volete che io lo sappia? — rispose Alice, che si meravigliava del suo coraggio. — È cosa che non mi riguarda.

La Regina diventò di porpora per la rabbia e, dopo di averla fissata selvaggiamente come una bestia feroce, gridò: — Tagliatele la testa, subito!...

— Siete matta! — rispose Alice a voce alta e con fermezza; e la Regina tacque.

Il Re mise la mano sul braccio della Regina, e disse timidamente: — Rifletti, cara mia, è una bambina!

La Regina irata gli voltò le spalle e disse al fante: — Voltateli!

Il fante obbedì, e con un piede voltò attentamente i giardinieri.

— Alzatevi! — gridò la Regina, e i tre giardinieri, si levarono immediatamente in piedi, inchinandosi innanzi al Re e alla Regina, ai principi reali, e a tutti gli altri.

— Basta! — strillò la regina. — Mi fate girare la testa. — E guardando il rosaio continuò: — Che facevate qui?

— Con buona grazia della Maestà vostra, — rispose Due umilmente, piegando il ginocchio a terra, tentavamo...

— Ho compreso! — disse la Regina, che aveva già osservato le rose, — Tagliate loro la testa! — E il corteo reale si rimise in moto, lasciando indietro tre soldati, per mozzare la testa agli sventurati giardinieri, che corsero da Alice per esserne protetti.

— Non vi decapiteranno! — disse Alice, e li mise in un grosso vaso da fiori accanto a lei. I tre soldati vagarono qua e là per qualche minuto in cerca di loro, e poi tranquillamente seguirono gli altri.

— Avete loro mozzata la testa? — gridò la Regina. — Maestà, le loro teste se ne sono andate! — risposero i soldati. — Bene! — gridò la Regina. — Si gioca il croquet?

The soldiers were silent, and looked at Alice, as the question was evidently meant for her.

'Yes!' shouted Alice.

'Come on, then!' roared the Queen, and Alice joined the procession, wondering very much what would happen next.

'It's—it's a very fine day!' said a timid voice at her side. She was walking by the White Rabbit, who was peeping anxiously into her face.

'Very,' said Alice: '—where's the Duchess?'

'Hush! Hush!' said the Rabbit in a low, hurried tone. He looked anxiously over his shoulder as he spoke, and then raised himself upon tiptoe, put his mouth close to her ear, and whispered 'She's under sentence of execution.'

'What for?' said Alice.

'Did you say "What a pity!"?' the Rabbit asked.

'No, I didn't,' said Alice: 'I don't think it's at all a pity. I said "What for?"'

She boxed the Queen's ears—' the Rabbit began. Alice gave a little scream of laughter. 'Oh, hush!' the Rabbit whispered in a frightened tone. 'The Queen will hear you! You see, she came rather late, and the Queen said—'

'Get to your places!' shouted the Queen in a voice of thunder, and people began running about in all directions, tumbling up against each other.

However, they got settled down in a minute or two, and the game began.

Alice thought she had never seen such a curious croquet-ground in her life; it was all ridges and furrows; the balls were live hedgehogs, the mallets live flamingoes, and the soldiers had to double themselves up and to stand on their hands and feet, to make the arches.

The chief difficulty Alice found at first was in managing her flamingo.

She succeeded in getting its body tucked away, comfortably enough, under her arm, with its legs hanging down, but generally, just as she had got its neck nicely straightened out, and was going to give the hedgehog a blow with its head, it would twist itself round and look up in her face, with such a puzzled expression that she could not help bursting out laughing:

and when she had got its head down, and was going to begin again, it was very provoking to find that the hedgehog had unrolled itself, and was in the act of crawling away:

besides all this, there was generally a ridge or furrow in the way wherever she wanted to send the hedgehog to, and, as the doubled-up soldiers were always getting up and walking off to other parts of the ground, Alice soon came to the conclusion that it was a very difficult game indeed.

The players all played at once without waiting for turns, quarrelling all the while, and fighting for the hedgehogs; and in a very short time the Queen was in a furious passion, and went stamping about, and shouting 'Off with his head!' or 'Off with her head!' about once in a minute.

Alice began to feel very uneasy: to be sure, she had not as yet had any dispute with the Queen, but she knew that it might happen any minute:

I soldati tacevano e guardavano Alice, pensando che la domanda fosse rivolta a lei.

— Sì! — gridò Alice.

Venite qui dunque! — urlò la Regina. E Alice seguì il corteo, curiosa di vedere il seguito.

— Che bel tempo! — disse una timida voce accanto a lei. Ella s'accorse di camminare accanto al Coniglio bianco, che la scrutava in viso con una certa ansia.

— Bene, — rispose Alice: — dov'è la Duchessa?

— St! st! — disse il Coniglio a voce bassa, con gran fretta. Si guardò ansiosamente d'intorno levandosi in punta di piedi, avvicinò la bocca all'orecchio della bambina: — È stata condannata a morte.

— Per qual reato? — domandò Alice.

— Hai detto: "Che peccato?" — chiese il Coniglio.

— Ma no, — rispose Alice: — Ho detto per che reato?

— Ha dato uno schiaffo alla Regina... —cominciò il coniglio. Alice ruppe in una risata. — Zitta! — bisbigliò il Coniglio tutto tremante. — Ti potrebbe sentire la Regina! Sai, è arrivata tardi, e la Regina ha detto...

— Ai vostri posti! — gridò la Regina con voce tonante. E gl'invitati si sparpagliarono in tutte le direzioni, l'uno rovesciando l'altro.

Finalmente, dopo un po', poterono disporsi in un certo ordine, e il giuoco cominciò.

Alice pensava che in vita sua non aveva mai veduto un terreno più curioso per giocare il croquet; era tutto a solchi e zolle; le palle erano ricci, i mazzapicchi erano fenicotteri vivi, e gli archi erano soldati vivi, che si dovevano curvare e reggere sulle mani e sui piedi.

La principale difficoltà consisteva in ciò, che Alice non sapeva come maneggiare il suo fenicottero.

Ma poi riuscì a tenerselo bene avviluppato sotto il braccio, con le gambe penzoloni; ma quando gli allungava il collo e si preparava a picchiare il riccio con la testa, il fenicottero girava il capo e poi si metteva a guardarla in faccia con una espressione di tanto stupore che ella non poteva tenersi dallo scoppiare dalle risa:

e dopo che gli aveva fatto abbassare la testa, e si preparava a ricominciare, ecco che il riccio si era svolto, e se n'andava via.

Oltre a ciò c'era sempre una zolla o un solco là dove voleva scagliare il riccio, e siccome i soldati incurvati si alzavano e andavan vagando qua e là, Alice si persuase che quel giuoco era veramente difficile.

I giocatori giocavano tutti insieme senza aspettare il loro turno, litigando sempre e picchiandosi a cagion dei ricci; e in breve la Regina diventò furiosa, e andava qua e là pestando i piedi e gridando: — Mozzategli la testa! — oppure: — Mozzatele la testa! — almeno una volta al minuto.

— Alice cominciò a sentirsi un po' a disagio: e vero che non aveva avuto nulla da dire con la Regina; ma poteva succedere da un momento all'altro, e pensò:

'and then,' thought she: 'what would become of me? They're dreadfully fond of beheading people here; the great wonder is, that there's any one left alive!'

She was looking about for some way of escape, and wondering whether she could get away without being seen, when she noticed a curious appearance in the air. It puzzled her very much at first, but, after watching it a minute or two, she made it out to be a grin, and she said to herself 'It's the Cheshire Cat: now I shall have somebody to talk to.'

'How are you getting on?' said the Cat, as soon as there was mouth enough for it to speak with.

Alice waited till the eyes appeared, and then nodded. 'It's no use speaking to it,' she thought: 'till its ears have come, or at least one of them.'

In another minute the whole head appeared, and then Alice put down her flamingo, and began an account of the game, feeling very glad she had someone to listen to her. The Cat seemed to think that there was enough of it now in sight, and no more of it appeared.

I don't think they play at all fairly,' Alice began, in rather a complaining tone:

'and they all quarrel so dreadfully one can't hear oneself speak—and they don't seem to have any rules in particular; at least, if there are, nobody attends to them—and you've no idea how confusing it is all the things being alive;

for instance, there's the arch I've got to go through next walking about at the other end of the ground—and I should have croqueted the Queen's hedgehog just now, only it ran away when it saw mine coming!'

'How do you like the Queen?' said the Cat in a low voice.

Not at all,' said Alice: 'she's so extremely—' Just then she noticed that the Queen was close behind her, listening: so she went on, '—likely to win, that it's hardly worth while finishing the game.'

The Queen smiled and passed on.

'Who are you talking to?' said the King, going up to Alice, and looking at the Cat's head with great curiosity.

It's a friend of mine—a Cheshire Cat,' said Alice: 'allow me to introduce it.'

'I don't like the look of it at all,' said the King: 'however, it may kiss my hand if it likes.'

'I'd rather not,' the Cat remarked.

Don't be impertinent,' said the King: 'and don't look at me like that!' He got behind Alice as he spoke.

'A cat may look at a king,' said Alice. 'I've read that in some book, but I don't remember where.'

Well, it must be removed,' said the King very decidedly, and he called the Queen, who was passing at the moment: 'My dear! I wish you would have this cat removed!'

The Queen had only one way of settling all difficulties, great or small. 'Off with his head!' she said, without even looking round.

'I'll fetch the executioner myself,' said the King eagerly, and he hurried off.

Alice thought she might as well go back, and see how the game was going on, as she heard the Queen's voice in the distance, screaming with passion.

"Che avverrà di me? Qui c'è la smania di troncar teste. Strano che vi sia ancora qualcuno che abbia il collo a posto!"

E pensava di svignarsela, quando scorse uno strano spettacolo in aria.

Prima ne restò sorpresa, ma dopo aver guardato qualche istante, vide un ghigno e disse fra sè: "È Ghignagatto: potrò finalmente parlare con qualcuno."

— Come va il giuoco? — disse il Gatto, appena ebbe tanto di bocca da poter parlare.

Alice aspettò che apparissero gli occhi, e poi fece un cenno col capo. "È inutile parlargli, — pensò, — aspettiamo che appaiano le orecchie, almeno una."

Tosto apparve tutta la testa, e Alice depose il suo fenicottero, e cominciò a raccontare le vicende del giuoco, lieta che qualcuno le prestasse attenzione. Il Gatto intanto dopo aver messa in mostra la testa, credè bene di non far apparire il resto del corpo.

— Non credo che giochino realmente, — disse Alice lagnandosi.

— Litigano con tanto calore che non sentono neanche la loro voce... non hanno regole nel giuoco; e se le hanno, nessuno le osserva... E poi c'è una tal confusione con tutti questi oggetti vivi; che non c'è modo di raccapezzarsi. Per esempio, ecco l'arco che io dovrei attraversare, che scappa via dall'altra estremità del terreno... Proprio avrei dovuto fare croquet col riccio della Regina, ma è fuggito non appena ha visto il mio.

— Ti piace la Regina? — domandò il Gatto a voce bassa.

— Per nulla! — rispose Alice; — essa è tanto... — Ma s'accorse che la Regina le stava vicino in ascolto, e continuò —...abile al giuoco, ch'è inutile finire la partita.

La Regina sorrise e passò oltre.

— Con chi parli? — domandò il Re che s'era avvicinato ad Alice, e osservava la testa del Gatto con grande curiosità.

— Con un mio amico... il Ghignagatto, — disse Alice; — vorrei presentarlo a Vostra Maestà.

— Quel suo sguardo non mi piace, — rispose il Re; — però se vuole, può baciarmi la mano.

— Non ho questo desiderio, — osservò il Gatto.

— Non essere insolente, — disse il Re, — e non mi guardare in quel modo. — E parlando si rifugiò dietro Alice.

— Un gatto può guardare in faccia a un re, — osservò Alice, — l'ho letto in qualche libro, ma non ricordo dove.

— Ma bisogna mandarlo via, — disse il Re risoluto; e chiamò la Regina che passava in quel momento: — Cara mia, vorrei che si mandasse via quel Gatto!

La Regina conosceva un solo modo per sciogliere tutte le difficoltà, grandi o piccole, e senza neppure guardare intorno, gridò: — Tagliategli la testa!

— Andrò io stesso a chiamare il carnefice, — disse il Re, e andò via a precipizio.

Alice pensò che intanto poteva ritornare per vedere il progresso del gioco, mentre udiva da lontano la voce della Regina che s'adirava urlando.

She had already heard her sentence three of the players to be executed for having missed their turns, and she did not like the look of things at all, as the game was in such confusion that she never knew whether it was her turn or not.

So she went in search of her hedgehog.

The hedgehog was engaged in a fight with another hedgehog, which seemed to Alice an excellent opportunity for croqueting one of them with the other:

the only difficulty was, that her flamingo was gone across to the other side of the garden, where Alice could see it trying in a helpless sort of way to fly up into a tree.

By the time she had caught the flamingo and brought it back, the fight was over, and both the hedgehogs were out of sight:

'but it doesn't matter much,' thought Alice: 'as all the arches are gone from this side of the ground.'

So she tucked it away under her arm, that it might not escape again, and went back for a little more conversation with her friend.

When she got back to the Cheshire Cat, she was surprised to find quite a large crowd collected round it: there was a dispute going on between the executioner, the King, and the Queen, who were all talking at once, while all the rest were quite silent, and looked very uncomfortable.

The moment Alice appeared, she was appealed to by all three to settle the question, and they repeated their arguments to her, though, as they all spoke at once, she found it very hard indeed to make out exactly what they said.

The executioner's argument was, that you couldn't cut off a head unless there was a body to cut it off from: that he had never had to do such a thing before, and he wasn't going to begin at his time of life.

The King's argument was, that anything that had a head could be beheaded, and that you weren't to talk nonsense.

The Queen's argument was, that if something wasn't done about it in less than no time she'd have everybody executed, all round. (It was this last remark that had made the whole party look so grave and anxious.)

Alice could think of nothing else to say but 'It belongs to the Duchess: you'd better ask her about it.'

'She's in prison,' the Queen said to the executioner: 'fetch her here.' And the executioner went off like an arrow.

The Cat's head began fading away the moment he was gone, and, by the time he had come back with the Duchess, it had entirely disappeared;

so the King and the executioner ran wildly up and down looking for it, while the rest of the party went back to the game.

Ella aveva sentito già condannare a morte tre giocatori che avevano perso il loro turno. Tutto ciò non le piaceva, perchè il gioco era diventato una tal confusione ch'ella non sapeva più se fosse la sua volta di tirare o no.

E si mise in cerca del suo riccio.

Il riccio stava allora combattendo contro un altro riccio; e questa sembrò ad Alice una buona occasione per batterli a croquet l'uno contro l'altro:

ma v'era una difficoltà: il suo fenicottero era dall'altro lato del giardino, e Alice lo vide sforzarsi inutilmente di volare su un albero.

Quando le riuscì d'afferrare il fenicottero e a ricondurlo sul terreno, la battaglia era finita e i due ricci s'erano allontanati.

"Non importa, — pensò Alice, — tanto tutti gli archi se ne sono andati dall'altro lato del terreno."

E se lo accomodò per benino sotto il braccio per non farselo scappare più, e ritornò dal Gatto per riattaccare discorso con lui.

Ma con sorpresa trovò una gran folla raccolta intorno al Ghignagatto; il Re, la Regina e il carnefice urlavano tutti e tre insieme, e gli altri erano silenziosi e malinconici.

Quando Alice apparve fu chiamata da tutti e tre per risolvere la questione. Essi le ripeterono i loro argomenti; ma siccome parlavano tutti in una volta, le fu difficile intendere che volessero.

Il carnefice sosteneva che non si poteva tagliar la testa dove mancava un corpo da cui staccarla; che non aveva mai avuto da fare con una cosa simile prima, e che non voleva cominciare a farne alla sua età.

L'argomento del Re, era il seguente: che ogni essere che ha una testa può essere decapitato, e che il carnefice non doveva dire sciocchezze.

L'argomento della Regina era questo: che se non si fosse eseguito immediatamente il suo ordine, avrebbe ordinato l'esecuzione di quanti la circondavano. (E quest'ingiunzione aveva dato a tutti quell'aria grave e piena d'ansietà.)

Alice non seppe dir altro che questo: — Il Gatto è della Duchessa: sarebbe meglio interrogarla.

— Ella è in prigione, — disse la Regina al carnefice: — Conducetela qui. — E il carnefice volò come una saetta.

Andato via il carnefice, la testa del Gatto cominciò a dileguarsi, e quando egli tornò con la Duchessa non ce n'era più traccia:

il Re e il carnefice corsero qua e là per ritrovarla, mentre il resto della brigata si rimetteva a giocare.

9. The Mock Turtle's Story

'You can't think how glad I am to see you again, you dear old thing!' said the Duchess, as she tucked her arm affectionately into Alice's, and they walked off together.

Alice was very glad to find her in such a pleasant temper, and thought to herself that perhaps it was only the pepper that had made her so savage when they met in the kitchen.

'When I'm a Duchess,' she said to herself, (not in a very hopeful tone though):

I won't have any pepper in my kitchen at all. Soup does very well without—Maybe it's always pepper that makes people hot-tempered,' she went on, very much pleased at having found out a new kind of rule:

'and vinegar that makes them sour—and camomile that makes them bitter—and—and barley-sugar and such things that make children sweet-tempered. I only wish people knew that: then they wouldn't be so stingy about it, you know—'

She had quite forgotten the Duchess by this time, and was a little startled when she heard her voice close to her ear.

'You're thinking about something, my dear, and that makes you forget to talk. I can't tell you just now what the moral of that is, but I shall remember it in a bit.'

'Perhaps it hasn't one,' Alice ventured to remark.

'Tut, tut, child!' said the Duchess. 'Everything's got a moral, if only you can find it.' And she squeezed herself up closer to Alice's side as she spoke.

Alice did not much like keeping so close to her: first, because the Duchess was very ugly; and secondly, because she was exactly the right height to rest her chin upon Alice's shoulder, and it was an uncomfortably sharp chin.

However, she did not like to be rude, so she bore it as well as she could.

'The game's going on rather better now,' she said, by way of keeping up the conversation a little.

'Tis so,' said the Duchess: 'and the moral of that is—"Oh: 'tis love: 'tis love, that makes the world go round!"'

Somebody said,' Alice whispered: 'that it's done by everybody minding their own business!'

Ah, well! It means much the same thing,' said the Duchess, digging her sharp little chin into Alice's shoulder as she added: 'and the moral of that is—"Take care of the sense, and the sounds will take care of themselves."'

'How fond she is of finding morals in things!' Alice thought to herself.

'I dare say you're wondering why I don't put my arm round your waist,' the Duchess said after a pause: 'the reason is, that I'm doubtful about the temper of your flamingo. Shall I try the experiment?'

'He might bite,' Alice cautiously replied, not feeling at all anxious to have the experiment tried.

Very true,' said the Duchess: 'flamingoes and mustard both bite. And the moral of that is—"Birds of a feather flock together."'

9. Storia della Falsa Testuggine

— Non puoi immaginare la mia gioia nel rivederti, bambina mia! — disse la Duchessa infilando affettuosamente il braccio in quello di Alice, e camminando insieme.

Alice fu lieta di vederla di buon umore, e pensò che quando l'aveva vista in cucina era stato il pepe, forse, a renderla intrattabile.

"Quando sarò Duchessa, — si disse (ma senza soverchia speranza),

— non vorrò avere neppure un granello di pepe in cucina. La minestra è saporosa anche senza pepe. È il pepe, certo, che irrita tanta gente, continuò soddisfatta d'aver scoperta una specie di nuova teoria,

— l'aceto la inacidisce... la camomilla la fa amara... e i confetti e i pasticcini addolciscono il carattere dei bambini. Se tutti lo sapessero, non lesinerebbero tanto in fatto di dolci."

In quell'istante aveva quasi dimenticata la Duchessa, e sussultò quando si sentì dire all'orecchio:

— Tu pensi a qualche cosa ora, cara mia, e dimentichi di parlarmi. Ora non posso dirti la morale, ma me ne ricorderò fra breve.

— Forse non ne ha, — Alice si arrischiò di osservare.

— Zitta! zitta! bambina! — disse la Duchessa. — Ogni cosa ha la sua morale, se si sa trovarla - .E le si strinse più da presso.

Ad Alice non piaceva esserle così vicina; primo; perchè la Duchessa era bruttissima; secondo, perché era così alta che poggiava il mento sulle spalle d'Alice, un mento terribilmente aguzzo!

Ma non volle mostrarsi scortese, e sopportò quella noia con molta buona volontà.

— Il giuoco va meglio, ora, — disse per alimentare un po' la conversazione.

— Eh sì, — rispose la Duchessa, — e questa è la morale: "È l'amore, è l'amore che fa girare il mondo."

— Ma qualcheduno ha detto invece, — bisbigliò Alice, — se ognuno badasse a sè, il mondo andrebbe meglio.

— Bene! È lo stesso, — disse la Duchessa, conficcando il suo mento aguzzo nelle spalle d'Alice: — E la morale è questa: "Guardate al senso; le sillabe si guarderanno da sè."

("Come si diletta a trovare la morale in tutto!" pensò Alice.)

— Scommetto che sei sorpresa, perchè non ti cingo la vita col braccio, — disse la Duchessa dopo qualche istante, — ma si è perchè non so di che carattere sia il tuo fenicottero. Vogliamo far la prova?

— Potrebbe morderla, — rispose Alice, che non desiderava simili esperimenti.

— È vero, — disse la Duchessa, — i fenicotteri e la mostarda non fanno che mordere, e la morale è questa: "Gli uccelli della stessa razza se ne vanno insieme."

'Only mustard isn't a bird,' Alice remarked.

'Right, as usual,' said the Duchess: 'what a clear way you have of putting things!'

'It's a mineral, I think,' said Alice.

Of course it is,' said the Duchess, who seemed ready to agree to everything that Alice said; 'there's a large mustard-mine near here. And the moral of that is—"The more there is of mine, the less there is of yours."'

Oh, I know!' exclaimed Alice, who had not attended to this last remark: 'it's a vegetable. It doesn't look like one, but it is.'

I quite agree with you,' said the Duchess; 'and the moral of that is—"Be what you would seem to be"—or if you'd like it put more simply—

Never imagine yourself not to be otherwise than what it might appear to others that what you were or might have been was not otherwise than what you had been would have appeared to them to be otherwise.'

I think I should understand that better,' Alice said very politely: 'if I had it written down: but I can't quite follow it as you say it.'

'That's nothing to what I could say if I chose,' the Duchess replied, in a pleased tone.

'Pray don't trouble yourself to say it any longer than that,' said Alice.

'Oh, don't talk about trouble!' said the Duchess. 'I make you a present of everything I've said as yet.'

'A cheap sort of present!' thought Alice. 'I'm glad they don't give birthday presents like that!' But she did not venture to say it out loud.

'Thinking again?' the Duchess asked, with another dig of her sharp little chin.

'I've a right to think,' said Alice sharply, for she was beginning to feel a little worried.

Just about as much right,' said the Duchess: 'as pigs have to fly; and the m—'

But here, to Alice's great surprise, the Duchess's voice died away, even in the middle of her favourite word 'moral,' and the arm that was linked into hers began to tremble.

Alice looked up, and there stood the Queen in front of them, with her arms folded, frowning like a thunderstorm.

'A fine day, your Majesty!' the Duchess began in a low, weak voice.

'Now, I give you fair warning,' shouted the Queen, stamping on the ground as she spoke; 'either you or your head must be off, and that in about half no time! Take your choice!'

The Duchess took her choice, and was gone in a moment.

'Let's go on with the game,' the Queen said to Alice; and Alice was too much frightened to say a word, but slowly followed her back to the croquet-ground.

The other guests had taken advantage of the Queen's absence, and were resting in the shade: however, the moment they saw her, they hurried back to the game, the Queen merely remarking that a moment's delay would cost them their lives.

All the time they were playing the Queen never left off quarrelling with the other players, and shouting 'Off with his head!' or 'Off with her head!'

— Ma la mostarda non è un uccello, — osservò Alice.

— Bene, come sempre, disse la Duchessa, — tu dici le cose con molta chiarezza!

— È un minerale, credo, — disse Alice.

— Già, — rispose la Duchessa, che pareva accettasse tutto quello che diceva Alice; — in questi dintorni c'è una miniera di mostarda e la morale è questa: "La miniera è la maniera di gabbar la gente intera."

— Oh lo so! — esclamò Alice, che non aveva badato a queste parole; — è un vegetale, benchè non sembri.

— Proprio così, — disse la Duchessa, — e la morale è questa: "Sii ciò che vuoi parere" o, se vuoi che te la dica più semplicemente:

"Non credere mai d'essere diversa da quella che appari agli altri di esser o d'esser stata, o che tu possa essere, e l'essere non è altro che l'essere di quell'essere ch'è l'essere dell'essere, e non diversamente."

— Credo che la intenderei meglio, — disse Alice con molto garbo, — se me la scrivesse; non posso seguir con la mente ciò che dice.

— Questo è nulla rimpetto a quel che potrei dire, se ne avessi voglia, — soggiunse la Duchessa.

— Non s'incomodi a dire qualche altra cosa più lunga, — disse Alice.

— Non mi parlar d'incomodo! — rispose la Duchessa. — Ti faccio un regalo di ciò che ho detto finora.

"Un regalo che non costa nulla, — pensò Alice; — meno male che negli onomastici e nei genetliaci non si fanno regali simili". — Ma non osò dirlo a voce alta.

— Sempre pensosa? — domandò la Duchessa, dando alla spalla della bambina un altro colpo del suo mento acuminato.

— N'ho ben ragione! — rispose vivamente Alice, perchè cominciava a sentirsi un po' seccata.

E la Duchessa: — La stessa ragione che hanno i porci di volare: e la mora...

A questo punto, con gran sorpresa d'Alice, la voce della Duchessa andò morendo e si spense in mezzo alla sua favorita parola: morale. Il braccio che era in quello d'Alice cominciò a tremare.

Alice alzò gli occhi, e vide la Regina ritta di fronte a loro due, le braccia conserte, le ciglia aggrottate, come un uragano.

— Maestà che bella giornata! — balbettò la Duchessa con voce bassa e fioca.

Vi avverto a tempo, — gridò la Regina, pestando il suolo; — o voi o la vostra testa dovranno andarsene immediatamente! Scegliete!

La Duchessa scelse e in un attimo sparì.

— Ritorniamo al giuoco, — disse la Regina ad Alice; ma Alice era troppo atterrita, e non rispose sillaba, seguendola lentamente sul terreno.

Gl'invitati intanto, profittando dell'assenza della Regina, si riposavano all'ombra: però appena la videro ricomparire, tornarono ai loro posti; la Regina accennò soltanto che se avessero ritardato un momento solo, avrebbero perduta la vita.

Mentre giocavano, la Regina continuava a querelarsi con gli altri giocatori, gridando sempre: — Tagliategli la testa! — oppure: — Tagliatele la testa! —

Those whom she sentenced were taken into custody by the soldiers, who of course had to leave off being arches to do this, so that by the end of half an hour or so there were no arches left, and all the players, except the King, the Queen, and Alice, were in custody and under sentence of execution.

Then the Queen left off, quite out of breath, and said to Alice: 'Have you seen the Mock Turtle yet?'

'No,' said Alice. 'I don't even know what a Mock Turtle is.'

'It's the thing Mock Turtle Soup is made from,' said the Queen.

I never saw one, or heard of one,' said Alice. 'Come on, then,' said the Queen: 'and he shall tell you his history,'

As they walked off together, Alice heard the King say in a low voice, to the company generally:

'You are all pardoned.' 'Come, that's a good thing!' she said to herself, for she had felt quite unhappy at the number of executions the Queen had ordered.

They very soon came upon a Gryphon, lying fast asleep in the sun. (If you don't know what a Gryphon is, look at the picture.)

'Up, lazy thing!' said the Queen: 'and take this young lady to see the Mock Turtle, and to hear his history. I must go back and see after some executions I have ordered'; and she walked off, leaving Alice alone with the Gryphon.

Alice did not quite like the look of the creature, but on the whole she thought it would be quite as safe to stay with it as to go after that savage Queen: so she waited.

The Gryphon sat up and rubbed its eyes: then it watched the Queen till she was out of sight: then it chuckled. 'What fun!' said the Gryphon, half to itself, half to Alice.

'What is the fun?' said Alice.

'Why, she,' said the Gryphon. 'It's all her fancy, that: they never executes nobody, you know. Come on!'

'Everybody says "come on!" here,' thought Alice, as she went slowly after it: 'I never was so ordered about in all my life, never!'

They had not gone far before they saw the Mock Turtle in the distance, sitting sad and lonely on a little ledge of rock, and, as they came nearer, Alice could hear him sighing as if his heart would break. She pitied him deeply.

'What is his sorrow?' she asked the Gryphon, and the Gryphon answered, very nearly in the same words as before:

'It's all his fancy, that: he hasn't got no sorrow, you know. Come on!'

So they went up to the Mock Turtle, who looked at them with large eyes full of tears, but said nothing.

This here young lady,' said the Gryphon: 'she wants for to know your history, she do.'

'I'll tell it her,' said the Mock Turtle in a deep, hollow tone: 'sit down, both of you, and don't speak a word till I've finished.'

So they sat down, and nobody spoke for some minutes. Alice thought to herself: 'I don't see how he can even finish, if he doesn't begin.' But she waited patiently.

Coloro ch'erano condannati a morte erano arrestati da soldati che dovevano servire d'archi al gioco, e così in meno di mezz'ora, non c'erano più archi, e tutti i giocatori, eccettuati il Re, la Regina e Alice, erano in arresto e condannati nel capo.

Finalmente la Regina lasciò il giuoco, senza più fiato, e disse ad Alice: — Non hai veduto ancora la Falsa-testuggine?

— No, — disse Alice. — Non so neppure che sia la Falsa-testuggine.

— È quella con cui si fa la minestra di Falsa-testuggine, — disse la Regina.

— Non ne ho mai veduto, nè udito parlare, — soggiunse Alice. — Vieni dunque, — disse la Regina, ed essa ti racconterà la sua storia.

Mentre andavano insieme, Alice sentì che il Re diceva a voce bassa a tutti i condannati:

— Faccio grazia a tutti. — Oh come sono contenta! — disse fra sè Alice, perchè era afflittissima per tutte quelle condanne ordinate dalla Regina.

Tosto arrivarono presso un Grifone sdraiato e addormentato al sole. (Se voi non sapete che sia un Grifone, guardate la figura.)

— Su, su, pigro! — disse la Regina, — conducete questa bambina a vedere la Falsa-testuggine che le narrerà la sua storia. Io debbo tornare indietro per assistere alle esecuzioni che ho ordinate. — E andò via lasciando Alice sola col Grifone.

Non piacque ad Alice l'aspetto della bestia, ma poi riflettendo che, dopo tutto, rimaner col Grifone era più sicuro che star con quella feroce Regina, rimase in attesa.

Il Grifone si levò, si sfregò gli occhi, aspettò che la Regina sparisse interamente e poi si mise a ghignare: — Che commedia! — disse il Grifone, parlando un po' per sè, un po' per Alice.

— Quale commedia? — domandò Alice.

— Quella della Regina, — soggiunse il Grifone. — È una sua mania, ma a nessuno viene tagliata la testa, mai. Vieni!

— Qui tutti mi dicono: "Vieni!" — osservò Alice, seguendolo lentamente. — Non sono mai stata comandata così in tutta la mia vita!

Non s'erano allontanati di molto che scorsero in distanza la Falsa-testuggine, seduta malinconicamente sull'orlo d'una rupe. Avvicinatisi un po' più, Alice la sentì sospirare come se le si rompesse il cuore. N'ebbe compassione.

— Che ha? — domandò al Grifone, e il Grifone rispose quasi con le stesse parole di prima: — È una mania che l'ha presa, ma non ha nulla. Vieni!

E andarono verso la Falsa-testuggine, che li guardò con certi occhioni pieni di lacrime, ma senza far motto.

— Questa bambina, — disse il Grifone, — vorrebbe sentire la tua storia, vorrebbe.

— Gliela dirò, — rispose la Falsa-testuggine, con voce profonda. — Sedete, e non dite sillaba, prima che io termini.

E sedettero e per qualche minuto nessuno parlò. Alice intanto osservò fra sè: "Come potrà mai finire se non comincia mai?" Ma aspettò pazientemente.

Once,' said the Mock Turtle at last, with a deep sigh: 'I was a real Turtle.'

These words were followed by a very long silence, broken only by an occasional exclamation of 'Hjckrrh!' from the Gryphon, and the constant heavy sobbing of the Mock Turtle.

Alice was very nearly getting up and saying: 'Thank you, sir, for your interesting story,' but she could not help thinking there must be more to come, so she sat still and said nothing.

When we were little,' the Mock Turtle went on at last, more calmly, though still sobbing a little now and then: 'we went to school in the sea. The master was an old Turtle—we used to call him Tortoise—'

'Why did you call him Tortoise, if he wasn't one?' Alice asked. 'We called him Tortoise because he taught us,' said the Mock Turtle angrily: 'really you are very dull!'

You ought to be ashamed of yourself for asking such a simple question,' added the Gryphon; and then they both sat silent and looked at poor Alice, who felt ready to sink into the earth.

At last the Gryphon said to the Mock Turtle: 'Drive on, old fellow! Don't be all day about it!' and he went on in these words:

Yes, we went to school in the sea, though you mayn't believe it—'

'I never said I didn't!' interrupted Alice.

'You did,' said the Mock Turtle.

'Hold your tongue!' added the Gryphon, before Alice could speak again. The Mock Turtle went on.

We had the best of educations—in fact, we went to school every day—'

'I've been to a day-school, too,' said Alice; 'you needn't be so proud as all that.'

'With extras?' asked the Mock Turtle a little anxiously.

Yes,' said Alice: 'we learned French and music.'

'And washing?' said the Mock Turtle.

'Certainly not!' said Alice indignantly.

Ah! then yours wasn't a really good school,' said the Mock Turtle in a tone of great relief. 'Now at ours they had at the end of the bill, "French, music, and washing—extra."'

'You couldn't have wanted it much,' said Alice; 'living at the bottom of the sea.'

'I couldn't afford to learn it.' said the Mock Turtle with a sigh. 'I only took the regular course.'

'What was that?' inquired Alice.

Reeling and Writhing, of course, to begin with,' the Mock Turtle replied; 'and then the different branches of Arithmetic— Ambition, Distraction, Uglification, and Derision.'

'I never heard of "Uglification,"' Alice ventured to say. 'What is it?'

— Una volta, — disse finalmente la Falsa-testuggine con un gran sospiro, — io ero una testuggine vera.

Quelle parole furono seguite da un lungo silenzio, interrotto da qualche "Hjckrrh!" del Grifone e da continui e grossi singhiozzi della Falsa-testuggine.

Alice stava per levarsi e dirle: — Grazie della vostra storia interessante, — quando pensò che ci doveva essere qualche altra cosa, e sedette tranquillamente senza dir nulla.

— Quando eravamo piccini, — riprese finalmente la Falsa-testuggine, un po' più tranquilla, ma sempre singhiozzando di quando in quando, — andavamo a scuola al mare. La maestra era una vecchia testuggine... — e noi la chiamavamo tartarug...

— Perchè la chiamavate tartaruga se non era tale? — domandò Alice. — La chiamavamo tartaruga, perchè c'insegnava, — disse la Falsa-testuggine con dispetto: Hai poco sale in zucca!

— Ti dovresti vergognare di fare domande così semplici, — aggiunse il Grifone; e poi tacquero ed entrambi fissarono gli occhi sulla povera Alice che avrebbe preferito sprofondare sotterra.

Finalmente il Grifone disse alla Falsa-testuggine: — Va innanzi, cara mia! e non ti dilungare tanto! E così la Falsa-testuggine continuò:

— Andavamo a scuola al mare, benchè tu non lo creda...

— Non ho mai detto questo! — interruppe Alice.

— Sì che l'hai detto, — disse la Falsa-testuggine .

— Zitta! — soggiunse il Grifone, prima che. Alice potesse rispondere. La Falsa-testuggine continuò:

— Noi fummo educate benissimo... infatti andavamo a scuola tutti i giorni...

Anch'io andavo a scuola ogni giorno, — disse Alice; — non serve inorgoglirsi per così poco.

— E avevate dei corsi facoltativi? — domandò la Falsa-testuggine con ansietà.

— Sì, — rispose Alice; — imparavamo il francese e la musica.

— E il bucato? — disse la Falsa-testuggine.

— No, il bucato, no, — disse Alice indignata.

— Ah! e allora che scuola era? — disse la Falsa-testuggine, come se si sentisse sollevata. — Nella nostra, c'era nella fine del programma: Corsi facoltativi: francese, musica, e bucato.

— E vivendo in fondo al mare, — disse Alice, — a che vi serviva?

— Non ebbi mai il mezzo per impararlo, — soggiunse sospirando la Falsa-testuggine; — così seguii soltanto i corsi ordinari.

— Ed erano? — domandò Alice.

— Annaspare e contorcersi, prima di tutto, — rispose la Falsa-testuggine. — E poi le diverse operazioni dell'aritmetica... ambizione, distrazione, bruttificazione, e derisione.

— Non ho mai sentito parlare della bruttificazione, — disse Alice. — Che cos'è?

The Gryphon lifted up both its paws in surprise. 'What! Never heard of uglifying!' it exclaimed. 'You know what to beautify is, I suppose?'

Yes,' said Alice doubtfully: 'it means—to—make—anything—prettier.'

Well, then,' the Gryphon went on: 'if you don't know what to uglify is, you are a simpleton.'

Alice did not feel encouraged to ask any more questions about it, so she turned to the Mock Turtle, and said 'What else had you to learn?'

Well, there was Mystery,' the Mock Turtle replied, counting off the subjects on his flappers: '—Mystery, ancient and modern, with Seaography: then Drawling—the Drawling-master was an old conger-eel, that used to come once a week: He taught us Drawling, Stretching, and Fainting in Coils.'

'What was that like?' said Alice.

'Well, I can't show it you myself,' the Mock Turtle said: 'I'm too stiff. And the Gryphon never learnt it.'

Hadn't time,' said the Gryphon: 'I went to the Classics master, though. He was an old crab, he was.'

'I never went to him,' the Mock Turtle said with a sigh: 'he taught Laughing and Grief, they used to say.'

'So he did, so he did,' said the Gryphon, sighing in his turn; and both creatures hid their faces in their paws.

And how many hours a day did you do lessons?' said Alice, in a hurry to change the subject.

'Ten hours the first day,' said the Mock Turtle: 'nine the next, and so on.'

'What a curious plan!' exclaimed Alice.

'That's the reason they're called lessons,' the Gryphon remarked: 'because they lessen from day to day.'

This was quite a new idea to Alice, and she thought it over a little before she made her next remark. 'Then the eleventh day must have been a holiday?'

'Of course it was,' said the Mock Turtle.

'And how did you manage on the twelfth?' Alice went on eagerly.

'That's enough about lessons,' the Gryphon interrupted in a very decided tone: 'tell her something about the games now.'

Il Grifone levò le due zampe in segno di sorpresa ed esclamò: — Mai sentito parlare di bruttificazione! Ma sai che significhi bellificazione, spero.

— Sì, — rispose Alice, ma un po' incerta: — significa... rendere... qualche cosa... più bella.

Ebbene, — continua il Grifone, — se non sai che significa bruttificazione mi par che ti manchi il comprendonio.

Alice non si sentiva incoraggiata a fare altre domande. Così si volse alla Falsa-testuggine e disse: — Che altro dovevate imparare?

— C'era il mistero, rispose la Falsa-testuggine, contando i soggetti sulle natatoie... — il mistero antico e moderno con la marografia: poi il disdegno... il maestro di disdegno era un vecchio grongo, e veniva una volta la settimana: c'insegnava il disdegno, il passaggio, e la frittura ad occhio.

— E che era? — disse Alice.

— Non te la potrei mostrare, — rispose la Falsa-testuggine, — perchè vedi son tutta d'un pezzo. E il Grifone non l'ha mai imparata.

— Non ebbi tempo, — rispose il Grifone: ma studiai le lingue classiche e bene. Ebbi per maestro un vecchio granchio, sapete.

— Non andai mai da lui, — disse la Falsa-testuggine con un sospiro: — dicevano che insegnasse Catino e Gretto.

— Proprio così, — disse il Grifone, sospirando anche lui, ed entrambe le bestie si nascosero la faccia tra le zampe.

— Quante ore di lezione al giorno avevate? — disse prontamente Alice per cambiar discorso.

— Dieci ore il primo giorno, — rispose la Falsa-testuggine: — nove il secondo, e così di seguito.

— Che strano metodo! — esclamò Alice.

— Ma è questa la ragione perchè si chiamano lezioni, — osservò il Grifone: — perchè c'è una lesione ogni giorno.

— Era nuovo per Alice, e ci pensò su un poco, prima di fare questa osservazione: — Allora l'undecimo giorno era vacanza?

— Naturalmente, — disse la Falsa-testuggine.

— E che si faceva il dodicesimo? — domandò vivamente Alice.

— Basta in quanto alle lezioni: dille ora qualche cosa dei giuochi, — interruppe il Grifone, in tono molto risoluto.

10. The Lobster's Quadrille

The Mock Turtle sighed deeply, and drew the back of one flapper across his eyes. He looked at Alice, and tried to speak, but for a minute or two sobs choked his voice. Same as if he had a bone in his throat,' said the Gryphon: and it set to work shaking him and punching him in the back.

At last the Mock Turtle recovered his voice, and, with tears running down his cheeks, he went on again:—

You may not have lived much under the sea—' ('I haven't,' said Alice)— 'and perhaps you were never even introduced to a lobster—' (Alice began to say 'I once tasted—' but checked herself hastily, and said 'No, never')

—so you can have no idea what a delightful thing a Lobster Quadrille is!'

'No, indeed,' said Alice. 'What sort of a dance is it?'

Why,' said the Gryphon: 'you first form into a line along the sea-shore—'

Two lines!' cried the Mock Turtle. 'Seals, turtles, salmon, and so on; then, when you've cleared all the jelly-fish out of the way—'

'That generally takes some time,' interrupted the Gryphon.

—you advance twice—'

'Each with a lobster as a partner!' cried the Gryphon.

Of course,' the Mock Turtle said: 'advance twice, set to partners—' '—change lobsters, and retire in same order,' continued the Gryphon.

Then, you know,' the Mock Turtle went on: 'you throw the—'

'The lobsters!' shouted the Gryphon, with a bound into the air.

—as far out to sea as you can—'

'Swim after them!' screamed the Gryphon.

'Turn a somersault in the sea!' cried the Mock Turtle, capering wildly about.

'Change lobster's again!' yelled the Gryphon at the top of its voice.

'Back to land again, and that's all the first figure,' said the Mock Turtle, suddenly dropping his voice; and the two creatures, who had been jumping about like mad things all this time, sat down again very sadly and quietly, and looked at Alice.

'It must be a very pretty dance,' said Alice timidly.

'Would you like to see a little of it?' said the Mock Turtle.

'Very much indeed,' said Alice.

'Come, let's try the first figure!' said the Mock Turtle to the Gryphon. 'We can do without lobsters, you know. Which shall sing?'

10. Il Ballo dei Gamberi

La Falsa-testuggine cacciò un gran sospiro e si passò il rovescio d'una natatoia sugli occhi. Guardò Alice, e cercò di parlare, ma per qualche istante ne fu impedita dai singhiozzi.
— Come se avesse un osso in gola, — disse il Grifone, e si mise a scuoterla e a batterle la schiena.

Finalmente la Falsa-testuggine ricuperò la voce e con le lacrime che le solcavano le gote, riprese:
— Forse tu non sei vissuta a lungo sott'acqua... (— Certo che no, — disse Alice) — e forse non sei mai stata presentata a un gambero... (Alice stava per dire: — Una volta assaggiai...
— ma troncò la frase e disse: — No mai):
— così tu non puoi farti un'idea della bellezza d'un ballo di gamberi?
— No, davvero, — rispose Alice. — Ma che è mai un ballo di gamberi?
— Ecco, — disse il Grifone, — prima di tutto si forma una linea lungo la spiaggia...
— Due! — gridò la Falsa-testuggine. — Foche, testuggini di mare, salmoni e simili: poi quando si son tolti dalla spiaggia i polipi...
— E generalmente così facendo si perde del tempo, — interruppe il Grifone.
— ...si fa un avant-deux.

— Ciascuno con un gambero per cavaliere, — gridò il Grifone.
— Eh già! — disse la Falsa-testuggine: — si fa un avant-deux, e poi un balancé... — Si scambiano i gamberi e si ritorna en place, — continuò il Grifone.
— E poi capisci? — continuò la Falsa-testuggine, — si scaraventano i...
— I gamberi! — urlo il Grifone, saltando come un matto.

...nel mare, più lontano che si può...
— Quindi si nuota dietro di loro! — strillò il Grifone.
— Si fa capitombolo in mare! — gridò la Falsa-testuggine, saltellando pazzamente qua e la.
— Si scambiano di nuovo i gamberi! — Vociò il Grifone.

— Si ritorna di nuovo a terra, e... e questa è la prima figura, — disse la Falsa-testuggine, abbassando di nuovo la voce. E le due bestie che poco prima saltavano come matte, si accosciarono malinconicamente e guardarono Alice.

— Vuoi vederne un saggio? — domandò la Falsa-testuggine.

— Mi piacerebbe molto, — disse Alice.

— Coraggio, proviamo la prima figura! disse la Falsa-testuggine al Grifone. — Possiamo farla senza gamberi. Chi canta?

'Oh, you sing,' said the Gryphon. 'I've forgotten the words.'

So they began solemnly dancing round and round Alice, every now and then treading on her toes when they passed too close, and waving their forepaws to mark the time, while the Mock Turtle sang this, very slowly and sadly:
— "'Will you walk a little faster?" said a whiting to a snail.
"There's a porpoise close behind us, and he's treading on my tail.
See how eagerly the lobsters and the turtles all advance! They are waiting on the shingle—
will you come and join the dance? Will you, won't you, will you, won't you, will you join the dance? Will you, won't you, will you, won't you, won't you join the dance? "You can really have no notion how delightful it will be When they take us up and throw us, with the lobsters, out to sea!"
But the snail replied "Too far, too far!" and gave a look askance— Said he thanked the whiting kindly, but he would not join the dance. Would not, could not, would not, could not, would not join the dance. Would not, could not, would not, could not, could not join the dance.
'Thank you, it's a very interesting dance to watch,' said Alice, feeling very glad that it was over at last: 'and I do so like that curious song about the whiting!'
Oh, as to the whiting,' said the Mock Turtle: 'they—you've seen them, of course?'
Yes,' said Alice: 'I've often seen them at dinn—' she checked herself hastily.
I don't know where Dinn may be,' said the Mock Turtle: 'but if you've seen them so often, of course you know what they're like.'
I believe so,' Alice replied thoughtfully. 'They have their tails in their mouths—and they're all over crumbs.'
You're wrong about the crumbs,' said the Mock Turtle: 'crumbs would all wash off in the sea. But they have their tails in their mouths; and the reason is—' here the Mock Turtle yawned and shut his eyes.—'Tell her about the reason and all that,' he said to the Gryphon.
The reason is,' said the Gryphon: 'that they would go with the lobsters to the dance. So they got thrown out to sea. So they had to fall a long way. So they got their tails fast in their mouths. So they couldn't get them out again. That's all.'

Thank you,' said Alice: 'it's very interesting. I never knew so much about a whiting before.'
And the Gryphon added 'Come, let's hear some of your adventures.'
I could tell you my adventures—beginning from this morning,' said Alice a little timidly: 'but it's no use going back to yesterday, because I was a different person then.'
'Explain all that,' said the Mock Turtle.

'No, no! The adventures first,' said the Gryphon in an impatient tone: 'explanations take such a dreadful time.'
So Alice began telling them her adventures from the time when she first saw the White Rabbit.
She was a little nervous about it just at first, the two creatures got so close to her, one on each side, and opened their eyes and mouths so very wide, but she gained courage as she went on.

— Canta tu, — disse il Grifone. — Io ho dimenticate le parole.
E cominciarono a ballare solennemente intorno ad Alice, pestandole i piedi di quando in quando, e agitando le zampe anteriori per battere il tempo. La Falsa-testuggine cantava adagio adagio malinconicamente:
Alla chiocciola il nasello: "Su, dicea, cammina presto; mi vien dietro un cavalluccio — che uno stinco m'ha già pesto:

vedi quante mai testuggini — qui s'accalcan per ballare!"

Presto vuoi, non vuoi danzare? Presto vuoi, non vuoi danzare? "Tu non sai quant'è squisita — come è dolce questa danza quando in mar ci scaraventano — senza un'ombra di esitanza!"

Ma la chiocciola rispose: — "Grazie, caro, è assai lontano, e arrivar colà non posso — camminando così piano." Non potea, volea danzare! Non potea, volea danzare!

— Grazie, è un bel ballo, — disse Alice, lieta che fosse finito; — e poi quel canto curioso del nasello mi piace tanto!

— A proposito di naselli, — disse la Falsa-testuggine, — ne hai veduti, naturalmente?
— Sì, — disse Alice, — li ho veduti spesso a tavo... — E si mangiò il resto.
— Non so dove sia Tavo, — disse la Falsa-testuggine — ma se li hai veduti spesso, sai che cosa sono.

— Altro! — rispose Alice meditabonda, — hanno la coda in bocca e sono mollicati.
— Ma che molliche! — soggiunse la Falsa-testuggine, — le molliche sarebbero spazzate dal mare. Però hanno la coda in bocca; e la ragione è questa... E a questo la Falsa-testuggine sbadigliò e chiuse gli occhi. — Digliela tu la ragione, — disse al Grifone.
— La ragione è la seguente, — disse il Grifone. — Essi vollero andare al ballo; e poi furono buttati in mare; e poi fecero il capitombolo molto al di là, poi tennero stretta la coda fra i denti; e poi non poterono distaccarsela più; e questo è tutto.
— Grazie, — disse Alice, — molto interessante. Non ne seppi mai tanto dei naselli.
— Presto facci un racconto delle tue avventure, — disse il Grifone.
— Ne potrei raccontare cominciando da stamattina, — disse timidamente Alice; — ma è inutile raccontarvi quelle di ieri, perchè... ieri io ero un altra.
— Come un'altra? Spiegaci, — disse la Falsa-testuggine.

— No, no! prima le avventure, — esclamò il Grifone impaziente; — le spiegazioni occupano tanto tempo.
Così Alice cominciò a raccontare i suoi casi, dal momento dell'incontro col Coniglio bianco;
ma tosto si cominciò a sentire un po' a disagio, chè le due bestie le si stringevano da un lato e l'altro, spalancando gli occhi e le bocche; ma la bambina poco dopo riprese coraggio.

Her listeners were perfectly quiet till she got to the part about her repeating 'You are old, Father William,' to the Caterpillar, and the words all coming different, and then the Mock Turtle drew a long breath, and said 'That's very curious.'

'It's all about as curious as it can be,' said the Gryphon.

'It all came different!' the Mock Turtle repeated thoughtfully. 'I should like to hear her try and repeat something now. Tell her to begin.' He looked at the Gryphon as if he thought it had some kind of authority over Alice.

'Stand up and repeat "'Tis the voice of the sluggard,"' said the Gryphon.

How the creatures order one about, and make one repeat lessons!' thought Alice; 'I might as well be at school at once.'

However, she got up, and began to repeat it, but her head was so full of the Lobster Quadrille, that she hardly knew what she was saying, and the words came very queer indeed:—

"Tis the voice of the Lobster; I heard him declare,

"You have baked me too brown, I must sugar my hair."

As a duck with its eyelids, so he with his nose Trims his belt and his buttons, and turns out his toes.'

'That's different from what I used to say when I was a child,' said the Gryphon.

'Well, I never heard it before,' said the Mock Turtle; 'but it sounds uncommon nonsense.'

Alice said nothing; she had sat down with her face in her hands, wondering if anything would ever happen in a natural way again.

'I should like to have it explained,' said the Mock Turtle.

'She can't explain it,' said the Gryphon hastily. 'Go on with the next verse.'

'But about his toes?' the Mock Turtle persisted. 'How could he turn them out with his nose, you know?'

'It's the first position in dancing.' Alice said; but was dreadfully puzzled by the whole thing, and longed to change the subject.

'Go on with the next verse,' the Gryphon repeated impatiently: 'it begins "I passed by his garden."'

Alice did not dare to disobey, though she felt sure it would all come wrong, and she went on in a trembling voice:—

I passed by his garden, and marked, with one eye, How the Owl and the Panther were sharing a pie—'

What is the use of repeating all that stuff,' the Mock Turtle interrupted: 'if you don't explain it as you go on? It's by far the most confusing thing I ever heard!'

'Yes, I think you'd better leave off,' said the Gryphon: and Alice was only too glad to do so.

'Shall we try another figure of the Lobster Quadrille?' the Gryphon went on. 'Or would you like the Mock Turtle to sing you a song?'

Oh, a song, please, if the Mock Turtle would be so kind,' Alice replied, so eagerly that the Gryphon said, in a rather offended tone: 'Hm! No accounting for tastes! Sing her "Turtle Soup," will you, old fellow?'

The Mock Turtle sighed deeply, and began, in a voice sometimes choked with sobs, to sing this:—

I suoi uditori si mantennero tranquilli sino a che ella giunse alla ripetizione del "Sei vecchio, caro babbo", da lei fatta al Bruco. Siccome le parole le venivano diverse dal vero originale, la Falsa-testuggine cacciò un gran sospiro, e disse:

— È molto curioso!

— È più curioso che mai! — esclamò il Grifone.

— È scaturito assolutamente diverso! — soggiunse la Falsa-testuggine, meditabonda. — Vorrei che ella ci recitasse qualche cosa ora. Dille di cominciare. E guardò il Grifone, pensando ch'egli avesse qualche specie d'autorità su Alice.

— Levati in piedi, — disse il Grifone, — e ripetici la canzone: "Trenta quaranta..."

— Oh come queste bestie danno degli ordini, e fanno recitar le lezioni! — pensò Alice; — sarebbe meglio andare a scuola subito!

A ogni modo, si levò, e cominciò a ripetere la canzone; ma la sua testolina era così piena di gamberi e di balli, che non sapeva che si dicesse, e i versi le venivano male:

"Son trenta e son quaranta," — il gambero già canta,

"M'ha troppo abbrustolito — mi voglio inzuccherare,

In faccia a questo specchio — mi voglio spazzolare, E voglio rivoltare — e piedi e naso in su!"

— Ma questo è tutto diverso da quello che recitavo da bambino, — disse il Grifone.

— È la prima volta che lo sento, — osservò la Falsa-testuggine; — ed è una vera sciocchezza!

Alice non rispose: se ne stava con la faccia tra le mani, sperando che le cose tornassero finalmente al loro corso naturale.

— Vorrei che me lo spiegassi, — disse la Falsa-testuggine.

— Non sa spiegarlo, — disse il Grifone; — comincia la seconda strofa.

— A proposito di piedi, — continuò la Falsa-testuggine, — come poteva rivoltarli, e col naso, per giunta?

— È la prima posizione nel ballo, — disse Alice; ma era tanto confusa che non vedeva l'ora di mutar discorso.

— Continua la seconda strofa, — replicò il Grifone con impazienza; — comincia: "Bianca la sera."

Alice non osò disubbidire, benchè sicura che l'avrebbe recitata tutt'al rovescio, e continuò tremante:

"Al nereggiar dell'alba — nel lor giardino, in fretta, tagliavano un pasticcio — l'ostrica e la civetta."

— Perchè recitarci tutta questa robaccia? interruppe la Falsa-testuggine; — se non ce la spieghi? Fai tanta confusione!

— Sì, sarebbe meglio smettere, — disse il Grifone. E Alice fu più che lieta di terminare.

— Vogliamo provare un'altra figura del ballo dei gamberi? — continuò il Grifone. — O preferiresti invece che la Falsa-testuggine cantasse lei?

— Oh, sì, se la Falsa-testuggine vorrà cantare! — rispose Alice; ma con tanta premura, che il Grifone offeso gridò: — Ah tutti i gusti sono gusti. Amica, cantaci la canzone della "Zuppa di testuggine."

La Falsa-testuggine sospirò profondamente, e con voce soffocata dai singhiozzi cantò così:

Beautiful Soup, so rich and green, Waiting in a hot tureen! Who for such dainties would not stoop? Soup of the evening, beautiful Soup! Soup of the evening, beautiful Soup! Beau—ootiful Soo—oop! Beau—ootiful Soo—oop! Soo—oop of the e—e—evening, Beautiful, beautiful Soup!

'Beautiful Soup! Who cares for fish, Game, or any other dish? Who would not give all else for two pennyworth only of beautiful Soup? Pennyworth only of beautiful Soup? Beau—ootiful Soo—oop! Beau—ootiful Soo—oop! Soo—oop of the e—e—evening, Beautiful, beauti—FUL SOUP!'

'Chorus again!' cried the Gryphon, and the Mock Turtle had just begun to repeat it, when a cry of 'The trial's beginning!' was heard in the distance.

'Come on!' cried the Gryphon, and, taking Alice by the hand, it hurried off, without waiting for the end of the song.

What trial is it?' Alice panted as she ran; but the Gryphon only answered 'Come on!' and ran the faster, while more and more faintly came, carried on the breeze that followed them, the melancholy words:—

Soo—oop of the e—e—evening, Beautiful, beautiful Soup!'

Bella zuppa così verde in attesa dentro il tondo chi ti vede e non si perde nel piacere più profondo? Zuppa cara, bella zuppa, zuppa cara, bella zuppa, bella zuppa, bella zuppa, zuppa cara, bella bella bella zuppa! Bella zuppa, chi è il meschino che vuol pesce, caccia od altro? Sol di zuppa un cucchiaino preferir usa chi è scaltro. Solo un cucchiain di zuppa, cara zuppa, bella zuppa, cara zuppa, bella zuppa, zuppa cara, bella bella bella zuppa! —

Ancora il coro! — gridò il Grifone. E la Falsa-testuggine si preparava a ripeterlo, quando si udì una voce in distanza: — Si comincia il processo!

— Vieni, vieni! — gridò il Grifone, prendendo Alice per mano, e fuggiva con lei senza aspettare la fine.

— Che processo? — domandò Alice; ma il Grifone le rispose: — Vieni! — e fuggiva più veloce, mentre il vento portava più flebili le melanconiche parole:

Zuppa cara, bella bella bella zuppa!

11. Who Stole the Tarts?

The King and Queen of Hearts were seated on their throne when they arrived, with a great crowd assembled about them—all sorts of little birds and beasts, as well as the whole pack of cards:

the Knave was standing before them, in chains, with a soldier on each side to guard him; and near the King was the White Rabbit, with a trumpet in one hand, and a scroll of parchment in the other.

In the very middle of the court was a table, with a large dish of tarts upon it: they looked so good, that it made Alice quite hungry to look at them—'I wish they'd get the trial done,' she thought: 'and hand round the refreshments!'

But there seemed to be no chance of this, so she began looking at everything about her, to pass away the time.

Alice had never been in a court of justice before, but she had read about them in books, and she was quite pleased to find that she knew the name of nearly everything there.

'That's the judge,' she said to herself: 'because of his great wig.'

The judge, by the way, was the King; and as he wore his crown over the wig, (look at the frontispiece if you want to see how he did it,) he did not look at all comfortable, and it was certainly not becoming.

And that's the jury-box,' thought Alice: 'and those twelve creatures,' (she was obliged to say 'creatures,' you see, because some of them were animals, and some were birds,) 'I suppose they are the jurors.'

She said this last word two or three times over to herself, being rather proud of it: for she thought, and rightly too, that very few little girls of her age knew the meaning of it at all. However: 'jury-men' would have done just as well.

The twelve jurors were all writing very busily on slates. 'What are they doing?' Alice whispered to the Gryphon. 'They can't have anything to put down yet, before the trial's begun.'

They're putting down their names,' the Gryphon whispered in reply: 'for fear they should forget them before the end of the trial.'

Stupid things!' Alice began in a loud, indignant voice, but she stopped hastily, for the White Rabbit cried out: 'Silence in the court!' and the King put on his spectacles and looked anxiously round, to make out who was talking.

Alice could see, as well as if she were looking over their shoulders, that all the jurors were writing down 'stupid things!' on their slates, and she could even make out that one of them didn't know how to spell 'stupid,' and that he had to ask his neighbour to tell him.

'A nice muddle their slates'll be in before the trial's over!' thought Alice.

One of the jurors had a pencil that squeaked. This of course, Alice could not stand, and she went round the court and got

11. Chi Ha Rubato le Torte?

Arrivati, videro il Re e la Regina di cuori seduti in trono, circondati da una gran folla di uccellini, di bestioline e da tutto il mazzo di carte:

il Fante stava davanti, incatenato, con un soldato da un lato e l'altro: accanto al Re stava il Coniglio bianco con una tromba nella destra e un rotolo di pergamena nella sinistra.

Nel mezzo della corte c'era un tavolo, con un gran piatto di torte d'apparenza così squisita che ad Alice venne l'acquolina in bocca. "Vorrei che si finisse presto il processo, — pensò Alice, — e che si servissero le torte!"

Ma nessuno si muoveva intanto, ed ella cominciò a guardare intorno per ammazzare il tempo.

Alice non aveva mai visto un tribunale, ma ne aveva letto qualche cosa nei libri, e fu lieta di riconoscere tutti quelli che vedeva.

"Quello è il giudice, — disse fra sè, — perchè porta quel gran parruccone.

(text not in original translation)

— E quello è il banco dei giurati, — osservò Alice, — e quelle dodici creature, — doveva dire "creature", perchè alcune erano quadrupedi, ed altre uccelli, — sono sicuramente i giurati."

E ripetè queste parole due o tre volte, superba della sua scienza, perchè giustamente si diceva che pochissime ragazze dell'età sua sapevano tanto.

I dodici giurati erano affaccendati a scrivere su delle lavagne.
— Che fanno? — bisbigliò Alice nell'orecchio del Grifone.
— Non possono aver nulla da scrivere se il processo non è ancora cominciato.
— Scrivono i loro nomi, — bisbigliò il Grifone; — temono di dimenticarseli prima della fine del processo.

— Che stupidi! — esclamò Alice sprezzante, ma tacque subito, perchè il Coniglio bianco, esclamò: — Silenzio in corte! — e il Re inforcò gli occhiali, mettendosi a guardare ansiosamente da ogni lato per scoprire i disturbatori.

Alice vedeva bene, come se fosse loro addosso, che scrivevano "stupidi", sulle lavagne: osservò altresì che uno di loro non sapeva sillabare "stupidi", e domandava al vicino come si scrivesse.

"Le lavagne saranno tutte uno scarabocchio prima della fine del processo!" pensò Alice.

Un giurato aveva una matita che strideva. Alice non potendo resistervi, girò intorno al tribunale, gli giunse alle spalle e gliela strappò di sorpresa.

behind him, and very soon found an opportunity of taking it away.

She did it so quickly that the poor little juror (it was Bill, the Lizard) could not make out at all what had become of it; so, after hunting all about for it, he was obliged to write with one finger for the rest of the day; and this was of very little use, as it left no mark on the slate.

'Herald, read the accusation!' said the King.

On this the White Rabbit blew three blasts on the trumpet, and then unrolled the parchment scroll, and read as follows:—

'The Queen of Hearts, she made some tarts, All on a summer day: The Knave of Hearts, he stole those tarts, And took them quite away!'

'Consider your verdict,' the King said to the jury.

'Not yet, not yet!' the Rabbit hastily interrupted. 'There's a great deal to come before that!'

Call the first witness,' said the King; and the White Rabbit blew three blasts on the trumpet, and called out: 'First witness!'

The first witness was the Hatter. He came in with a teacup in one hand and a piece of bread-and-butter in the other.

'I beg pardon, your Majesty,' he began: 'for bringing these in: but I hadn't quite finished my tea when I was sent for.'

'You ought to have finished,' said the King. 'When did you begin?'

The Hatter looked at the March Hare, who had followed him into the court, arm-in-arm with the Dormouse. 'Fourteenth of March, I think it was,' he said.

'Fifteenth,' said the March Hare.

'Sixteenth,' added the Dormouse.

'Write that down,' the King said to the jury, and the jury eagerly wrote down all three dates on their slates, and then added them up, and reduced the answer to shillings and pence.

'Take off your hat,' the King said to the Hatter.

'It isn't mine,' said the Hatter.

'Stolen!' the King exclaimed, turning to the jury, who instantly made a memorandum of the fact.

'I keep them to sell,' the Hatter added as an explanation; 'I've none of my own. I'm a hatter.'

Here the Queen put on her spectacles, and began staring at the Hatter, who turned pale and fidgeted.

'Give your evidence,' said the King; 'and don't be nervous, or I'll have you executed on the spot.'

This did not seem to encourage the witness at all: he kept shifting from one foot to the other, looking uneasily at the Queen, and in his confusion he bit a large piece out of his teacup instead of the bread-and-butter.

Just at this moment Alice felt a very curious sensation, which puzzled her a good deal until she made out what it was: she was beginning to grow larger again, and she thought at first she would get up and leave the court; but on second thoughts she decided to remain where she was as long as there was room for her.

'I wish you wouldn't squeeze so.' said the Dormouse, who was sitting next to her. 'I can hardly breathe.'

Lo fece con tanta rapidità che il povero giurato (era Guglielmo, la lucertola) non seppe più che fosse successo della matita. Dopo aver girato qua e là per ritrovarla, fu costretto a scrivere col dito tutto il resto della giornata. Ma a che pro, se il dito non lasciava traccia sulla lavagna?

— Usciere! leggete l'atto d'accusa, — disse il Re.

Allora il Coniglio diè tre squilli di tromba, poi spiegò il rotolo della pergamena, e lesse così:

"La Regina di cuori fece le torte in tutto un dì d'estate: Tristo, il Fante di cuori di nascosto le torte ha trafugate!"

— Ponderate il vostro verdetto! — disse il Re ai giurati.

— Non ancora, non ancora ! — interruppe vivamente il Coniglio. — Vi son molte cose da fare prima!

— Chiamate il primo testimone, — disse il Re; e il Coniglio bianco diè tre squilli di tromba, e chiamò: — Il primo testimone!

Il testimone era il Cappellaio. S'avanzò con una tazza di tè in una mano, una fetta di pane imburrato nell'altra.

— Domando perdono alla maestà vostra, disse, — se vengo con le mani impedite; ma non avevo ancora finito di prendere il tè quando sono stato chiamato.

— Avreste dovuto finire, — rispose il Re. Quando avete cominciato a prenderlo?

Il Cappellaio guardò la Lepre di Marzo che lo aveva seguito in corte, a braccetto col Ghiro. — Credo che fosse il quattordici di marzo, — disse il Cappellaio.

— Il quindici, — esclamò la Lepre di Marzo.

— Il sedici, — soggiunse il Ghiro.

— Scrivete questo, — disse il Re ai giurati. E i giurati si misero a scrivere prontamente sulle lavagne, e poi sommarono i giorni riducendoli a lire e centesimi.

— Cavatevi il cappello, — disse il Re al Cappellaio.

— Non è mio, — rispose il Cappellaio.

— È rubato allora! — esclamò il Re volgendosi ai giurati, i quali subito annotarono il fatto.

— Li tengo per venderli, — soggiunse il Cappellaio per spiegare la cosa: — Non ne ho di miei. Sono cappellaio.

La Regina inforcò gli occhiali, e cominciò a fissare il Cappellaio, che diventò pallido dallo spavento.

— Narraci quello che sai, — disse il Re, — e non aver paura... ti farò decapitare immediatamente.

Queste parole non incoraggiarono il testimone, che non si reggeva più in piedi. Guardava angosciosamente la Regina, e nella confusione addentò la tazza invece del pane imburrato.

Proprio in quel momento, Alice provò una strana sensazione, che la sorprese molto finchè non se ne diede ragione: cominciava a crescere di nuovo; pensò di lasciare il tribunale, ma poi riflettendoci meglio volle rimanere finchè per lei ci fosse spazio.

— Perchè mi urti così? — disse il Ghiro che le sedeva da presso. — Mi manca il respiro.

'I can't help it,' said Alice very meekly: 'I'm growing.'

'You've no right to grow here,' said the Dormouse.

'Don't talk nonsense,' said Alice more boldly: 'you know you're growing too.'

'Yes, but I grow at a reasonable pace,' said the Dormouse: 'not in that ridiculous fashion.' And he got up very sulkily and crossed over to the other side of the court.

All this time the Queen had never left off staring at the Hatter, and, just as the Dormouse crossed the court, she said to one of the officers of the court:

'Bring me the list of the singers in the last concert!' on which the wretched Hatter trembled so, that he shook both his shoes off.

Give your evidence,' the King repeated angrily: 'or I'll have you executed, whether you're nervous or not.'

I'm a poor man, your Majesty,' the Hatter began, in a trembling voice: '—and I hadn't begun my tea—not above a week or so—and what with the bread-and-butter getting so thin—and the twinkling of the tea—'

'The twinkling of the what?' said the King.

'It began with the tea,' the Hatter replied.

'Of course twinkling begins with a T!' said the King sharply. 'Do you take me for a dunce? Go on!'

I'm a poor man,' the Hatter went on: 'and most things twinkled after that—only the March Hare said—'

'I didn't!' the March Hare interrupted in a great hurry.

'You did!' said the Hatter.

'I deny it!' said the March Hare.

'He denies it,' said the King: 'leave out that part.'

Well, at any rate, the Dormouse said—' the Hatter went on, looking anxiously round to see if he would deny it too: but the Dormouse denied nothing, being fast asleep.

After that,' continued the Hatter: 'I cut some more bread-and-butter—'

'But what did the Dormouse say?' one of the jury asked.

'That I can't remember,' said the Hatter.

You must remember,' remarked the King: 'or I'll have you executed.'

The miserable Hatter dropped his teacup and bread-and-butter, and went down on one knee. 'I'm a poor man, your Majesty,' he began.

'You're a very poor speaker,' said the King.

Here one of the guinea-pigs cheered, and was immediately suppressed by the officers of the court.

(As that is rather a hard word, I will just explain to you how it was done. They had a large canvas bag, which tied up at the mouth with strings: into this they slipped the guinea-pig, head first, and then sat upon it.)

I'm glad I've seen that done,' thought Alice. 'I've so often read in the newspapers, at the end of trials, "There was some attempts at applause, which was immediately suppressed by the officers of the court," and I never understood what it meant till now.'

'If that's all you know about it, you may stand down,' continued the King.

— Che ci posso fare? — disse affabilmente Alice. — Sto crescendo.

— Tu non hai diritto di crescere qui, — urlò il Ghiro.

— Non dire delle sciocchezze, — gridò Alice, — anche tu cresci.

— Sì, ma io cresco a un passo ragionevole, soggiunse il Ghiro, — e non in quella maniera ridicola. — E brontolando si levò e andò a mettersi dall'altro lato.

Intanto la Regina non aveva mai distolto lo sguardo dal Cappellaio e mentre il Ghiro attraversava la sala del tribunale, disse a un usciere:

- Dammi la lista dei cantanti dell'ultimo concerto! A quest'ordine il Cappellaio si mise a tremare così che le scarpe gli sfuggirono dai piedi.

— Narraci quello che sai, — ripetè adirato il Re, — o ti farò tagliare la testa, abbi o no paura.

— Maestà: sono un povero disgraziato, — cominciò il Cappellaio con voce tremante, — e ho appena cominciato a prendere il tè... non è ancora una settimana... e in quanto al pane col burro che si assottiglia... e il tremolio del tè.

— Che tremolio? — esclamò il re.

Il tremolio cominciò col tè, — rispose il Cappellaio.

— Sicuro che "tremolio" comincia con un T! — disse vivamente il Re. — M'hai preso per un allocco? Continua.

— Sono un povero disgraziato, — continuò il Cappellaio, — e dopo il tè tremavamo tutti... solo la Lepre di Marzo disse...

— Non dissi niente! — interruppe in fretta la Lepre di Marzo.

— Sì che lo dicesti! — disse il Cappellaio.

— Lo nego! — replicò la Lepre di Marzo.

— Lo nega, — disse il Re: — ebbene, lascia andare.

— Bene, a ogni modo il Ghiro disse... E il Cappellaio guardò il Ghiro per vedere se anche lui volesse dargli una smentita: ma quegli, profondamente addormentato, non negava nulla.

— Dopo di ciò, — continuò il Cappellaio, — mi preparai un'altra fetta di pane col burro...

— Ma che cosa disse il Ghiro? — domandò un giurato.

— Non lo posso ricordare, — disse il Cappellaio.

— Lo devi ricordare, — disse il Re, — se no ti farò tagliare la testa.

L'infelice Cappellaio si lasciò cadere la tazza, il pane col burro e le ginocchia a terra, e implorò: — Sono un povero mortale!

— Sei un povero oratore, — disse il Re.

Qui un Porcellino d'India diè un applauso, che venne subito represso dagli uscieri del tribunale.

(Ed ecco come: fu preso un sacco che si legava con due corde all'imboccatura; vi si fece entrare a testa in giù il Porcellino, e gli uscieri vi si sedettero sopra.)

— Sono contenta d'avervi assistito, — pensò Alice. — Ho letto tante volte nei giornali, alla fine dei processi: "Vi fu un tentativo di applausi, subito represso dal presidente"; ma non avevo mai compreso che cosa volesse dire.

— Se è questo tutto quello che sai, — disse il Re, — puoi ritirarti.

'I can't go no lower,' said the Hatter: 'I'm on the floor, as it is.'

'Then you may sit down,' the King replied.

Here the other guinea-pig cheered, and was suppressed.

'Come, that finished the guinea-pigs!' thought Alice. 'Now we shall get on better.'

'I'd rather finish my tea,' said the Hatter, with an anxious look at the Queen, who was reading the list of singers.

'You may go,' said the King, and the Hatter hurriedly left the court, without even waiting to put his shoes on.

—and just take his head off outside,' the Queen added to one of the officers: but the Hatter was out of sight before the officer could get to the door.

'Call the next witness!' said the King.

The next witness was the Duchess's cook. She carried the pepper-box in her hand, and Alice guessed who it was, even before she got into the court, by the way the people near the door began sneezing all at once.

'Give your evidence,' said the King.

'Shan't,' said the cook.

The King looked anxiously at the White Rabbit, who said in a low voice: 'Your Majesty must cross-examine this witness.'

'Well, if I must, I must,' the King said, with a melancholy air, and, after folding his arms and frowning at the cook till his eyes were nearly out of sight, he said in a deep voice, 'What are tarts made of?'

'Pepper, mostly,' said the cook.

'Treacle,' said a sleepy voice behind her.

'Collar that Dormouse,' the Queen shrieked out. 'Behead that Dormouse! Turn that Dormouse out of court! Suppress him! Pinch him! Off with his whiskers!'

For some minutes the whole court was in confusion, getting the Dormouse turned out, and, by the time they had settled down again, the cook had disappeared.

Never mind!' said the King, with an air of great relief. 'Call the next witness.' And he added in an undertone to the Queen: 'Really, my dear, you must cross-examine the next witness. It quite makes my forehead ache!'

Alice watched the White Rabbit as he fumbled over the list, feeling very curious to see what the next witness would be like: '—for they haven't got much evidence yet,' she said to herself. Imagine her surprise, when the White Rabbit read out, at the top of his shrill little voice, the name 'Alice!'

— Non posso ritirarmi, — disse il Cappellaio, — sono già sul pavimento.

— Allora siediti, — disse il Re.

Qui un altro Porcellino d'India diè un applauso, ma fu represso.

— Addio Porcellini d'India! Non vi vedrò più! — disse Alice.

— Ora si andrà innanzi meglio.

— Vorrei piuttosto finire il tè, — disse il Cappellaio, guardando con ansietà la Regina, la quale leggeva la lista dei cantanti.

— Puoi andare, — disse il Re, e il Cappellaio lasciò frettolosamente il tribunale, senza nemmeno rimettersi le scarpe.

—...E tagliategli la testa, — soggiunse la Regina, volgendosi a un ufficiale; ma il Cappellaio era già sparito prima che l'ufficiale arrivasse alla porta.

— Chiamate l'altro testimone! — gridò il Re.

L'altro testimone era la cuoca della Duchessa. Aveva il vaso del pepe in mano, e Alice indovinò chi fosse anche prima di vederla, perchè tutti quelli vicini all'ingresso cominciarono a starnutire.

— Che cosa sai? — disse il Re.

— Niente, — rispose la cuoca.

Il Re guardò con ansietà il Coniglio bianco che mormorò:— Maestà, fatele delle domande.

— Bene, se debbo farle, le farò, — disse il Re, e dopo aver incrociate le braccia sul petto, e spalancati gli occhi sulla cuoca, disse con voce profonda:

— Di che cosa sono composte le torte?

— Di pepe per la maggior parte, — rispose la cuoca.

— Di melassa, — soggiunse una voce sonnolenta dietro di lei.

— Afferrate quel Ghiro! — gridò la Regina. — Tagliategli il capo! Fuori quel Ghiro! Sopprimetelo! pizzicatelo! Strappategli i baffi!

Durante qualche istante il tribunale fu una Babele, mentre il Ghiro veniva afferrato; e quando l'ordine fu ristabilito, la cuoca era scomparsa.

— Non importa, — disse il Re con aria di sollievo. — Chiamate l'altro testimone. — E bisbigliò alla Regina: — Cara mia, l'altro testimone dovresti esaminarlo tu. A me duole il capo.

Alice stava osservando il Coniglio che esaminava la lista, curiosa di vedere chi fosse mai l'altro testimone, — perchè non hanno ancora una prova, — disse fra sè. Figurarsi la sua sorpresa, quando il Coniglio bianco chiamò con voce stridula: Alice!

12. Alice's Evidence

'Here!' cried Alice, quite forgetting in the flurry of the moment how large she had grown in the last few minutes, and she jumped up in such a hurry that she tipped over the jury-box with the edge of her skirt, upsetting all the jurymen on to the heads of the crowd below, and there they lay sprawling about, reminding her very much of a globe of goldfish she had accidentally upset the week before.

'Oh, I beg your pardon!' she exclaimed in a tone of great dismay, and began picking them up again as quickly as she could, for the accident of the goldfish kept running in her head, and she had a vague sort of idea that they must be collected at once and put back into the jury-box, or they would die.

The trial cannot proceed,' said the King in a very grave voice: 'until all the jurymen are back in their proper places— all,' he repeated with great emphasis, looking hard at Alice as he said do.

Alice looked at the jury-box, and saw that, in her haste, she had put the Lizard in head downwards, and the poor little thing was waving its tail about in a melancholy way, being quite unable to move.

She soon got it out again, and put it right; 'not that it signifies much,' she said to herself; 'I should think it would be quite as much use in the trial one way up as the other.'

As soon as the jury had a little recovered from the shock of being upset, and their slates and pencils had been found and handed back to them, they set to work very diligently to write out a history of the accident, all except the Lizard, who seemed too much overcome to do anything but sit with its mouth open, gazing up into the roof of the court.

'What do you know about this business?' the King said to Alice.

'Nothing,' said Alice.

'Nothing whatever?' persisted the King.

'Nothing whatever,' said Alice.

That's very important,' the King said, turning to the jury. They were just beginning to write this down on their slates, when the White Rabbit interrupted:

'Unimportant, your Majesty means, of course,' he said in a very respectful tone, but frowning and making faces at him as he spoke.

Unimportant, of course, I meant,' the King hastily said, and went on to himself in an undertone:

'important—unimportant— unimportant—important—' as if he were trying which word sounded best.

Some of the jury wrote it down 'important,' and some 'unimportant.' Alice could see this, as she was near enough to look over their slates; 'but it doesn't matter a bit,' she thought to herself.

12. La Testimonianza di Alice

— Presente! — rispose Alice. Dimenticando, nella confusione di quell'istante di esser cresciuta enormemente, saltò con tanta fretta che rovesciò col lembo della veste il banco de' giurati, i quali capitombolarono con la testa in giù sulla folla, restando con le. gambe in aria. Questo le rammentò l'urtone dato la settimana prima a un globo di cristallo con i pesciolini d'oro.

— Oh, vi prego di scusarmi! — ella esclamò con voce angosciata e cominciò a raccoglierli con molta sollecitudine, perchè invasa dall'idea dei pesciolini pensava di doverli prontamente raccogliere e rimettere sul loro banco se non li voleva far morire.

— Il processo, — disse il Re con voce grave, — non può andare innanzi se tutti i giurati non saranno al loro posto... dico tutti, — soggiunse con energia, guardando fisso Alice.

Alice guardò il banco de' giurati, e vide che nella fretta avea rimessa la lucertola a testa in giù. La poverina agitava melanconicamente la coda, non potendosi muovere.

Subito la raddrizzò. "Non già perchè significhi qualche cosa, — disse fra sè, — perchè ne la testa nè la coda gioveranno al processo."

Appena i giurati si furono rimessi dalla caduta e riebbero in consegna le lavagne e le matite, si misero a scarabocchiare con molta ansia la storia del loro ruzzolone, tranne la lucertola, che era ancora stordita e sedeva a bocca spalancata, guardando il soffitto.

— Che cosa sai di quest'affare? — domandò il Re ad Alice.

— Niente, — rispose Alice.

— Proprio niente? — replicò il Re.

— Proprio niente, — soggiunse Alice.

— È molto significante, — disse il Re, volgendosi ai giurati. Essi si accingevano a scrivere sulle lavagne, quando il Coniglio bianco li interruppe:

— Insignificante, intende certamente vostra Maestà, — disse con voce rispettosa, ma aggrottando le ciglia e facendo una smorfia mentre parlava.

— Insignificante, già, è quello che intendevo — soggiunse in fretta il Re; e poi si mise a dire a bassa voce:

"significante, insignificante, significante..." — come se volesse provare quale delle due parole sonasse meglio.

Alcuni dei giurati scrissero "significante", altri "insignificante." Alice potè vedere perchè era vicina, e poteva sbirciare sulle lavagne: "Ma non importa", pensò.

At this moment the King, who had been for some time busily writing in his note-book, cackled out 'Silence!' and read out from his book:

'Rule Forty-two. All persons more than a mile hight to leave the court.'

Everybody looked at Alice.

'I'm not a mile high,' said Alice.

'You are,' said the King. 'Nearly two miles high,' added the Queen.

'Well, I shan't go, at any rate,' said Alice: 'besides, that's not a regular rule: you invented it just now.'

'It's the oldest rule in the book,' said the King.

'Then it ought to be Number One,' said Alice.

The King turned pale, and shut his note-book hastily. 'Consider your verdict,' he said to the jury, in a low, trembling voice.

'There's more evidence to come yet, please your Majesty,' said the White Rabbit, jumping up in a great hurry; 'this paper has just been picked up.'

'What's in it?' said the Queen.

I haven't opened it yet,' said the White Rabbit: 'but it seems to be a letter, written by the prisoner to—to somebody.'

It must have been that,' said the King: 'unless it was written to nobody, which isn't usual, you know.'

'Who is it directed to?' said one of the jurymen.

'It isn't directed at all,' said the White Rabbit; 'in fact, there's nothing written on the outside.' He unfolded the paper as he spoke, and added 'It isn't a letter, after all: it's a set of verses.'

'Are they in the prisoner's handwriting?' asked another of they jurymen.

No, they're not,' said the White Rabbit: 'and that's the queerest thing about it.' (The jury all looked puzzled.)

'He must have imitated somebody else's hand,' said the King. (The jury all brightened up again.)

Please your Majesty,' said the Knave: 'I didn't write it, and they can't prove I did: there's no name signed at the end.'

If you didn't sign it,' said the King: 'that only makes the matter worse. You must have meant some mischief, or else you'd have signed your name like an honest man.'

There was a general clapping of hands at this: it was the first really clever thing the King had said that day.

'That proves his guilt,' said the Queen.

'It proves nothing of the sort!' said Alice. 'Why, you don't even know what they're about!'

'Read them,' said the King.

The White Rabbit put on his spectacles. 'Where shall I begin, please your Majesty?' he asked.

Begin at the beginning,' the King said gravely: 'and go on till you come to the end: then stop.'

These were the verses the White Rabbit read:—

'They told me you had been to her, And mentioned me to him: She gave me a good character, But said I could not swim.

Allora il Re, che era stato occupatissimo a scrivere nel suo taccuino, gridò: — Silenzio! — e lesse dal suo libriccino:

"Norma quarantaduesima: — Ogni persona, la cui altezza supera il miglio deve uscire dal tribunale."
Tutti guardarono Alice.

— Io non sono alta un miglio, — disse Alice.

— Sì che lo sei, — rispose il Re. — Quasi due miglia d'altezza, — aggiunse la Regina.

— Ebbene non m'importa, ma non andrò via, — disse Alice.

— Inoltre quella è una norma nuova; l'avete inventata or ora.

— Che! è la più vecchia norma del libro! — rispose il Re.

— Allora dovrebbe essere la prima, — disse Alice.

Allora il Re diventò pallido e chiuse in fretta il libriccino. — Ponderate il vostro verdetto, — disse volgendosi ai giurati, ma con voce sommessa e tremante.

— Maestà, vi sono altre testimonianze, — disse il Coniglio bianco balzando in piedi. — Giusto adesso abbiamo trovato questo foglio.

— Che contiene? — domandò la Regina

Non l'ho aperto ancora, disse il Coniglio bianco; — ma sembra una lettera scritta dal prigioniero a... a qualcuno.

— Dev'essere così — disse il Re, — salvo che non sia stata scritta a nessuno, il che generalmente non avviene.

— A chi è indirizzata — domandò uno dei giurati.

— Non ha indirizzo, — disse il Coniglio bianco, — infatti non c'è scritto nulla al di fuori. — E aprì il foglio mentre parlava, e soggiunse: — Dopo tutto, non è una lettera; è una filastrocca in versi.

— Sono di mano del prigioniero? — domandò un giurato.

— No, no, —rispose Il Coniglio bianco, questo è ancora più strano. (I giurati si guardarono confusi.)

— Forse ha imitato la scrittura di qualcun altro, — disse il Re.(I giurati si schiarirono.)

— Maestà, — disse il Fante, — io non li ho scritti, e nessuno potrebbe provare il contrario. E poi non c'è alcuna firma in fondo.

— Il non aver firmato, — rispose il Re, non fa che aggravare il tuo delitto. Tu miravi certamente a un reato; se no, avresti lealmente firmato il foglio.

Vi fu un applauso generale, e a ragione, perchè quella era la prima frase di spirito detta dal Re in quel giorno.

— Questo prova la sua colpa, — affermò la Regina.

— Non prova niente, — disse Alice. — Ma se non sai neppure ciò che contiene il foglio!

— Leggilo! — disse il re.

Il Coniglio bianco si mise gli occhiali e domandò: — Maestà, di grazia, di dove debbo incominciare ?

— Comincia dal principio, — disse il Re solennemente... — e continua fino alla fine, poi fermati.

Or questi erano i versi che il Coniglio bianco lesse:

"Mi disse che da lei te n'eri andato, ed a lui mi volesti rammentar; lei poi mi diede il mio certificato dicendomi: ma tu non sai nuotar.

He sent them word I had not gone (We know it to be true):
If she should push the matter on, What would become of you?
I gave her one, they gave him two, You gave us three or more; They all returned from him to you, Though they were mine before.
If I or she should chance to be Involved in this affair, He trusts to you to set them free, Exactly as we were.

My notion was that you had been (Before she had this fit) An obstacle that came between Him, and ourselves, and it.

Don't let him know she liked them best, For this must ever be A secret, kept from all the rest, Between yourself and me.'

That's the most important piece of evidence we've heard yet,' said the King, rubbing his hands; 'so now let the jury—'
If any one of them can explain it,' said Alice, (she had grown so large in the last few minutes that she wasn't a bit afraid of interrupting him,)
'I'll give him sixpence. _I_ don't believe there's an atom of meaning in it.'
The jury all wrote down on their slates: 'She doesn't believe there's an atom of meaning in it,' but none of them attempted to explain the paper.
If there's no meaning in it,' said the King: 'that saves a world of trouble, you know, as we needn't try to find any. And yet I don't know,' he went on, spreading out the verses on his knee, and looking at them with one eye;
'I seem to see some meaning in them, after all. "-said I could not swim—" you can't swim, can you?' he added, turning to the Knave.
The Knave shook his head sadly. 'Do I look like it?' he said. (Which he certainly did not, being made entirely of cardboard.)
All right, so far,' said the King, and he went on muttering over the verses to himself: '"We know it to be true—" that's the jury, of course— "I gave her one, they gave him two—" why, that must be what he did with the tarts, you know—'
'But, it goes on "they all returned from him to you,"' said Alice.
Why, there they are!' said the King triumphantly, pointing to the tarts on the table. 'Nothing can be clearer than that. Then again—"before she had this fit—" you never had fits, my dear, I think?' he said to the Queen.

Never!' said the Queen furiously, throwing an inkstand at the Lizard as she spoke.
(The unfortunate little Bill had left off writing on his slate with one finger, as he found it made no mark; but he now hastily began again, using the ink, that was trickling down his face, as long as it lasted.)

'Then the words don't fit you,' said the King, looking round the court with a smile. There was a dead silence.
It's a pun!' the King added in an offended tone, and everybody laughed: 'Let the jury consider their verdict,' the King said, for about the twentieth time that day.
No, no!' said the Queen. 'Sentence first—verdict afterwards.'

Egli poi disse che non ero andato (e non si può negar, chi non lo sa?) e se il negozio sarà maturato, oh dimmi allor di te che mai sarà?
Una a lei diedi, ed essi due le diero, tu me ne desti tre, fors'anche più; ma tutte si rinvennero, — o mistero! ed eran tutte mie, non lo sai tu?
Se lei ed io per caso in questo affare misterioso involti ci vedrem, egli ha fiducia d'esser liberato e con noi stare finalmente insiem.
Ho questa idea che prima dell'accesso, (già tu sai che un accesso la colpì), un ostacol per lui, per noi, per esso fosti tu solo in quel fatale dì.
Ch'egli non sappia chi lei predilige (il segreto bisogna mantener); sia segreto per tutti, chè qui vige la impenetrabile legge del mister."
— Questo è il più importante documento di accusa, — disse il Re stropicciandosi le mani; — ora i giurati si preparino.
— Se qualcuno potesse spiegarmelo, — disse Alice (la quale era talmente cresciuta in quegli ultimi minuti che non aveva più paura d'interrompere il Re)
— gli darei mezza lira. Non credo che ci sia in esso neppure un atomo di buon senso.
I giurati scrissero tutti sulla lavagna: "Ella non crede che vi sia in esso neppure un atomo di buon senso".Ma nessuno cercò di spiegare il significato del foglio.
— Se non c'è un significato, — disse il Re, — noi usciamo da un monte di fastidi, perchè non è necessario trovarvelo. E pure non so, — continuò aprendo il foglio sulle ginocchia e sbirciandolo,
— ma mi pare di scoprirvi un significato, dopo tutto...
"Disse... non sai mica nuotar." Tu non sai nuotare, non è vero? — continuò volgendosi al Fante.
Il Fante scosse tristemente la testa e disse: — Vi pare che io possa nuotare? (E certamente, no, perchè era interamente di cartone).
— Bene, fin qui,—, disse il Re, e continuò: — "E questo è il vero, e ognun di noi io sa." Questo è senza dubbio per i giurati. — "Una a lei diedi, ed essi due gli diero." — Questo spiega l'uso fatto delle torte, capisci...
Ma, — disse Alice, — continua con le parole: "Ma tutte si rinvennero".
— Già, esse son la, —disse il Re con un'aria di trionfo, indicando le torte sul tavolo. — Nulla di più chiaro.
Continua:"Già tu sai che un accesso la colpì",— tu non hai mai avuto degli attacchi nervosi, cara mia, non è vero?— soggiunse volgendosi alla Regina.
— Mai! — gridò furiosa la Regina, e scaraventò un calamaio sulla testa della lucertola.
(Il povero Guglielmo! aveva cessato di scrivere sulla lavagna col dito, perchè s'era accorto che non ne rimaneva traccia; e in quell'istante si rimise sollecitamente all'opera, usando l'inchiostro che gli scorreva sulla faccia, e l'usò finche ne ebbe.)
— Dunque a te questo verso non si attacca, — disse il Re, guardando con un sorriso il tribunale. E vi fu gran silenzio.
È un bisticcio — soggiunse il Re con voce irata, e tutti allora risero. — Che i giurati ponderino il loro verdetto — ripetè il Re, forse per la ventesima volta quel giorno.
— No, disse la Regina. — Prima la sentenza, poi il verdetto.

'Stuff and nonsense!' said Alice loudly. 'The idea of having the sentence first!'

'Hold your tongue!' said the Queen, turning purple.

'I won't!' said Alice.

'Off with her head!' the Queen shouted at the top of her voice. Nobody moved.

'Who cares for you?' said Alice, (she had grown to her full size by this time.) 'You're nothing but a pack of cards!'

At this the whole pack rose up into the air, and came flying down upon her: she gave a little scream, half of fright and half of anger, and tried to beat them off, and found herself lying on the bank, with her head in the lap of her sister, who was gently brushing away some dead leaves that had fluttered down from the trees upon her face.

Wake up, Alice dear!' said her sister; 'Why, what a long sleep you've had!'

'Oh, I've had such a curious dream!' said Alice, and she told her sister, as well as she could remember them, all these strange Adventures of hers that you have just been reading about; and when she had finished, her sister kissed her, and said,

It was a curious dream, dear, certainly: but now run in to your tea; it's getting late.'

So Alice got up and ran off, thinking while she ran, as well she might, what a wonderful dream it had been.

But her sister sat still just as she left her, leaning her head on her hand, watching the setting sun, and thinking of little Alice and all her wonderful Adventures, till she too began dreaming after a fashion, and this was her dream:—

First, she dreamed of little Alice herself, and once again the tiny hands were clasped upon her knee, and the bright eager eyes were looking up into hers.

She could hear the very tones of her voice, and see that queer little toss of her head to keep back the wandering hair that would always get into her eyes.

And still, as she listened, or seemed to listen, the whole place around her became alive the strange creatures of her little sister's dream.

The long grass rustled at her feet as the White Rabbit hurried by—the frightened Mouse splashed his way through the neighbouring pool—she could hear the rattle of the teacups as the March Hare and his friends shared their never-ending meal, and the shrill voice of the Queen ordering off her unfortunate guests to execution—once more the pig-baby was sneezing on the Duchess's knee, while plates and dishes crashed around it—once more the shriek of the Gryphon, the squeaking of the Lizard's slate-pencil, and the choking of the suppressed guinea-pigs, filled the air, mixed up with the distant sobs of the miserable Mock Turtle.

So she sat on, with closed eyes, and half believed herself in Wonderland, though she knew she had but to open them again, and all would change to dull reality—the grass would be only rustling in the wind, and the pool rippling to the waving of the reeds—the rattling teacups would change to tinkling sheep-bells, and the Queen's shrill cries to the voice of the shepherd boy—and the sneeze of the baby, the shriek of the Gryphon, and all the other queer noises, would change (she knew) to the confused clamour of the busy

— È una stupidità — esclamò Alice. — Che idea d'aver prima la sentenza!

— Taci! — gridò la Regina, tutta di porpora in viso.

— Ma che tacere! — disse Alice.

— Tagliatele la testa! urlò la Regina con quanta voce aveva. Ma nessuno si mosse.

— Chi si cura di te? — disse Alice, (allora era cresciuta fino alla sua statura naturale.); — Tu non sei che la Regina d'un mazzo di carte.

A queste parole tutto il mazzo si sollevò in aria vorticosamente e poi si rovesciò sulla fanciulla: essa diede uno strillo di paura e d'ira, e cercò di respingerlo da sè, ma si trovò sul poggio, col capo sulle ginocchia di sua sorella, la quale le toglieva con molta delicatezza alcune foglie secche che le erano cadute sul viso.

— Risvegliati, Alice cara,— le disse la sorella, — da quanto tempo dormi, cara!

— Oh! ho avuto un sogno così curioso! — disse Alice, e raccontò alla sorella come meglio potè, tutte le strane avventure che avete lette; e quando finì, la sorella la baciò e le disse:

— È stato davvero un sogno curioso, cara ma ora, va subito a prendere il tè; è già tardi. —

E così Alice si levò; e andò via, pensando, mentre correva, al suo sogno meraviglioso.

Sua sorella rimase colà con la testa sulla palma, tutta intenta a guardare il sole al tramonto, pensando alla piccola Alice, e alle sue avventure meravigliose finchè anche lei si mise a sognare, e fece un sogno simile a questo:

Prima di tutto sognò la piccola, Alice, con le sue manine delicate congiunte sulle ginocchia di lei e coi grandi occhioni lucenti fissi in lei.

Le sembrava di sentire il vero suono della sua voce, e di vedere quella caratteristica mossa della sua testolina quando rigettava indietro i capelli che volevano velarle gli occhi.

Mentre ella era tutta intenta ad ascoltare, o sembrava che ascoltasse, tutto il. luogo d'intorno si popolò delle strane creature del sogno di sua sorella.

L'erba rigogliosa stormiva ai suoi piedi, mentre il Coniglio passava trotterellando e il Topo impaurito s'apriva a nuoto una via attraverso lo stagno vicino. Ella poteva sentire il rumore delle tazze mentre la Lepre di Marzo e gli amici suoi partecipavano al pasto perpetuo; udiva la stridula voce della Regina che mandava i suoi invitati a morte. Ancora una volta il bimbo Porcellino starnutiva sulle ginocchia della Duchessa, mentre i tondi e i piatti volavano e s'infrangevano d'intorno e l'urlo del Grifone, lo stridore della matita della Lucertola sulla lavagna, la repressione dei Porcellini d'India riempivano l'aria misti ai singhiozzi lontani della Falsa-testuggine.

Si sedette, con gli occhi a metà velati e quasi si credè davvero nel Paese delle Meraviglie; benchè sapesse che aprendo gli occhi tutto si sarebbe mutato nella triste realtà. Avrebbe sentito l'erba stormire al soffiar del vento, avrebbe veduto lo stagno incresparsi all'ondeggiare delle canne. L'acciottolio, delle tazze si sarebbe mutato nel tintinnio della campana delle pecore, e la stridula voce della Regina nella voce del pastorello, e gli starnuti del bimbo, l'urlo del Grifone e tutti gli altri curiosi rumori si sarebbero mutati (lei lo sapeva) nel

farm-yard—while the lowing of the cattle in the distance would take the place of the Mock Turtle's heavy sobs.

Lastly, she pictured to herself how this same little sister of hers would, in the after-time, be herself a grown woman; and how she would keep, through all her riper years, the simple and loving heart of her childhood: and how she would gather about her other little children, and make their eyes bright and eager with many a strange tale, perhaps even with the dream of Wonderland of long ago: and how she would feel with all their simple sorrows, and find a pleasure in all their simple joys, remembering her own child-life, and the happy summer days.

rumore confuso d'una fattoria, e il muggito lontano degli armenti avrebbe sostituito i profondi singhiozzi della Falsa-testuggine.

Finalmente essa immaginò come sarebbe stata la sorellina già cresciuta e diventata donna: Alice avrebbe conservato nei suoi anni maturi il cuore affettuoso e semplice dell'infanzia e avrebbe raccolto intorno a sè altre fanciulle e avrebbe fatto loro risplendere gli occhi, beandole con molte strane storielle e forse ancora col suo sogno di un tempo: le sue avventure nel Paese delle Meraviglie. Con quanta tenerezza avrebbe ella stessa partecipato alle loro innocenti afflizioni, e con quanta gioia alle loro gioie, riandando i beati giorni della infanzia e le felici giornate estive!

Italian-English Frequency Dictionary

Rank	Italian-Part of Speech	Translation
1	**il*** lo, l', la, i, gli, le-art	the
2	**che**-con; prn; adj	that; which, who; what
3	**di***del, dello, dell', della, dei, degli, delle-prp	of, to; than, and
4	**non**-adv	not, non
5	**a***al, allo, all', alla, ai, agli, alla-prp	to, in, at
6	**un, uno, una**-art; prn	a, an; one
7	**dire**-vb	say
8	**ma**-con	but
9	**si**-prn	one-, its-, thems-, him-, her-, yourself
10	**con**-prp; con	with, by
11	**in***nel, nello, nell', nella, nei, negli, nelle-prp	in, into
12	**per**-prp; adv	for, to, by, in
13	**essere**-vb; gli	be; being
14	**se**-con	if
15	**come**-adv; prn; prp; con	as, how
16	**rispondere**-vb	answer
17	**più**-adj; i; adv; con	more, most
18	**al**-art	a
19	**perché**-con; adv; prp	because, why; why
20	**mi**-prn	me
21	**da***dal, dallo, dall', dalla, dai, dagli, dalle-prp	from
22	**della**-adj	any
23	**onde**-adv; conj; prn	hence, whence; so that, so as; of which, whose
24	**regina**-la	queen
25	**ciò**-prn	that, it
26	**voce**-la	entry, voice, item
27	**quando**-adv; con	when
28	**re**-il	king
29	**ne**-adj; prn	any; of it, of them
30	**così**-adv; con	so, thus; that
31	**io**-prn; gli	I
32	**cosa**-prn; la	what; thing
33	**o**-con	or
34	**mai**-adv	never
35	**poi**-adv; con	then
36	**cappellaio**-il	hatter
37	**falso**-adj; il	false
38	**pensare**-vb	think
39	**lei**-prn	she, her
40	**voi**-prn	you
41	**fra**-prp; adv	between, among
42	**grifone**-il	griffin
43	**vi**-prn; adv	you; there
44	**quello**-adj; prn	one
45	**via**-prp; adv; la	via, by; away; street
46	**coniglio**-il	rabbit
47	**tanto**-adv; adj	much, so
48	**qualche**-adj; prn	some, few, any; a few
49	**capo**-il	boss
50	**loro**-prn	their
51	**mentre**-con; adv; gli	while, as, whereas
52	**sorcio**-il	mouse
53	**tutto**-adj; il	all
54	**bene**-adv; il; adj	very; well, good; good, asset
55	**suo**-adj; prn	your; its
56	**questo**-adj; prn	this; such, this one
57	**duchessa**-la	duchess
58	**ella**-prn	she
59	**avere**-vb	have
60	**continuare**-vb	continue
61	**illustrazione**-la	illustration
62	**domandare**-vb	ask, request
63	**chi**-prn	who
64	**prima**-adv; art	first, before; before
65	**soggiungere**-vb	add
66	**due**-I; num	two
67	**ora**-adv; con; la	now; now; now, time, hour
68	**ghiro**-il	dormouse
69	**poco**-adj; adv; gli	little; a litte, not much; bit
70	**oh**-int	oh
71	**tempo**-il	time, weather
72	**volta**-la	time, turn
73	**no**-adv; il	no, not; no
74	**subito**-adv	immediately, at once
75	**senza**-prp	without

#	Italian	English
76	**gridare**-*vb*	shout
77	**occhio**-*il*	eye
78	**gatto**-*il*	cat
79	**lepre**-*la*	hare
80	**molto**-*adj; adv; gli*	very, much
81	**bruco**-*il*	caterpillar
82	**stare**-*vb*	stay
83	**davvero**-*adv*	really
84	**fare**-*vb*	do
85	**modo**-*il*	way, manner
86	**tre**-*l; num*	three
87	**uno**-*art; adj; prn; nn*	a; one; any; a man
88	**parola**-*la*	word
89	**dopo**-*adv; prp*	after
90	**giù**-*adv*	down
91	**osservare**-*vb*	observe, see
92	**dire**-*vb*	say
93	**allora**-*adv*	then
94	**forse**-*adv*	perhaps
95	**mio**-*prn*	my
96	**certo**-*adj; adv*	certain; of course
97	**nuovo**-*adj*	new
98	**quale**-*adj; prn; con*	what, which; which; as
99	**sentire**-*vb*	feel, hear
100	**mettere**-*vb*	put
101	**piede**-*il*	foot
102	**già**-*adv*	already
103	**ogni**-*adj*	every
104	**tu**-*prn*	you
105	**sempre**-*adv*	always
106	**testare**-*vb*	test
107	**proprio**-*adj; il; prn; adv*	one's own; own; its; just, exactly
108	**altro**-*adj; prn; adv; gli*	other, more
109	**quanto**-*adv; con; il*	as, how much; than
110	**torre**-*la*	tower
111	**sopra**-*adv; prp; le*	above, on
112	**cominciare**-*vb; lo*	begin
113	**giurare**-*vb*	swear
114	**appena**-*adv; adj*	just, (as) soon (as)
115	**vedere**-*vb*	see
116	**ci**-*adv; prn*	ourselves, us
117	**me**-*prn*	me
118	**meglio**-*adv*	better, best
119	**volere**-*vb*	want
120	**casa**-*la*	house, home
121	**fuori**-*adv*	out, outside
122	**punto**-*il*	point
123	**bianco**-*adj; il*	white
124	**guardare**-*vb*	look, watch
125	**gran**-*adj*	great
126	**parlare**-*vb*	speak, talk
127	**nulla**-*il; prn*	nothing; nothing, anything
128	**mezzo**-*il; adj*	half, middle, means; half, middle
129	**li**-*prn*	them
130	**stesso**-*adj; prn; lo*	same; itself
131	**verso**-*prp; il*	to, towards; direction, way
132	**stare**-*vb*	stay
133	**finalmente**-*adv*	finally
134	**mano**-*la*	hand
135	**là**-*adv*	there
136	**sì**-*int*	yes, yeah
137	**tè**-*il*	tea
138	**istante**-*il*	instant
139	**coda**-*la*	queue, tail
140	**assai**-*adv*	very
141	**vero**-*adj*	true
142	**giorno**-*il*	day
143	**sapere**-*vb*	know
144	**ecco**-*adv*	here
145	**fa**-*adv*	ago
146	**lì**-*adv*	there
147	**terra**-*la*	land, earth
148	**meno**-*adj; adv; prp; lo; con*	less; less; unless; no so (much as)
149	**niente**-*lo; prn*	nothing, anything; any, none
150	**statura**-*la*	stature
151	**andare**-*vb*	go, move, proceed, run
152	**vicino**-*adj; adv; il*	close, near
153	**intorno**-*adv*	around, round
154	**tribunale**-*il*	court
155	**anche**-*adv*	also, even; anchor
156	**dunque**-*adv*	therefore
157	**sotto**-*adv; prp; adj*	under, below; under
158	**giardino**-*il*	garden
159	**quasi**-*adv; pfx*	almost, nearly
160	**tavola**-*la*	table
161	**sei**-*num*	six
162	**gambero**-*il*	crayfish

163	**dietro**-*prp; il; adj; adv*	behind; back, rear; after; after
164	**credo**-*lo*	creed, credo
165	**bocca**-*la*	mouth
166	**mare**-*il*	sea, seaside
167	**lui**-*prn*	him, he
168	**trovare**-*vb*	find
169	**colombo**-*il*	pigeon
170	**potere**-*vb; il*	be able; power
171	**soltanto**-*adv*	only, solely
172	**troppo**-*adv; con; adj*	too much
173	**maestà**-*la*	majesty
174	**ancora**-*adv; con; le*	yet, still, more; more
175	**essa**-*prn*	it
176	**te**-*prn*	you
177	**dentro**-*adv; prp*	in, inside
178	**servire**-*vb*	serve
179	**bimbo**-*il*	baby, child
180	**capitolo**-*il*	chapter
181	**pane**-*il*	bread
182	**pure**-*adv*	also
183	**presto**-*adv*	soon, early
184	**innanzi**-*prp; adv*	before; forward
185	**ragione**-*la; adj*	reason
186	**neppure**-*adv; con*	not even, neither
187	**curioso**-*adj*	curious
188	**noi**-*prn*	we
189	**vostro**-*adj*	your (pl)
190	**cuoco**-*il*	cook
191	**guanto**-*il*	glove, gauntlet
192	**paura**-*la*	fear
193	**tale**-*adj; prn; art; phr*	such; such; a, an
194	**fanciulla**-*la*	girl
195	**stagno**-*il; adj*	pond; watertight
196	**braccio**-*il*	arm
197	**domanda**-*la*	demand, question
198	**lungo**-*adj; prp; il*	long; along; length
199	**indietro**-*adv*	back
200	**cantare**-*vb*	sing
201	**volgere**-*vb*	turn
202	**dove**-*adv; con*	where; where
203	**sala**-*la*	room
204	**fretta**-*la*	hurry
205	**eppure**-*con*	and yet
206	**silenziare**-*vb*	mute
207	**contro**-*adv; prp; il*	against, counter; against, versus
208	**affatto**-*adv*	at all, quite
209	**aspettare**-*vb*	wait
210	**rivolgere**-*vb*	turn, direct
211	**replicare**-*vb*	replicate, reply
212	**sorprendere**-*vb*	surprise
213	**perciò**-*con; adv*	therefore; accordingly
214	**importante**-*adj*	important
215	**cercare**-*vb*	search
216	**soldato**-*il*	soldier
217	**ventaglio**-*il*	fan
218	**lieto**-*adj*	happy
219	**insieme**-*adv; il/la*	together; set, whole
220	**cui**-*prn; con*	which
221	**saio**-*il*	habit
222	**alto**-*adj; lo*	high, tall
223	**povero**-*adj; il*	poor; the poor
224	**eh**-*int*	huh
225	**lacrima**-*la*	tear
226	**restare**-*vb*	stay, remain, maintain
227	**senso**-*il*	direction, sense, meaning
228	**mondo**-*il; adj*	world
229	**fungo**-*il*	mushroom
230	**grazia**-*la*	grace, pardon
231	**parere**-*vb*	think, seem; opinion
232	**vecchio**-*adj; il*	old; old (wo)man
233	**foresta**-*la*	forest
234	**pepe**-*il*	pepper
235	**caro**-*adj*	dear, expensive; dear
236	**bello**-*adj*	beautiful
237	**pozzo**-*il*	well
238	**spalla**-*la*	shoulder
239	**porcellino**-*il*	piggy, little pig
240	**male**-*adv; il*	bad, evil
241	**lezione**-*la*	lesson
242	**presso**-*prp; adv; adj*	at, in; near; close
243	**fante**-*il*	knave, infantryman
244	**siccome**-*con*	since
245	**piccolo**-*adj; il*	little, small
246	**sembrare**-*vb*	seem, look, sound
247	**importare**-*vb*	import
248	**egli**-*prn*	he
249	**naso**-*il*	nose
250	**naturale**-*adj*	natural

251	**presa**-*la*	outlet
252	**essi**-*prn*	they, them
253	**primo**-*num; adj*	first
254	**buono**-*adj; il*	good; voucher, coupon
255	**simile**-*adj*	similar, alike
256	**burro**-*il*	butter
257	**storia**-*la*	history, story
258	**orecchio**-*il*	ear
259	**inutile**-*adj*	useless, unnecessary
260	**ah**-*int*	ha
261	**ce**-*prn*	us
262	**rincominciare**-*vb*	start again
263	**parte**-*la*	part
264	**timidamente**-*adv*	shyly
265	**lavagna**-*la*	blackboard
266	**però**-*con; adv*	but, yet; however
267	**morale**-*adj; la*	moral
268	**porgere**-*vb*	extend
269	**cinque**-*num*	five
270	**lato**-*il; adj*	side
271	**uccello**-*il*	bird
272	**almeno**-*adv*	at least
273	**torcere**-*vb*	twist
274	**grande**-*adj*	great, great
275	**dettare**-*vb*	dictate
276	**momento**-*il*	moment
277	**confusione**-*la*	confusion
278	**bambino**-*il*	child, baby, boy/girl
279	**crescere**-*vb*	grow
280	**collare**-*il; vb*	collar; size
281	**vita**-*la*	life, waist
282	**interrompere**-*vb*	stop, interrupt
283	**finestra**-*la*	window
284	**giardiniere**-*il*	gardener
285	**processo**-*il*	process
286	**piacere**-*vb*	pleasure; like
287	**aprire**-*vb*	open
288	**sera**-*la*	evening
289	**matto**-*adj; il*	crazy; madman
290	**cuore**-*il*	heart, core
291	**fine**-*la; adj*	purpose; end; fine
292	**giungere**-*vb*	reach
293	**conversazione**-*la*	conversation
294	**bisbigliare**-*vb*	whisper
295	**tardi**-*adv*	late
296	**discorso**-*il*	speech
297	**porre**-*vb*	put, place
298	**contentare**-*vb*	satisfy
299	**strano**-*adj*	strange
300	**scuola**-*la*	school
301	**serpente**-*il*	snake, serpent
302	**ansietà**-*la*	anxiety
303	**riprendere**-*vb*	resume
304	**coro**-*il*	choir
305	**scrivere**-*vb*	write
306	**basso**-*adj; il*	low, bottom, lower; bass
307	**altezza**-*le*	height
308	**sorella**-*la*	sister
309	**uscio**-*il*	door
310	**ebbene**-*adv*	so, well
311	**riccio**-*adj; il*	curly; hedgehog
312	**fondo**-*il; adj*	background, bottom, fund; deep
313	**davanti**-*adj; adv; prp; gli*	front; in front
314	**mento**-*il*	chin
315	**bestia**-*la*	beast
316	**curiosità**-*la*	curiosity
317	**nome**-*il*	name
318	**uscire**-*vb*	go out, leave
319	**giusto**-*adj; adv*	right, just, fair; correctly
320	**ve**-*prn*	you
321	**zuppo**-*adj*	soaked
322	**furiosamente**-*adv*	furiously
323	**talmente**-*adv*	so
324	**resto**-*il*	rest
325	**minuto**-*adj; il*	minute
326	**venire**-*vb*	come
327	**morire**-*vb; phr*	die
328	**finire**-*vb*	end, finish
329	**avventura**-*le*	adventure
330	**sette**-*i*	seven
331	**temere**-*vb*	fear, be afraid
332	**cadere**-*vb*	fall
333	**ghigno**-*il*	fleer
334	**mangiare**-*vb; il*	eat
335	**rammentare**-*vb*	remind
336	**riguardare**-*vb*	concern
337	**grosso**-*adj*	big, thick
338	**dieci**-*num*	ten
339	**caso**-*il*	case
340	**gola**-*la*	throat

341	**tazza**-*la*	cup
342	**oro**-*il*	gold
343	**correre**-*vb*	run
344	**guaio**-*il*	trouble
345	**racconto**-*il*	(short) story
346	**sedere**-*vb*	sit down
347	**levare**-*vb; il*	upbeat
348	**quattro**-*num*	four
349	**spiaggia**-*la*	beach
350	**India**-*la*	India
351	**dovere**-*il; vb; av*	have to, must; duty
352	**stato**-*il*	state
353	**dare**-*vb*	give
354	**contraddanza**-*la*	contredanse
355	**cristallo**-*il*	crystal
356	**entrambi**-*adj*	both, either
357	**gente**-*la*	people
358	**dito**-*il*	finger
359	**metà**-*la*	half
360	**peccare**-*vb*	sin
361	**libro**-*il*	book
362	**idea**-*la*	idea
363	**foglio**-*il*	sheet, leaf
364	**foglia**-*la*	leaf
365	**corso**-*il*	course
366	**difficoltà**-*le*	difficulties, difficulty, trouble
367	**minestra**-*la*	soup
368	**alcun**-*adj*	any
369	**significare**-*vb*	mean
370	**terreno**-*il; adj*	ground, soil; earthly
371	**leggere**-*vb*	read
372	**pollice**-*il*	inch
373	**piccina**-*la*	kiddie
374	**rumore**-*il*	noise
375	**lucertola**-*la*	lizard
376	**intanto**-*adv*	in the meantime
377	**un'**-*art*	a
378	**provare**-*vb*	try
379	**attenzione**-*le*	caution
380	**bisognare**-*vb*	must
381	**poverino**-*il*	poor darling
382	**solo**-*adj; adv*	only
383	**bere**-*vb; il*	drinking
384	**benchè**-*con*	although
385	**fuggire**-*vb*	flee
386	**passare**-*vb*	pass, spend, switch
387	**pipa**-*la*	pipe
388	**lentamente**-*adv*	slowly
389	**nostro**-*prn*	our
390	**pezzettino**-*il*	snippet
391	**sogno**-*il*	dream
392	**difficile**-*adj*	difficult
393	**fiore**-*il*	flower
394	**accorgersi**-*vb*	notice, realize
395	**dubbio**-*il; adj*	doubtful; doubt
396	**ognuno**-*adj; prn*	each
397	**urlare**-*vb*	scream
398	**causa**-*la*	cause
399	**capello**-*il*	hair
400	**picchiare**-*vb*	beat
401	**zampa**-*la*	paw
402	**spesso**-*adv; adj*	often; thick
403	**cagnolino**-*il*	puppy, doggie
404	**entrare**-*vb*	enter
405	**partire**-*vb*	leave
406	**testimone**-*il/la*	witness
407	**prendere**-*vb*	take
408	**ripetere**-*vb*	repeat
409	**qual**-*adv; prn*	everytime, whenever; what, which
410	**nuotare**-*vb*	swim
411	**cogliere**-*vb*	take, catch
412	**lontano**-*adv; adj; prp*	far
413	**caminetto**-*il*	fireplace
414	**viso**-*il*	face
415	**secondo**-*adj; adv; num; prp; con*	according to; second
416	**scossa**-*la*	shock
417	**sciocchezza**-*la*	foolishness
418	**mutamento**-*il*	change
419	**rose**-*adj*	rose
420	**tuono**-*il*	thunder
421	**qualcheduno**-*il*	someone
422	**vivamente**-*adv*	vividly
423	**distanza**-*la*	distance
424	**invece**-*adv*	instead
425	**scommettere**-*vb*	bet
426	**esse**-*prn*	they
427	**ritornare**-*vb*	return
428	**osare**-*vb*	dare
429	**altrimenti**-*adv*	otherwise
430	**nove**-*num*	nine

431	l'-*art*	the
432	albero-*il*	tree
433	tuo-*adj*	your
434	aria-*la*	air, song
435	principio-*il*	principle
436	mazzo-*il*	deck, bunch
437	badare-*vb*	look after
438	miglior-*adj*	best
439	nottola-*la*	noctule
440	sospiro-*il*	sigh
441	canzonare-*vb*	tease
442	grazie-*int*	thank you
443	singhiozzo-*il*	sob
444	teste-*il, la*	witness
445	saltare-*vb*	skip, jump
446	tetto-*il*	roof
447	bimba-*la*	infant
448	destro-*adj; il*	right
449	vecchio-*adj; il*	old; old (wo)man
450	dodici-*num*	twelve
451	razza-*la*	race, breed, stingray
452	pelo-*il*	hair, fur, coat
453	lontananza-*la*	distance
454	indicare-*vb*	indicate, show
455	mattina-*la*	morning
456	stanco-*adj*	tired
457	versare-*vb*	pour, spill
458	capire-*vb*	understand
459	bestiolina-*f*	peewee
460	conserto-*adj*	crossed
461	esempio-*gli*	example
462	maniera-*la*	way, manner
463	sonno-*il*	sleep
464	mozzare-*vb*	cut off
465	tartaruga-*la*	tortoise
466	cucina-*la*	kitchen
467	sorta-*la*	kind
468	strofa-*la*	stanza
469	talvolta-*adv*	at times
470	proposito-*il*	purpose, intention
471	grave-*adj*	serious, severe
472	riuscire-*vb*	succeed, able
473	rassomigliare-*vb*	resemble
474	ballare-*vb*	dance
475	soppressata-*la*	headcheese
476	ginocchio-*il*	knee
477	uovo-*lo*	egg
478	tosto-*il; adj*	toast; bad-ass
479	testimonianza-*la*	testimony
480	verdetto-*il*	verdict, judgment
481	sollecitamente-*adv*	solicitously
482	totalmente-*adv*	totally
483	astro-*gli*	star
484	sparire-*vb*	disappear
485	rimettere-*vb*	replace, return
486	conigliera-*la*	rabbit hutch
487	bambina-*la*	child
488	oltre-*adv; prp*	over; over, more than, beyond
489	scala-*la*	ladder, scale, stairs
490	colorare-*vb*	color
491	dimenticare-*vb*	forget
492	ricordare-*vb*	remember
493	premura-*la*	care
494	argomento-*gli*	topic, subject, argument
495	valere-*vb*	be worth
496	meschino-*adj*	petty, mean
497	puntare-*vb*	point, aim
498	accoccolarsi-*vb*	curl up
499	lingua-*la*	tongue, language
500	riflettere-*vb*	reflect
501	ieri-*adv; lo*	yesterday
502	speranza-*la*	hope
503	cervello-*il*	brain
504	gatta-*la*	cat
505	ramo-*il*	branch, bough
506	francese-*adj; il*	French
507	alcune-*prn*	several, some
508	folla-*la*	crowd
509	cartello-*il*	cartel, sign
510	spaventare-*vb*	scare, frighten
511	tuonare-*vb*	thunder
512	testimoniare-*vb*	witness, testify
513	generalmente-*adv*	generally, as a rule
514	solenne-*adj*	solemn, impressive
515	mente-*la*	mind
516	sentenza-*la*	judgment, sentence
517	sospirare-*vb*	sigh
518	giovanetto-*il*	lad
519	tremante-*adj*	trembling, shaking
520	esso-*prn*	it, he
521	acuto-*adj; il*	acute; high note

522	**girare**-*vb*	turn	
523	**ormai**-*adv*	by now, almost, by then	
524	**processione**-*la*	procession	
525	**dianzi**-*adv*	just now	
526	**alzare**-*vb*	raise	
527	**osservazione**-*le*	observation, remark	
528	**ditale**-*il*	thimble	
529	**deporre**-*vb*	lay, testify	
530	**pesce**-*il*	fish	
531	**intendere**-*vb*	hear, mean, intend	
532	**regola**-*la*	rule	
533	**conoscere**-*vb*	know	
534	**tremare**-*vb*	tremble, shake	
535	**spiegare**-*vb*	explain	
536	**conservare**-*vb*	keep, preserve	
537	**inutilmente**-*adv*	uselessly	
538	**rendere**-*vb*	make	
539	**propizio**-*adj*	favorable	
540	**accadere**-*vb*	happen	
541	**diverso**-*adj*	different	
542	**danzare**-*vb*	dance	
543	**appoggiare**-*vb*	support, rest	
544	**persona**-*la*	person	
545	**riverenza**-*la*	reverence	
546	**seguire**-*vb*	follow	
547	**scritto**-*adj; lo*	written	
548	**amore**-*il*	(my) love	
549	**sinistra**-*la*	left	
550	**affrettare**-*vb*	hasten, expedite	
551	**muovere**-*vb*	move	
552	**motto**-*il*	motto	
553	**arco**-*lo*	bow	
554	**battere**-*vb*	beat	
555	**scioccare**-*vb*	shock	
556	**spazio**-*lo*	space	
557	**orlo**-*ill*	hem	
558	**buca**-*la*	hole, pit	
559	**buon**-*adj*	delicious	
560	**quaggiù**-*adv*	hither	
561	**notte**-*la*	night	
562	**breve**-*adj; la*	short	
563	**delitto**-*il*	crime	
564	**cielo**-*il*	sky	
565	**veramente**-*adv*	really	
566	**papa**-*il*	Pope	
567	**settimana**-*la*	week	

568	**vento**-*il*	wind	
569	**tavolino**-*il*	table	
570	**nemmeno**-*adv; con*	not even, neither	
571	**disprezzo**-*il*	contempt	
572	**pena**-*la*	penalty	
573	**porco**-*il*	pig	
574	**sicuro**-*adj; lo*	sure, safe, secure	
575	**discorrere**-*vb*	talk	
576	**imparare**-*vb*	learn	
577	**cane**-*il*	dog	
578	**giudice**-*il*	judge	
579	**posto**-*il*	place, spot, location	
580	**scambiare**-*vb*	exchange, swap	
581	**eccomi**-*int*	coming!	
582	**abituato**-*adj*	wont	
583	**babbo**-*il*	dad, father	
584	**appresso**-*prp; adv*	near; lateral	
585	**pronto**-*adj; adv*	ready	
586	**cioè**-*adv; abr*	i.e., that is, namely	
587	**inforcare**-*vb*	get on	
588	**afferrare**-*vb*	grab, grasp	
589	**attimo**-*lo*	moment, instant	
590	**oggi**-*adv; il*	today	
591	**profondamente**-*adv*	deeply	
592	**attorno**-*adv*	about; around	
593	**profondo**-*adj*	deep	
594	**persuadere**-*vb*	persuade, convince	
595	**sopprimere**-*vb*	abolish	
596	**colà**-*adv*	there	
597	**frase**-*la*	phrase, sentence	
598	**palchetto**-*il*	shelf	
599	**corridoio**-*il*	aisle, hallway	
600	**ballo**-*il*	dance, ball	
601	**luogo**-*il*	place	
602	**dormire**-*vb*	sleep	
603	**tondo**-*adj; il*	round; round	
604	**delicatezza**-*la*	delicacy, gentleness	
605	**dente**-*il*	tooth	
606	**circolare**-*adj; la; vb*	circular; circular; circulate	
607	**specie**-*le*	species, kind	
608	**matita**-*la*	pencil	
609	**possibile**-*adj*	possible	
610	**bastare**-*vb*	suffice	
611	**campo**-*il*	field	
612	**questione**-*la*	question	

613	**cannocchiale**-*il*	telescope
614	**signore**-*il/la; abr*	Mr. / Mrs.
615	**sommesso**-*adj*	low
616	**comune**-*adj; il*	common; community, town
617	**rimanere**-*vb*	stay
618	**carta**-*la*	paper, card, map
619	**mutare**-*vb*	change, slough
620	**indovinare**-*vb*	guess
621	**offeso**-*adj*	offended
622	**supporre**-*vb*	suppose
623	**irato**-*adj*	angry
624	**studiare**-*vb*	study
625	**carezzevole**-*adj*	caressing
626	**tornare**-*vb*	return
627	**sperare**-*vb*	hope
628	**dispetto**-*lo*	spite, annoyance
629	**abitare**-*vb*	live
630	**premiare**-*vb*	reward
631	**traverso**-*adj*	cross, oblique
632	**perdere**-*vb*	lose
633	**purchè**-*con*	provided
634	**mese**-*il*	month
635	**musica**-*la*	music
636	**avvenire**-*adj; il; vb*	future; future; occur
637	**erba**-*le*	grass, pot, herb
638	**librare**-*vb*	weight
639	**chiamare**-*vb*	call
640	**confuso**-*adj*	confused, fuzzy
641	**ritrovare**-*vb*	find
642	**zampino**-*il*	claw
643	**gamba**-*la*	leg
644	**figurare**-*vb*	appear, figure
645	**starnutire**-*vb*	sneeze
646	**corpo**-*il*	body
647	**verga**-*la*	rod
648	**costo**-*il*	cost
649	**vociare**-*vb*	shout
650	**chiamata**-*la*	(telephone) call
651	**credere**-*vb*	believe
652	**trarre**-*vb*	draw, get
653	**indi**-*adv*	therefrom
654	**lista**-*la*	list
655	**arruffare**-*vb*	ruffle
656	**alcun**-*adj*	any
657	**alcuno**-*adj*	any, some
658	**richiamare**-*vb*	call, recall

659	**tromba**-*la*	trumpet, bugle
660	**ala**-*le*	wing
661	**piano**-*il; adj; adv*	plan, floor, piano; plane, flat
662	**piatto**-*adj; il*	dish, plate
663	**forzare**-*vb*	force, compel
664	**forte**-*adj; il; adv*	strong; forte; loudly
665	**forma**-*la*	form
666	**pieno**-*adj; il*	full
667	**allorchè**-*con*	when
668	**signorina**-*la; abr*	young lady
669	**appunto**-*adv; i*	just
670	**sciocco**-*adj; lo*	silly
671	**gravemente**-*adv*	seriously, sorely
672	**interessante**-*adj*	interesting
673	**rapidamente**-*adv*	quickly
674	**lustro**-*il; adj*	shine; shiny
675	**lesto**-*adj*	quick
676	**stupido**-*adj; lo*	stupid
677	**invito**-*lo*	invitation
678	**veduta**-*la*	view
679	**lesso**-*adj; il*	boiled; boiled meat
680	**ranocchio**-*il*	frog
681	**debole**-*adj; il/la*	weak
682	**autorevole**-*adj*	authoritative
683	**pur**-*adv*	while
684	**tratto**-*il*	stretch
685	**carino**-*adj*	cute, nice, pretty
686	**spazioso**-*adj*	spacious
687	**anno**-*gli*	year
688	**udire**-*vb*	hear
689	**occhiali**-*gli*	glasses
690	**gomito**-*il*	elbow
691	**immediatamente**-*adv*	immediately
692	**marzo**-*gli*	March
693	**chiunque**-*prn*	anyone
694	**senape**-*la*	mustard
695	**disdegnare**-*vb*	disdain
696	**benissimo**-*adv*	very well, fine
697	**reale**-*adj*	real, actual
698	**livrea**-*la*	livery
699	**addio**-*il*	goodbye, farewell
700	**labbro**-*il*	lip
701	**taschino**-*il*	pocket
702	**miglio**-*il*	mile
703	**probabilmente**-*adv*	probably

704	**affare**-*il*	deal, business, affair
705	**paese**-*il*	country, village
706	**storiella**-*la*	joke
707	**creatura**-*la*	creature
708	**petto**-*il*	chest
709	**confetto**-*il*	candy
710	**scappare**-*vb*	escape
711	**secco**-*adj*	dry
712	**umore**-*il*	mood, humor
713	**fontana**-*la*	fountain
714	**cantonata**-*la*	corner
715	**camminare**-*vb*	walk
716	**avvicinare**-*vb*	approach
717	**fiamma**-*la*	flame
718	**acqua**-*le*	water
719	**concertare**-*vb*	concert
720	**severo**-*adj; il*	severe; martinet
721	**bianco**-*adj; il*	white
722	**scaraventare**-*vb*	hurl
723	**diventare**-*vb*	become
724	**giusto**-*adj; adv*	right, just, fair; correctly
725	**pezzo**-*il*	piece
726	**segnare**-*vb*	score, sign
727	**segno**-*il*	sign
728	**veleno**-*il*	poison
729	**anitra**-*la*	duck
730	**risata**-*la*	laugh
731	**cetriolo**-*il*	cucumber
732	**focolare**-*il; il*	hearth; astronomer
733	**passo**-*il*	passage, step, pace, stride
734	**mollo**-*adj*	soaked, flabby
735	**starnuto**-*lo*	sneeze
736	**starnutare**-*vb*	sneeze
737	**quindici**-*num*	fifteen
738	**guaire**-*vb*	yelp
739	**trono**-*il*	throne
740	**fuso**-*adj; il*	melted; spindle
741	**compassione**-*la*	compassion, sympathy
742	**divorare**-*vb*	devour
743	**gemito**-*il*	groan, whine
744	**patata**-*la*	potato, pussy (coll)
745	**tremulo**-*adj*	trembling
746	**stanotte**-*adv*	tonight
747	**cascare**-*vb*	fall
748	**dialogo**-*il*	dialogue, conversation
749	**recitare**-*vb*	recite
750	**presentare**-*vb*	present, submit
751	**sguardo**-*lo*	look
752	**sbadigliare**-*vb*	yawn
753	**rispetto**-*il*	respect
754	**apertamente**-*adv*	openly
755	**semplicemente**-*adv*	simply
756	**occhione**-*il*	stone curlew
757	**candela**-*la*	candle, spark plug
758	**pronunziare**-*vb*	speak
759	**granchio**-*il*	crab
760	**serie**-*la*	series, set
761	**straordinario**-*adj; lo*	extraordinary; overtime
762	**opera**-*le*	opera
763	**globo**-*il*	globe, orb
764	**applauso**-*il*	applause
765	**vinto**-*il; adj*	loser; defeated
766	**violenza**-*la*	violence
767	**ascoltare**-*vb*	listen
768	**firmare**-*vb*	sign
769	**rabbioso**-*adj*	angry, rabid
770	**furia**-*la*	fury, rampage
771	**teco**-*prn*	with you
772	**staccare**-*vb*	remove, separate
773	**romanzo**-*il*	novel, romance
774	**imprimere**-*vb*	give, impress
775	**stropicciare**-*vb*	rub
776	**salto**-*il*	leap, jump
777	**genere**-*il*	gender, kind, genre
778	**salvo**-*prp; adj*	save, but; safe
779	**virtù**-*le*	virtue
780	**scoppiare**-*vb*	burst, break out
781	**scoprire**-*vb*	discover
782	**creanza**-*la*	civility
783	**ritorno**-*il*	return
784	**contare**-*vb*	count
785	**urlo**-*gli*	yell, cry, shout
786	**abbastanza**-*adv; adj*	enough
787	**singhiozzare**-*vb*	sob
788	**iscrizione**-*le*	entry, registration
789	**rifiutare**-*vb*	refuse
790	**promettere**-*vb*	promise
791	**paio**-*il*	pair
792	**rivoltare**-*vb*	turn over

793	**domani**-*adv; gli*	tomorrow
794	**grattare**-*vb*	scratch, scrape
795	**gusto**-*il*	taste
796	**quieto**-*adj*	quiet
797	**topo**-*il*	mouse
798	**giro**-*il*	tour
799	**commedia**-*la*	comedy
800	**beccare**-*vb*	peck, catch
801	**trasformare**-*vb*	transform, turn
802	**razzo**-*il*	rocket, squib
803	**ricominciare**-*vb*	recommence
804	**annoiare**-*vb*	bore, get bored
805	**soave**-*adj*	sweet
806	**coltello**-*il*	knife
807	**tasca**-*la*	pocket
808	**zittire**-*vb*	silence
809	**cavare**-*vb*	get, dig
810	**sensazione**-*la*	sensation
811	**pasticciare**-*vb*	mess up, mull
812	**pasticcino**-*il*	pastry
813	**dirigere**-*vb*	direct
814	**camino**-*il*	fireplace
815	**caccia**-*la*	hunting
816	**cacciare**-*vb*	hunt, throw out
817	**apparire**-*vb*	appear, show
818	**contento**-*adj*	happy
819	**vetro**-*il*	glass
820	**penzoloni**-*il; adv*	hanging; dingle-dangle
821	**vivente**-*adj*	living, living being
822	**liberare**-*vb*	release
823	**autorità**-*le*	authority
824	**cortigiano**-*il*	courtier
825	**prorompere**-*vb*	burst
826	**croquet**-*il*	croquet
827	**sonnacchioso**-*adv*	sleepily
828	**circa**-*adv; prp*	about
829	**rovescio**-*adj; il*	reverse; back
830	**mormorare**-*vb*	murmur, whisper
831	**incontrare**-*vb*	meet
832	**sognare**-*vb*	dream
833	**chiaramente**-*adv*	clearly
834	**impaziente**-*adj*	impatient
835	**fiatare**-*vb*	breathe
836	**fiato**-*il*	breath
837	**capitale**-*adj; la*	capital
838	**lumaca**-*la*	snail

839	**tocco**-*il; adj*	touch
840	**ultimo**-*adj*	last, latest
841	**poggio**-*il*	hillock
842	**capitare**-*vb*	happen, occur
843	**ricomparire**-*vb*	reappear
844	**rabbia**-*la*	anger
845	**bagno**-*il*	bathroom
846	**mezz'ora**-*la*	half an hour
847	**risvegliare**-*vb*	awaken, revive
848	**baffo**-*il*	whiskers
849	**feroce**-*adj*	fierce, savage
850	**respiro**-*il*	breath
851	**sommo**-*adj*	highest
852	**sollevare**-*vb*	lift, raise
853	**maestro**-*il; adj*	master, teacher, meastro
854	**rosso**-*adj; il*	red
855	**figliare**-*vb*	calve
856	**cenno**-*il*	sign
857	**pensieroso**-*adj*	thoughtful
858	**ordine**-*gli*	order
859	**ampolla**-*la*	ampoule
860	**applaudire**-*vb*	applaud, cheer
861	**libriccino**-*il*	booklet
862	**ameno**-*adj*	pleasant
863	**disperato**-*adj*	desperate
864	**invitare**-*vb*	invite
865	**donnola**-*la*	weasel
866	**cerca**-*la*	search
867	**comprendere**-*vb*	understand
868	**tagliare**-*vb*	cut
869	**tagliare**-*vb*	cut
870	**fresco**-*adj; il*	fresh, cool
871	**lungi**-*adv*	far
872	**accorto**-*adj*	shrewd
873	**lasciare**-*vb*	leave
874	**terminare**-*vb*	end, conclude
875	**minimo**-*adj; il*	minimum
876	**meraviglia**-*la*	wonder
877	**meravigliare**-*vb*	wonder, surprise
878	**braccetto**-*il*	arm
879	**giammai**-*adv*	never
880	**sventurato**-*adj*	unfortunate
881	**pergamena**-*la*	parchment
882	**ridere**-*vb*	laugh
883	**granduca**-*il*	Grand Duke
884	**trionfare**-*vb*	triumph

885	**aggiungere**-*vb*	add
886	**tranquillamente**-*adv*	quietly
887	**vincere**-*vb*	win
888	**corona**-*la*	crown, wreath
889	**mistero**-*il*	mystery
890	**fracasso**-*il*	din, crash
891	**suonare**-*vb*	play (music or instrument), sound, ring
892	**avvertimento**-*il*	warning, caution
893	**faccenda**-*la*	affair
894	**briciolo**-*lo*	bit
895	**apparecchiare**-*vb*	lay
896	**cardo**-*il*	thistle
897	**fanciullezza**-*la*	childhood
898	**occasione**-*le*	opportunity
899	**calderone**-*il*	cauldron
900	**calcio**-*il*	football, soccer
901	**sepolcrale**-*adj*	sepulchral
902	**voltare**-*vb*	turn
903	**urtare**-*vb*	bump, strike
904	**ghignare**-*vb*	sneer
905	**sdegnoso**-*adj*	disdainful
906	**dato**-*adj; il*	given; fact, datum
907	**giurare**-*vb*	swear
908	**inghiottire**-*vb*	swallow, gulp
909	**rubare**-*vb*	steal
910	**secernere**-*vb*	secrete
911	**medesimo**-*adj*	same
912	**borbottare**-*vb*	mutter
913	**vergognarsi**-*vb*	be ashamed
914	**mostrare**-*vb*	show
915	**prontamente**-*adv*	readily
916	**avanti**-*adv*	forward, ahead, on
917	**compare**-*gli*	gaffer
918	**selvaggio**-*adj; il*	wild
919	**ancorchè**-*con*	although
920	**attaccato**-*adj*	attached
921	**profittare**-*vb*	profit
922	**correttamente**-*adv*	correctly
923	**traversare**-*vb*	navigate
924	**civile**-*adj; lo*	civil; civilian
925	**fetta**-*la*	slice, cut
926	**attacco**-*lo*	attack
927	**accingere**-*vb*	wrap
928	**dimenticato**-*adj*	forgotten
929	**strillare**-*vb*	scream, shriek
930	**nuovamente**-*adv*	again
931	**sconsolare**-*vb*	discourage
932	**carezza**-*la*	caress
933	**smettere**-*vb*	stop
934	**apparenza**-*le*	appearance, guise
935	**testolina**-*la*	small head
936	**vaso**-*il*	vase
937	**sorellina**-*la*	litte sister, younger sister, baby sister
938	**allungare**-*vb*	stretch, lengthen
939	**moglie**-*la*	wife
940	**pesciolino**-*il*	minnow
941	**preparare**-*vb*	prepare
942	**oppure**-*con*	or, or else
943	**consiglio**-*il*	advice, council, board
944	**sassolino**-*il*	pebble
945	**perdono**-*il*	pardon, forgiveness
946	**colpire**-*vb*	hit
947	**effetto**-*il*	effect
948	**colpo**-*il*	hit
949	**precipizio**-*il*	precipice
950	**servitore**-*il*	servant
951	**intiero**-*adj*	entire
952	**chiedere**-*vb*	ask (for), enquire
953	**duro**-*adj; il*	hard
954	**vile**-*adj; il*	vile; dastard
955	**vino**-*il*	wine
956	**moto**-*il*	motion, motorbike
957	**vivo**-*adj; lo*	alive, live
958	**trasformazione**-*la*	transformation
959	**prigioniero**-*il; adj*	prisoner
960	**movimento**-*il*	movement
961	**subitaneo**-*adj*	sudden
962	**adagio**-*il; adv*	adage; adagio
963	**schiena**-*la*	back
964	**corto**-*adj*	short
965	**succedere**-*vb*	happen, occur, succeed
966	**verità**-*la*	truth
967	**estremità**-*le*	end, butt
968	**usciere**-*il*	usher
969	**linea**-*la*	line, figure
970	**età**-*le*	age
971	**italiano**-*adj; lo*	Italian
972	**arrabbiato**-*adj*	angry
973	**condannare**-*vb*	convict
974	**miniera**-*la*	mine

975	**ammalato**-*adj; il*	sick; sick person	
976	**volare**-*vb*	fly	
977	**premere**-*vb*	press, depress	
978	**sfilare**-*vb*	parade	
979	**attendere**-*vb*	wait for	
980	**anelare**-*vb*	yearn	
981	**ricondurre**-*vb*	bring back	
982	**carrettata**-*la*	cartful	
983	**opportunità**-*le*	opportunity	
984	**paladino**-*il*	paladin	
985	**appartenere**-*vb*	belong	
986	**scortese**-*adj*	rude, impolite	
987	**grugnire**-*vb*	grunt	
988	**poesia**-*la*	poetry	
989	**vivere**-*vb*	live	
990	**collera**-*la*	anger, rage	
991	**resa**-*la*	yield	
992	**steccato**-*i*	steccato	
993	**impazienza**-*le*	impatience	
994	**aquilotto**-*il*	eaglet	
995	**lettera**-*la*	letter	
996	**erudizione**-*le*	erudition	
997	**mortalmente**-*adv*	mortally	
998	**uso**-*lo*	use, usage	
999	**portare**-*vb*	bring	
1000	**proverbio**-*il*	proverb, saying	
1001	**padella**-*la*	pan	
1002	**scavare**-*vb*	dig	
1003	**delizioso**-*adj*	delicious	
1004	**cotanto**-*adj*	so	
1005	**tracciare**-*vb*	draw	
1006	**giornata**-*la*	day	
1007	**spaventato**-*adj*	afraid	
1008	**chiuso**-*adj; lo*	closed	
1009	**chiusa**-*le*	close, lock, sluice	
1010	**quaranta**-*num*	forty	
1011	**ruzzo**-*il*	romp	
1012	**fermare**-*vb*	stop	
1013	**gustare**-*vb*	enjoy, taste	
1014	**diritto**-*il; adj; adv*	right, law; straight; straight	
1015	**consistere**-*vb*	consist	
1016	**latitudine**-*la*	latitude	
1017	**malandrino**-*il*	rogue	
1018	**bottiglia**-*la*	bottle	
1019	**furioso**-*adj*	furious, mad	
1020	**nessun**-*adj*	no	
1021	**austero**-*adj*	austere	
1022	**capitombolo**-*il*	tumble	
1023	**prego**-*int*	please, you're welcome	
1024	**raccontare**-*vb*	tell	
1025	**soletta**-*la*	insole	
1026	**ritirare**-*vb; adv*	withdraw; throw again	
1027	**taccuino**-*il*	notebook	
1028	**piccino**-*adj; il*	little; child	
1029	**piangere**-*vb*	cry	
1030	**invano**-*adv; adj*	in vain; no purpose	
1031	**peggio**-*adj; il; adv*	worse	
1032	**dorato**-*adj*	golden, gold-plated	
1033	**mesto**-*adj*	sad	
1034	**servizievole**-*adj*	helpful	
1035	**cucciolo**-*il*	puppy	
1036	**mostra**-*la*	show	
1037	**cantante**-*il/la; adj*	singer; singing	
1038	**specchio**-*il*	mirror	
1039	**qua**-*adv*	here	
1040	**centesimo**-*il*	hundredth; cent	
1041	**sin**-*con*	since	
1042	**servizio**-*il*	service, report	
1043	**regale**-*adj*	kingly	
1044	**regalo**-*il*	gift, present	
1045	**latte**-*nm*	milk	
1046	**nasello**-*il*	hake	
1047	**scatola**-*la*	box	
1048	**parolone**-*il*	long word	
1049	**addossare**-*vb*	lean	
1050	**entrata**-*la*	entrance	
1051	**produrre**-*vb*	produce	
1052	**longitudine**-*la*	longitude	
1053	**ragazzina**-*la*	little girl	
1054	**squillo**-*lo*	ring	
1055	**dovunque**-*adv; con*	anywhere	
1056	**triste**-*adj*	sad	
1057	**siepe**-*la*	hedge	
1058	**adagiare**-*vb*	lay down	
1059	**maneggiare**-*vb*	handle, use	
1060	**altrui**-*adj*	others	
1061	**trottare**-*vb*	trot	
1062	**ragazzo**-*il*	boy(friend)/girl(friend)	
1063	**ragazza**-*la*	girl	
1064	**allegrezza**-*la*	joyfulness	
1065	**bisogno**-*il*	need	
1066	**intento**-*adj; il*	intent; aim	

1067	**pianto**-*il; adj*	tears; lamented
1068	**nessuno**-*adj; prn*	no; nobody, anyone
1069	**scarpa**-*la*	shoe
1070	**porporino**-*adj*	purplish
1071	**filo**-*il*	wire
1072	**costoro**-*prn*	them
1073	**creaturina**-*la*	bundle, heap
1074	**brutto**-*adj; il*	ugly, bad; bad, ugliness
1075	**ponderare**-*vb*	ponder
1076	**imbarazzare**-*vb*	embarrass, perplex
1077	**solito**-*adj; il*	usual
1078	**animale**-*adj; il*	animal
1079	**giovare**-*vb*	profit
1080	**spalancare**-*vb*	open wide
1081	**titolo**-*il*	title
1082	**guardare**-*vb*	look, watch
1083	**progredire**-*vb*	progress
1084	**comprare**-*vb*	buy
1085	**sangue**-*il*	blood
1086	**fianco**-*il*	side
1087	**sdrucciolevole**-*adj*	slippery
1088	**nominare**-*vb*	appoint, name
1089	**equilibrio**-*lo*	equilibrium
1090	**prigione**-*la*	prison
1091	**assumere**-*vb*	take, assume
1092	**seccare**-*vb*	dry, bother
1093	**sgabello**-*lo*	stool
1094	**sottile**-*adj*	thin, slim
1095	**asciugare**-*vb*	dry, wipe
1096	**candido**-*adj; il*	white; white
1097	**panciotto**-*il*	waistcoat
1098	**agitare**-*vb*	shake, stir
1099	**scorrere**-*vb*	slide, flow
1100	**allettare**-*vb*	lure
1101	**quinto**-*adj*	fifth
1102	**palla**-*la*	ball
1103	**novelletta**-*la*	novelette
1104	**pavimento**-*il*	floor
1105	**convenire**-*vb*	agree
1106	**stupefare**-*vb*	stupefy, stun
1107	**prudente**-*adj*	prudent
1108	**uccellino**-*il*	birdie
1109	**ammazzare**-*vb*	kill
1110	**prudenza**-*la*	prudence, caution
1111	**nocca**-*la*	knuckle
1112	**sufficiente**-*adj*	enough, sufficient
1113	**quindi**-*adv*	then
1114	**grongo**-*il*	conger
1115	**crisalide**-*la*	chrysalis
1116	**processare**-*vb*	try
1117	**pressochè**-*adv*	almost
1118	**incomodo**-*adj*	uncomfortable
1119	**occupare**-*vb*	occupy
1120	**naturalmente**-*adv*	naturally
1121	**pizzicare**-*vb*	pinch, pluck
1122	**severamente**-*adv*	severely
1123	**baciare**-*vb*	kiss
1124	**mantenere**-*vb*	keep, maintain
1125	**divenire**-*vb*	become
1126	**tacere**-*vb*	be silent
1127	**sfolgorante**-*adj*	blazing
1128	**enorme**-*adj*	huge
1129	**riempire**-*vb*	fill
1130	**brivido**-*il*	thrill, prickle
1131	**panno**-*il*	cloth
1132	**cipolla**-*la*	onion
1133	**mo'**-*adv*	now
1134	**od**-*con*	or
1135	**dolere**-*vb*	ache, be sorry
1136	**pepaiola**-*la*	pepperpot
1137	**passaggio**-*il*	passage
1138	**amico**-*lo*	friend
1139	**impaurire**-*vb*	frighten, get frightened
1140	**sostenuto**-*adj*	fast
1141	**imitare**-*vb*	imitate, mimic
1142	**guanciale**-*nn*	pillow
1143	**eseguire**-*vb*	perform, execute
1144	**abbandonare**-*vb*	abandon sth, leave sth.
1145	**impiccare**-*vb*	hang
1146	**fiacco**-*adj*	weak
1147	**quattordici**-*num*	fourteen
1148	**poveretto**-*adj; il*	poor; poor thing
1149	**altresì**-*adv*	moreover
1150	**ultimamente**-*adv*	lately
1151	**imperturbabilità**-*la*	equability
1152	**tuttavia**-*adv; con*	however, nevertheless; but, yet
1153	**audace**-*adj*	bold, daring
1154	**amichevolmente**-*adv*	amicably
1155	**riandare**-*vb*	go again
1156	**schifoso**-*adj*	lousy (fa schifo= it sucks)

1157	**origliare**-*vb*	eavesdrop
1158	**convertire**-*vb*	convert
1159	**appiccicare**-*vb*	stick
1160	**ingannare**-*vb*	deceive, fool
1161	**geografia**-*la*	geography
1162	**pasto**-*il*	meal
1163	**durante**-*prp*	during, in, over; while
1164	**pregare**-*vb*	pray
1165	**corrucciata**-*adj*	frowning, annoyed
1166	**offrire**-*vb*	offer
1167	**chiedere**-*vb*	ask (for), enquire
1168	**avventare**-*vb*	fling, hurl
1169	**impazzare**-*vb*	go crazy
1170	**scuotere**-*vb*	shake, shook
1171	**maturo**-*adj*	mature, adult
1172	**arrivare**-*vb*	arrive
1173	**ornato**-*adj; il*	adorned; embellishment
1174	**assottigliare**-*vb*	thin
1175	**uditorio**-*il; adj*	audience; auditory
1176	**squadrare**-*vb*	square
1177	**dispiacere**-*il; vb*	dislike, be sorry
1178	**conficcare**-*vb*	stick, drive
1179	**procacciare**-*vb*	procure
1180	**distribuire**-*vb*	distribute, deliver
1181	**querelare**-*vb*	sue
1182	**sacco**-*il; adv*	bag, sack; a lot
1183	**pentirsi**-*vb*	repent
1184	**vegliare**-*vb*	watch over
1185	**rompere**-*vb*	break
1186	**balbettare**-*vb*	stutter, babble
1187	**fumo**-*il*	smoke
1188	**assomigliare**-*vb*	look like, resemble
1189	**nascondere**-*vb*	hide
1190	**fune**-*la*	cable, wire; rope, linen
1191	**giacere**-*vb*	lie
1192	**angosciato**-*adj*	distressed
1193	**terribile**-*adj*	terrible
1194	**avvedersi**-*vb*	notice
1195	**involti**-*gli*	bundle
1196	**adottare**-*vb*	adopt
1197	**desolante**-*adj*	distressing
1198	**grazioso**-*adj; adv*	pretty; pretty
1199	**cullare**-*vb*	rock
1200	**cipiglio**-*il*	frown
1201	**tegola**-*la*	tile
1202	**angusto**-*adj*	narrow

1203	**dolore**-*il*	ache, pain
1204	**accettare**-*vb*	accept
1205	**seguitare**-*vb*	continue
1206	**sinistro**-*adj*	left
1207	**annoiato**-*adj*	bored
1208	**vantaggio**-*il*	advantage
1209	**rapire**-*vb*	kidnap
1210	**comandata**-*la*	squad
1211	**visitare**-*vb*	visit, see
1212	**cameretta**-*la*	little room
1213	**strepito**-*il*	barking
1214	**comandare**-*vb*	command
1215	**saettare**-*vb*	dart
1216	**risposare**-*vb*	remarry
1217	**moscone**-*il*	bluebottle
1218	**ambizione**-*le*	ambition
1219	**ganascia**-*la*	jaw
1220	**rifare**-*vb*	redo, rebuild
1221	**allontanare**-*vb*	remove, avert
1222	**frullare**-*vb*	whisk, flutter
1223	**capovolgere**-*vb*	invert, reverse
1224	**colorire**-*vb*	color
1225	**dimorare**-*vb*	dwell, reside
1226	**coraggio**-*il*	courage
1227	**governare**-*vb*	govern, steer
1228	**sicuramente**-*adv*	certainly
1229	**attraente**-*adj*	attractive
1230	**accusa**-*la*	accusation, charge, prosecution
1231	**citare**-*vb*	quote, mention
1232	**vacanza**-*la*	holiday, vacation
1233	**burbero**-*adj; il*	gruff; curmudgeon
1234	**ardito**-*adj*	bold
1235	**inciso**-*adj*	incidentally
1236	**osso**-*il*	bone
1237	**magico**-*adj*	magical
1238	**decapitare**-*vb*	decapitate
1239	**fantasticare**-*vb*	daydream
1240	**altrove**-*adv*	elsewhere
1241	**fanciullo**-*il*	child
1242	**lagnarsi**-*vb*	complain
1243	**contenere**-*vb*	contain
1244	**morto**-*adj; il*	dead, died
1245	**trasalire**-*vb*	wince
1246	**armare**-*vb*	arm
1247	**maggio**-*gli*	May
1248	**scegliere**-*vb*	choose

1249	**visione**-*la*	vision
1250	**avventurare**-*vb*	venture
1251	**sonnolento**-*adj*	sleepy
1252	**insegnare**-*vb*	teach
1253	**fuoco**-*il*	fire
1254	**distrazione**-*la*	distraction
1255	**giocondo**-*adj*	jocund
1256	**seguente**-*adj*	following, next
1257	**tentare**-*vb*	attempt, try, tempt
1258	**curvatura**-*la*	curvature, bending
1259	**quadro**-*il*	painting, picture, panel, square
1260	**tenere**-*vb*	hold, keep
1261	**violento**-*adj*	violent
1262	**pazzo**-*adj; il; phr*	crazy
1263	**cavaliere**-*il*	knight
1264	**magnifico**-*adj*	magnificent
1265	**termine**-*il*	term
1266	**arrosto**-*adj; il*	roast; roast meet
1267	**rilucente**-*adj*	shining
1268	**inopinato**-*adj*	unexpected
1269	**telescopio**-*il*	telescope
1270	**gentile**-*adj*	kind, gentle
1271	**smorzare**-*vb*	dampen
1272	**disfare**-*vb*	undo, unpack
1273	**ricoprire**-*vb*	cover, hold
1274	**ippopotamo**-*il*	hippopotamus
1275	**deliziare**-*vb*	delight
1276	**mobiliare**-*adj; vb*	movable; furnish
1277	**ruminare**-*vb*	ruminate
1278	**paletta**-*la*	scoop
1279	**lavare**-*vb*	wash
1280	**caduto**-*adj*	fallen
1281	**indicare**-*vb*	indicate, show
1282	**bisbiglio**-*il*	whisper
1283	**sopportare**-*vb*	bear
1284	**riavere**-*vb*	get back
1285	**malcontento**-*adj; il*	discontent; dissatisfaction
1286	**muggito**-*adj; il*	lowing; roar
1287	**stellare**-*adj*	stellar
1288	**mangiata**-*la*	feed
1289	**soffrire**-*vb*	suffer
1290	**attaccare**-*vb*	attack
1291	**sfracellare**-*vb*	smash
1292	**estrarre**-*vb*	extract, pull out
1293	**seriamente**-*adv*	seriously
1294	**salsa**-*la*	sauce
1295	**pericoloso**-*adj*	dangerous
1296	**eccettuare**-*vb*	except
1297	**truppa**-*la*	troop
1298	**tirare**-*vb*	pull
1299	**ripassare**-*vb*	revise
1300	**soffitto**-*il*	ceiling
1301	**taglio**-*il*	cut, cutting
1302	**buco**-*il*	hole
1303	**risolvere**-*vb*	solve
1304	**cranio**-*il*	skull
1305	**dilatare**-*vb*	dilate
1306	**luminoso**-*adj*	bright, light
1307	**patibolo**-*il*	scaffold
1308	**grossezza**-*la*	thickness
1309	**immenso**-*adj*	immense
1310	**gradire**-*vb*	like
1311	**misura**-*la*	measure
1312	**sibilante**-*adj; la*	sibilant; sibilant
1313	**metodo**-*il*	method
1314	**mandare**-*vb*	send
1315	**aspetto**-*lo*	appearance, look, aspect
1316	**orecchio**-*il*	ear
1317	**teoria**-*la*	theory
1318	**bastonare**-*vb*	beat, club
1319	**seggiolone**-*il*	high chair
1320	**pagare**-*vb*	pay
1321	**bagnare**-*vb*	wet, soak
1322	**soffice**-*adj*	soft
1323	**sensibilità**-*la*	feeling, sensibility
1324	**bisticciare**-*vb*	quarrel
1325	**delicato**-*adj*	delicate, gentle
1326	**ciocca**-*la*	lock
1327	**follemente**-*adv*	madly, wildly
1328	**cifra**-*la*	figure, number
1329	**schizzare**-*vb*	splash, squirt
1330	**consultare**-*vb*	consult, examine
1331	**diamante**-*il*	diamond
1332	**strappare**-*vb*	rip, tear
1333	**veglia**-*la*	vigil
1334	**programma**-*il*	program
1335	**negare**-*vb*	deny, negate
1336	**principino**-*il*	prince
1337	**alfine**-*adv*	in order
1338	**approvazione**-*la*	approval, endorsement
1339	**angoscia**-*le*	anguish

1340	**verdeggiante**-*adj*	verdant	
1341	**tredici**-*num*	thirteen	
1342	**gravità**-*la; abr*	severity; G	
1343	**pace**-*la*	peace	
1344	**popolare**-*adj; vb; abr*	populair; to populate	
1345	**pompare**-*vb*	pump	
1346	**inventare**-*vb*	invent	
1347	**penetrare**-*vb*	penetrate, enter	
1348	**inquieto**-*adj*	restless, worried	
1349	**riempire**-*vb*	fill	
1350	**polipo**-*il*	octopus	
1351	**pari**-*adj; il*	equal	
1352	**operazione**-*le*	operation	
1353	**disegnare**-*vb*	draw, sketch	
1354	**pitoccare**-*vb*	beg	
1355	**impiegare**-*vb*	use, take	
1356	**sprofondare**-*vb*	collapse	
1357	**romano**-*adj; il*	Roman; Roman	
1358	**supplicare**-*vb*	beg, plead	
1359	**beati**-*adj*	blessed	
1360	**ferrovia**-*la*	railway, rail	
1361	**latrare**-*vb*	bark	
1362	**diamine**-*int*	heck	
1363	**sedici**-*num*	sixteen	
1364	**occupato**-*adj*	busy	
1365	**increspare**-*vb*	ruffle	
1366	**lesione**-*la*	lesion, injury	
1367	**giro**-*il*	tour	
1368	**civettare**-*vb*	flirt, jilt	
1369	**squarciagola**-*adv*	lustily	
1370	**tentativo**-*il*	attempt	
1371	**gocciolare**-*vb*	drip	
1372	**saltellare**-*vb*	hop	
1373	**venti**-*i*	twenty	
1374	**terrazzino**-*il*	balcony	
1375	**briga**-*la*	bother, trouble	
1376	**riconoscere**-*vb*	recognize	
1377	**Pasqua**-*la*	Easter	
1378	**appassire**-*vb*	wither	
1379	**raggiro**-*il*	swindle	
1380	**prestare**-*vb*	loan, give	
1381	**impressione**-*le*	impression	
1382	**verde**-*adj; il*	green	
1383	**brodoso**-*adj*	watery	
1384	**stomaco**-*lo*	stomach	
1385	**toscano**-*adj; il*	Tuscan; Tuscan	

1386	**cremare**-*vb*	cremate	
1387	**impertinente**-*adj*	impertinent, naughty	
1388	**apparizione**-*le*	appearance	
1389	**addolcire**-*vb*	sweeten	
1390	**vendere**-*vb*	sell	
1391	**birba**-*la*	brat	
1392	**sguazzare**-*vb*	wallow	
1393	**abbassare**-*vb*	lower	
1394	**giudicare**-*vb*	judge	
1395	**tentennare**-*vb*	waver	
1396	**cala**-*la*	cove	
1397	**pretesto**-*il*	pretext, excuse	
1398	**lestezza**-*la*	deftness	
1399	**facile**-*adj; adv*	easy	
1400	**spicciolo**-*lo*	change	
1401	**sponda**-*la*	bank	
1402	**diminuire**-*vb*	decrease, reduce	
1403	**ristoro**-*il*	refreshment	
1404	**sorridente**-*adj*	smiling	
1405	**piuttosto**-*adv*	rather, quite, pretty	
1406	**cingere**-*vb*	encircle	
1407	**principale**-*adj; il*	main	
1408	**porta**-*nn*	door, port	
1409	**verme**-*il*	worm, maggot	
1410	**vendetta**-*la*	vengeance	
1411	**generale**-*adj; il*	general	
1412	**parlamento**-*il*	parliament	
1413	**ripieno**-*il; adj*	filling; stuffed	
1414	**decapitato**-*adj*	beheaded	
1415	**truffare**-*vb*	cheat, defraud	
1416	**gota**-*la*	cheek	
1417	**pulcino**-*il*	chick	
1418	**ninnare**-*vb*	lullaby	
1419	**animare**-*vb*	animate	
1420	**soffocare**-*vb*	choke, smother	
1421	**minacciare**-*vb*	threaten, impend	
1422	**buttare**-*vb*	throw	
1423	**animo**-*il*	mind	
1424	**famiglia**-*la*	family	
1425	**aritmetica**-*la*	arithmetic	
1426	**distinguere**-*vb*	distinguish, differentiate	
1427	**velocemente**-*adv*	quickly	
1428	**esistere**-*vb*	exist	
1429	**internare**-*vb*	intern	
1430	**aguzzare**-*vb*	sharpen	
1431	**aggiornare**-*vb*	update	

1432	**camomilla**-*la*	chamomile	
1433	**spettare**-*vb*	belong	
1434	**ceffo**-*il*	mug	
1435	**strada**-*la*	(large) street, road	
1436	**cinguettare**-*vb*	chirp	
1437	**imbarazzo**-*il*	embarrassment	
1438	**lampada**-*la*	lamp	
1439	**eccoti**-*int*	here you are	
1440	**imbarazzante**-*adj*	embarrassing	
1441	**raggiungere**-*vb*	reach	
1442	**secolo**-*il*	century	
1443	**inteso**-*adj*	understood	
1444	**intero**-*adj; i*	entire, full, whole; whole	
1445	**scricchiolare**-*vb*	creak	
1446	**mascella**-*la*	jaw, maxilla	
1447	**capriola**-*la*	somersault	
1448	**dilungato**-*adj*	pulled out	
1449	**carico**-*il; adj*	load, freight	
1450	**regolare**-*adj; vb*	regular; adjust	
1451	**sviare**-*vb*	divert	
1452	**andito**-*lo*	corridor	
1453	**dubitare**-*vb*	doubt	
1454	**personale**-*il; adj*	staff	
1455	**scaffale**-*lo*	shelf	
1456	**rovesciare**-*vb*	overthrow, topple	
1457	**coraggioso**-*adj*	courageous	
1458	**visita**-*la*	visit	
1459	**pigliare**-*vb*	grab, take	
1460	**arancia**-*la*	orange	
1461	**scordare**-*vb*	forget	
1462	**cappello**-*il*	hat	
1463	**viso**-*il*	face	
1464	**galantuomo**-*il*	gentleman	
1465	**scritturare**-*vb*	engage	
1466	**velare**-*vb; adj*	veil; velar	
1467	**eccitare**-*vb*	excite, energize	
1468	**classico**-*adj; il*	classic	
1469	**cessare**-*vb*	cease	
1470	**vapore**-*il*	steam, vapor	
1471	**sbagliare**-*vb*	make a mistake	
1472	**cielo**-*il*	sky	
1473	**vagare**-*vb*	wander, roam	
1474	**cima**-*la*	top	
1475	**posa**-*la*	pose, laying	
1476	**miserabile**-*adj; il*	miserable; wretch	
1477	**punzecchiare**-*vb*	prick	

1478	**ricercare**-*vb*	search, search for	
1479	**ingiusto**-*adj*	unfair, wrongful	
1480	**credenza**-*la*	belief, sideboard	
1481	**sfolgorare**-*vb*	blaze	
1482	**ridicolo**-*adj; il*	ridiculous	
1483	**deferenza**-*la*	deference	
1484	**ficcare**-*vb*	poke, stick	
1485	**contegno**-*il*	behavior, manner	
1486	**acuminato**-*adj*	sharp	
1487	**spazzolare**-*vb*	brush	
1488	**usare**-*vb*	use	
1489	**ripetizione**-*la*	repetition, private lesson	
1490	**arcigno**-*adj*	surly	
1491	**ruzzolare**-*vb*	tumble	
1492	**assemblea**-*le*	assembly, meeting	
1493	**libero**-*adj*	free	
1494	**liberò**-*adj*	free	
1495	**disturbo**-*il*	disorder	
1496	**solco**-*il*	groove	
1497	**recare**-*vb*	cause	
1498	**appianare**-*vb*	smooth	
1499	**fiero**-*adj*	proud	
1500	**esaminare**-*vb*	examine, study	
1501	**uccello**-*il*	bird	
1502	**casseruola**-*le*	casserole	
1503	**comunicare**-*vb*	communicate	
1504	**percorrere**-*vb*	travel, walk	
1505	**dileguare**-*vb*	vanish	
1506	**lealmente**-*adv*	loyally	
1507	**lancetta**-*la*	hand	
1508	**educare**-*vb*	educate, bring up	
1509	**antipatia**-*la*	dislike	
1510	**divertire**-*vb*	entertain	
1511	**crudo**-*adj*	raw, piping	
1512	**rinfrescare**-*vb*	refresh, cool	
1513	**rimproverare**-*vb*	reproach, blame	
1514	**accanto**-*adv*	next	
1515	**letizia**-*la*	joy	
1516	**fidanzare**-*vb*	affiance	
1517	**eccellente**-*adj*	excellent	
1518	**slargare**-*vb*	broaden, widen	
1519	**accadere**-*vb*	happen	
1520	**scarabocchio**-*lo*	scribble	
1521	**colare**-*vb*	strain, drip	
1522	**curvare**-*vb*	bend	
1523	**catino**-*il*	basin	

1524	**grandine**-*la*	hailstorm		1570	**perduto**-*adj*	lost
1525	**ufficiale**-*adj; il*	official		1571	**grasso**-*adj; il*	fat
1526	**impacciare**-*vb*	hinder		1572	**raccogliere**-*vb*	gather
1527	**lira**-*la*	lira		1573	**ridiventare**-*vb*	come again
1528	**cameriera**-*la*	waitress		1574	**legare**-*vb*	tie
1529	**realtà**-*la*	reality		1575	**piedino**-*il*	toothsie
1530	**timidezza**-*la*	shyness		1576	**ira**-*le*	anger, rage
1531	**unghia**-*le*	nail		1577	**affogare**-*vb*	drown
1532	**abbisognare**-*vb*	be in need of		1578	**vegetale**-*adj*	vegetable
1533	**sdegnare**-*vb*	disdain		1579	**ricordo**-*lo*	memory
1534	**cenere**-*la*	ash		1580	**vicenda**-*la*	event
1535	**ideare**-*vb*	design		1581	**nitido**-*adj*	clear
1536	**elevare**-*vb*	raise, rise		1582	**toppa**-*la*	patch
1537	**ciliegia**-*la*	cherry		1583	**idiota**-*adj; il, la*	idiotic, stupid; idiot
1538	**variante**-*la*	variant		1584	**permettere**-*vb*	allow
1539	**stroppia (il troppo ...)**-*exp*	to much of a good thing		1585	**ingoiare**-*vb*	gobble
				1586	**tuffare**-*vb*	dive, dip
1540	**invitato**-*il*	guest		1587	**piemontese**-*adj*	piedmontese
1541	**lucente**-*adj*	shiny, lucent		1588	**nettare**-*il; vb*	nectar; clean
1542	**zitto**-*adj*	silent, quiet		1589	**timore**-*il*	fear, awe
1543	**bramare**-*vb*	long		1590	**stralunare**-*vb*	roll
1544	**detestare**-*vb*	loathe		1591	**parete**-*la*	wall
1545	**adatto**-*adj*	suitable		1592	**schiaffeggiare**-*vb*	slap
1546	**affettuoso**-*adj*	affectionate, loving		1593	**innumerevole**-*adj*	countless, numerous
1547	**sorte**-*la*	fate		1594	**stupire**-*vb*	amaze, astonish
1548	**notare**-*vb*	note		1595	**ricoverare**-*vb*	shelter
1549	**disubbidire**-*vb*	disobey		1596	**dividere**-*vb*	divide, share
1550	**abbaiare**-*vb*	bark		1597	**magari**-*adv*	maybe, perhaps, even
1551	**togliere**-*vb*	remove, take off		1598	**inzuppare**-*vb*	soak
1552	**perenne**-*adj*	perennial, perpetual		1599	**gonnellino**-*il*	kilt
1553	**grado**-*il*	degree		1600	**broncio**-*il*	pout, sulk
1554	**tartagliare**-*vb*	stutter		1601	**soppressione**-*la*	abolition
1555	**giovinezza**-*la*	youth, girlhood		1602	**scherzare**-*vb*	joke
1556	**zanzara**-*la*	mosquito		1603	**sillabare**-*vb*	syllabify
1557	**veridico**-*adj*	truthful		1604	**pazzerello**-*il*	daft
1558	**evitare**-*vb; il*	avoid		1605	**lamina**-*la*	foil
1559	**zuppiera**-*la*	tureen		1606	**fisso**-*adj; adv*	fixed; fixedly
1560	**impossibile**-*adj*	impossible		1607	**acquavite**-*la*	brandy
1561	**guardata**-*la*	slant		1608	**stelo**-*lo*	stem
1562	**malinconico**-*adj*	melancholy, pensive		1609	**firma**-*la*	signature
1563	**malinconico**-*adj*	melancholy, pensive		1610	**sfondare**-*vb*	break through, stave
1564	**quattrocento**-*num*	four hundred		1611	**mestare**-*vb*	stir
1565	**fioco**-*adj*	dim		1612	**calza**-*la*	stocking
1566	**spaccato**-*adj; lo*	split; cutaway		1613	**guadagnare**-*vb*	earn, gain
1567	**incastrare**-*vb*	fit		1614	**sonnellino**-*il*	nap, doze
1568	**vetrino**-*il*	slide		1615	**certamente**-*adv*	of course
1569	**vetrina**-*la*	showcase				

1616	**dimenare**-*vb*	wiggle
1617	**grido**-*il*	cry
1618	**fuggevole**-*adj*	fleeting
1619	**cognizione**-*la*	cognition, acquaintance
1620	**fiume**-*il*	river
1621	**innamorato**-*adj; il*	in love; lover
1622	**memoria**-*la*	storage
1623	**punire**-*vb*	punish
1624	**pazienza**-*la*	patience
1625	**brontolare**-*vb*	grumble
1626	**raccattare**-*vb*	pick up
1627	**surrogato**-*il; adj*	surrogate; ersatz
1628	**enfasi**-*le*	emphasis
1629	**nervoso**-*adj*	nervous
1630	**fondamento**-*il*	foundation, grounding
1631	**extra**-*adj*	extra
1632	**canna**-*la*	cane, barrel, rod
1633	**salutare**-*adj; vb*	healthy; greet, say goodbye to
1634	**ordinare**-*vb*	order
1635	**accerchiare**-*vb*	encircle
1636	**sposare**-*vb*	marry
1637	**misurare**-*vb*	measure, gauge
1638	**confidare**-*vb*	trust, rely
1639	**loggione**-*il*	gallery
1640	**signora**-*la; abr*	lady, Mrs.
1641	**signore**-*il/la; abr*	Mr. / Mrs.
1642	**unire**-*vb*	unite
1643	**raramente**-*adv*	rarely
1644	**scoppiettare**-*vb*	crackle
1645	**incolpare**-*vb*	blame, accuse
1646	**facilmente**-*adv*	easily
1647	**disdegnoso**-*adj*	disdainful
1648	**ingollare**-*vb*	gobble
1649	**consigliere**-*il*	advisor, councilor
1650	**aspro**-*adj*	sour, harsh
1651	**spegnere**-*vb*	switch off, turn off
1652	**desiderare**-*vb*	wish
1653	**ridurre**-*vb*	reduce
1654	**mestizia**-*la*	mournfulness
1655	**stima**-*la*	estimate, esteem
1656	**mordere**-*vb*	bite
1657	**spezzare**-*vb*	break
1658	**figliuolo**-*il*	son
1659	**alimentare**-*adj; vb*	alimentary; feed
1660	**aceto**-*il*	vinegar
1661	**energico**-*adj*	energetic
1662	**contraddire**-*vb*	contradict
1663	**brillare**-*vb*	shine, glitter
1664	**accomodare**-*vb*	accommodate
1665	**affondare**-*vb*	sink, founder
1666	**pizzicotto**-*il*	nip
1667	**scomporre**-*vb*	decompose
1668	**ruzzoloni**-*il*	tumble
1669	**ruzzolone**-*il*	tumble
1670	**carro**-*il*	wagon
1671	**dispettoso**-*adj*	spiteful
1672	**sonnecchiare**-*vb*	doze
1673	**affissare**-*vb*	direct, fix
1674	**approdare**-*vb*	land
1675	**risplendente**-*adj*	resplendent
1676	**sostenere**-*vb*	support, bear
1677	**sghignazzare**-*vb*	sneer
1678	**continuo**-*adj*	continuous
1679	**unguento**-*il*	ointment
1680	**profferire**-*vb*	proffer
1681	**assopimento**-*il*	drowsiness
1682	**impensierire**-*vb*	worry
1683	**scarabocchiare**-*vb*	doodle, scribble
1684	**intenzione**-*le*	intention
1685	**consegnare**-*vb*	deliver
1686	**impeto**-*il*	impetus, fit
1687	**elegante**-*adj*	elegant
1688	**offendere**-*vb*	offend
1689	**distaccare**-*vb*	detach, second
1690	**riparare**-*vb*	repair
1691	**coprire**-*vb*	cover
1692	**coperto**-*adj; lo*	covered
1693	**stazione**-*la*	station
1694	**gretto**-*adj*	narrow
1695	**litigare**-*vb*	quarrel
1696	**direzione**-*la*	direction, management
1697	**accozzaglia**-*la*	jumble
1698	**occulto**-*adj*	occult, hidden
1699	**partecipare**-*vb*	take part
1700	**vantare**-*vb*	claim
1701	**motivare**-*vb*	motivate
1702	**premiato**-*adj; il*	prize; prizewinner
1703	**oltremodo**-*adv*	exceedingly
1704	**ghirlanda**-*la*	garland
1705	**ristabilire**-*vb*	restore, re-establish
1706	**torrone**-*gli*	nougat
1707	**sbranare**-*vb*	savage

1708	**adeguato**-*adj*	adequate	
1709	**ritratto**-*il*	portrait	
1710	**guardia**-*la*	guard	
1711	**mano**-*la*	hand	
1712	**respingere**-*vb*	reject, dismiss	
1713	**toccare**-*vb*	touch	
1714	**appetito**-*il*	appetite, hunger	
1715	**angolo**-*lo*	angle, corner	
1716	**angolare**-*adj*	angular	
1717	**sapore**-*il*	flavor, taste	
1718	**fissare**-*vb*	fix, secure	
1719	**avviluppare**-*vb*	envelop	
1720	**sbrogliare**-*vb*	unravel	
1721	**duodecimo**-*num*	twelfth	
1722	**premio**-*il*	prize	
1723	**abito**-*il*	dress, suit, attire	
1724	**imbroglio**-*il*	cheat, imbroglio	
1725	**sturare**-*vb*	unblock	
1726	**preferire**-*vb*	prefer	
1727	**pastorello**-*lo*	swain	
1728	**accrescere**-*vb*	increase	
1729	**spiegazione**-*la*	explanation	
1730	**abile**-*adj*	skillful, able	
1731	**pasticcio**-*il*	mess, pie	
1732	**indirizzare**-*vb*	address	
1733	**semichiusi**-*adj*	half-closed	
1734	**tirchio**-*adj; il*	stingy; miser	
1735	**meritare**-*vb*	deserve	
1736	**sorreggere**-*vb*	support	
1737	**fianco**-*il*	side	
1738	**trattare**-*vb*	treat	
1739	**sbirciare**-*vb*	peek	
1740	**conformare**-*vb*	conform	
1741	**strillo**-*lo*	scream, squeal	
1742	**timoroso**-*adj*	afraid	
1743	**fratello**-*il*	brother	
1744	**chiodo**-*il*	nail	
1745	**incrociare**-*vb*	cross, meet	
1746	**utile**-*adj; il*	helpful, useful; profit	
1747	**sottomissione**-*la*	submission, subjection	
1748	**sforzo**-*lo*	effort	
1749	**occhio**-*il*	eye	
1750	**scendere**-*vb*	get off	
1751	**risoluto**-*adj*	resolute	
1752	**polvere**-*la*	dust	
1753	**amo**-*lo*	hook, bait	

1754	**illustre**-*adj*	illustrious, distinguished
1755	**empio**-*adj*	impious
1756	**amare**-*vb*	love
1757	**liquore**-*il*	liquor, liqueur
1758	**zappare**-*vb*	hoe
1759	**parruccone**-*adj; il*	blimpish; mossback
1760	**composto**-*adj; il*	composed; compound
1761	**comporre**-*vb*	compose, dial
1762	**latina**-*adj; la*	latina; latina
1763	**dritto**-*adj; adv*	straight, upright; right
1764	**interesse**-*lo*	interest
1765	**rizzare**-*vb*	raise
1766	**incoraggiare**-*vb*	encourage, foster
1767	**impazzata**-*la*	madness
1768	**timido**-*adj; il*	shy; milksop
1769	**incatenare**-*vb*	enchain
1770	**bontà**-*la*	goodness
1771	**ascella**-*le*	armpit, lath
1772	**mentire**-*vb*	lie
1773	**scivolare**-*vb*	slip, slide
1774	**rigoglioso**-*adj*	luxuriant
1775	**chiave**-*la*	key
1776	**tulipano**-*il*	tulip
1777	**chiaro**-*adj; adv*	clear; light
1778	**parolina**-*la*	a quick word
1779	**eco**-*gli*	echo
1780	**narrare**-*vb*	tell, relate
1781	**confondere**-*vb*	confound
1782	**colle**-*il*	hill
1783	**inginocchiarsi**-*vb*	kneel
1784	**stringere**-*vb*	tighten
1785	**fendere**-*vb*	cleave, slit
1786	**personalità**-*la*	personality
1787	**sotterra**-*adv*	underground
1788	**innocente**-*adj*	innocent
1789	**omero**-*il*	humerus
1790	**piattino**-*il*	saucer
1791	**ciarlare**-*vb*	chatter
1792	**languido**-*adj*	languid
1793	**immaginare**-*vb*	imagine
1794	**piagnucolare**-*vb*	whine, whimper
1795	**abbandonato**-*adj*	abandoned, forsaken
1796	**ricrescere**-*vb*	grow back
1797	**marino**-*adj*	marine, sea; marina, marine, navy
1798	**frettoloso**-*adj*	hasty

№	Italian	English
1799	**bellino**-*adj*	pretty
1800	**bricco**-*il*	jug
1801	**botto**-*il*	blow, hit; explosion
1802	**inanellato**-*adj*	annulate
1803	**assassinio**-*il*	murder, assasination
1804	**sollievo**-*il*	relief, solace
1805	**inchiodare**-*vb*	nail, rivet
1806	**salone**-*il*	lounge
1807	**morsicare**-*vb*	bite
1808	**rotoloni (cadere ..)**-*exp*	tumble down
1809	**pestare**-*vb*	pound, beat
1810	**ottone**-*il*	brass
1811	**sdraiare**-*vb*	lie down
1812	**scottare**-*vb*	burn, scald
1813	**cacciata**-*la*	dislodgement
1814	**abituare**-*vb*	accustom
1815	**favore**-*il*	favor
1816	**stamane**-*adv*	this morning
1817	**coccodrillo**-*il*	crocodile
1818	**impedire**-*vb*	prevent, impede
1819	**micio**-*il*	pussy, tomcat
1820	**parrucca**-*la*	wig
1821	**franco**-*il; adj*	frank, free; franc
1822	**rallegrare**-*vb*	cheer, brighten
1823	**arrampicare**-*vb*	climb
1824	**stridulo**-*adj*	shrill
1825	**bisticcio**-*il*	quarrel
1826	**combattimento**-*il*	combat
1827	**inverno**-*il*	winter
1828	**aiuola**-*la*	flowerbed
1829	**campanello**-*il*	bell
1830	**seggio**-*il*	seat
1831	**coppia**-*la*	couple
1832	**figuro**-*il*	character
1833	**rimpiccolire**-*vb*	make smaller
1834	**moderazione**-*la*	moderation
1835	**proporre**-*vb*	propose, put forward
1836	**luccicante**-*adj*	shimmering
1837	**concedere**-*vb*	grant
1838	**sbattere**-*vb*	slam, beat
1839	**garbo**-*il*	politeness
1840	**adesso**-*adv*	now
1841	**raschiare**-*vb*	scrape
1842	**menare**-*vb*	lead
1843	**corvo**-*il*	crow, rook
1844	**matrona**-*la*	matron
1845	**originale**-*adj; il*	original
1846	**friggere**-*vb*	fry
1847	**scampare**-*vb*	escape
1848	**rotondo**-*adj*	round
1849	**ranuncolo**-*il*	buttercup
1850	**sdrucciolare**-*vb*	slip
1851	**slanciare**-*vb*	hurl, fling
1852	**rassegnare**-*vb*	resign oneself
1853	**migliore**-*adj; il*	best
1854	**tacchino**-*il*	turkey
1855	**pallido**-*adj*	pale, faint
1856	**riposare**-*vb*	rest
1857	**uragano**-*il*	hurricane
1858	**svoltare**-*vb*	turn
1859	**superare**-*vb*	exceed
1860	**piegare**-*vb*	fold
1861	**donna**-*la*	woman
1862	**pigiare**-*vb*	press
1863	**ammasso**-*il*	cluster
1864	**oca**-*le*	goose
1865	**discernere**-*vb*	discern, descry
1866	**ostacolo**-*il*	obstacle, hurdle
1867	**zolla**-*la*	plate
1868	**uccidere**-*vb*	kill
1869	**acchiappare**-*vb*	catch
1870	**costa**-*la*	coast, coastline
1871	**scosso**-*il; adj*	shaken; upset
1872	**saggio**-*adj; il*	wise; test
1873	**riapparire**-*vb*	reappear
1874	**sbalzare**-*vb*	throw
1875	**cuscino**-*il*	pillow
1876	**volo**-*il*	flight
1877	**ripensare**-*vb*	think back
1878	**comare**-*la*	godmother
1879	**muta**-*la*	pack
1880	**muto**-*adj; il*	silent; mute
1881	**tremarella**-*la*	shivers
1882	**armento**-*il*	herd
1883	**ruota**-*la*	wheel
1884	**scusare**-*vb*	excuse
1885	**scusa**-*la*	sorry
1886	**grammatico**-*il*	grammarian
1887	**fronte**-*la*	front, forehead
1888	**stiracchiare**-*vb*	stretch
1889	**concavo**-*adj; il*	concave; concave
1890	**prudentemente**-*adv*	prudently

1891	lasciata-*adj*	left, dropped	
1892	volgare-*adj*	vulgar, gross	
1893	covare-*vb*	hatch, sit	
1894	ristringere-*vb*	shrink again	
1895	foca-*la*	seal	
1896	agire-*vb*	act	
1897	filastrocca-*la*	doggerel	
1898	scodella-*le*	bowl	
1899	silenzioso-*adj*	silent	
1900	mille-*i; adj*	one thousand	
1901	strozzato-*adj*	choking	
1902	rappresentare-*vb*	represent	
1903	scorso-*adj*	last	
1904	accentare-*vb*	accent	
1905	comodo-*adj; il*	comfortable	
1906	comunque-*adv; con*	anyway; though	
1907	padrone-*il, la*	boss, master, owner, host/mistress, hostess	
1908	bocconcino-*il*	morsel	
1909	società-*la*	society	
1910	legno-*il*	wood	
1911	apice-*il*	apex, peak	
1912	stranezza-*la*	strangeness	
1913	rigettare-*vb*	reject	
1914	meditabondo-*adj*	musing	
1915	centro-*il*	center	
1916	gazza-*la*	magpie	
1917	affannato-*adj*	breathless	
1918	affannare-*vb*	trouble	
1919	difetto-*il*	defect, default	
1920	destrezza-*la*	dexterity	
1921	stretto-*adj; lo*	strict, strait; narrow	
1922	acerba-*adj*	unripe	
1923	arruffato-*adj*	ruffled	
1924	infilare-*vb*	insert, thread	
1925	derisione-*la*	derision	
1926	suolo-*il*	soil	
1927	suono-*il*	sound	
1928	fattoria-*la*	farm	
1929	documentare-*vb*	document	
1930	svanire-*vb*	fade, vanish	
1931	scempiaggini-*la*	foolery	
1932	riso-*il*	rice	
1933	atto-*gli; adj*	act	
1934	desinare-*lo; vb*	dinner; dine	
1935	alquanto-*adv*	somewhat, a few	
1936	ritardare-*vb*	delay, defer	
1937	comparire-*vb*	appear	
1938	vocina-*la*	small voice	
1939	spaventevole-*adj*	frightful	
1940	cantata-*la*	cantata	
1941	soggetto-*adj; il*	subject	
1942	assenza-*le*	absence	
1943	affaticare-*vb*	fatigue	
1944	rondella-*la*	washer	
1945	condurre-*vb*	lead, carry out	
1946	stridere-*vb*	screech, squeal	
1947	disperatamente-*adv*	desperately	
1948	prediligere-*vb*	prefer	
1949	segnale-*il*	signal, sign	
1950	rasserenare-*vb*	cheer up	
1951	deludere-*vb*	disappoint	
1952	quartina-*la*	quatrain	
1953	adunghiare-*vb*	grab with nails	
1954	importo-*il*	amount	
1955	luccicone-*il*	large tear	
1956	indovinare-*vb*	guess	
1957	avanzare-*vb*	advance, put forward	
1958	discendere-*vb*	descend, drop	
1959	discesa-*la*	descent	
1960	affacciare-*vb*	show	
1961	rispettivo-*adj*	respective	
1962	derelitto-*adj*	derelict	
1963	fermezza-*la*	firmness	
1964	orribile-*adj*	horrible	
1965	ahi-*int*	ouch	
1966	ventesimo-*adj*	twentieth, twentieth	
1967	decollare-*vb*	take off, decollate	
1968	appellare-*vb*	appeal	
1969	riporre-*vb*	put	
1970	giornale-*il*	newspaper, journal	
1971	viscoso-*adj*	viscous	
1972	strisciare-*vb*	crawl, slither	
1973	misto-*adj; il*	mixed; mixture	
1974	fattore-*il*	factor, consideration	
1975	posizione-*la*	position	
1976	pecora-*la*	sheep	
1977	sentenziare-*vb*	moralize	
1978	passato-*adj; il*	past	
1979	circondare-*vb*	surround, encircle	
1980	legaccio-*il*	string	
1981	amorino-*il*	cherub	

1982	**piantato**-*adj*	planted	
1983	**sollecitare**-*vb*	urge	
1984	**abbrustolire**-*vb*	toast	
1985	**smarrito**-*adj*	lost	
1986	**smarrire**-*vb*	lose, get lost	
1987	**pellegrino**-*il*	pilgrim	
1988	**protetto**-*adj*	safe	
1989	**cucchiaino**-*il*	teaspoon	
1990	**incollare**-*vb*	paste, stick	
1991	**turco**-*adj; il*	Turkish; Turk	
1992	**formare**-*vb*	form, train	
1993	**est**-*lo*	East	
1994	**opposto**-*adj; il*	opposite; opposite	
1995	**assaporare**-*vb*	savor	
1996	**elce**-*il*	ilex	
1997	**bucare**-*vb*	puncture	
1998	**stupore**-*lo*	amazement, wonder	
1999	**fingere**-*vb*	pretend	
2000	**forbire**-*vb*	furbish	
2001	**assassinare**-*vb*	assassinate	
2002	**sgarbatezza**-*la*	rudeness	
2003	**vasetto**-*il*	jar	
2004	**meraviglioso**-*adj*	wonderful	
2005	**pigro**-*adj; il*	lazy; idler	
2006	**prato**-*il*	meadow	
2007	**lussureggiante**-*adj*	lush	
2008	**gonzo**-*il*	dupe	
2009	**letto**-*il*	bed	
2010	**codesto**-*adj*	that, this	
2011	**mostruosità**-*le*	monstrosity	
2012	**pennellate**-*le*	brushstrokes	
2013	**indovinello**-*il*	riddle, quiz	
2014	**piovere**-*vb*	rain	
2015	**guizzare**-*vb*	flicker	
2016	**rupe**-*la*	cliff	
2017	**nido**-*il*	nest	
2018	**ubbidire**-*vb*	obey	
2019	**ivi**-*adv*	therein	
2020	**sforzare**-*vb*	strain, force	
2021	**cortina**-*la*	curtain	
2022	**rispettoso**-*adj*	respectful	
2023	**ciascuna**-*prn*	each	
2024	**mortale**-*adj; adv*	mortal; deadly, fatal; deathly	
2025	**velluto**-*il*	velvet	
2026	**undecimo**-*num*	eleventh	
2027	**avvedutezza**-*la*	foresight	

2028	**garbato**-*adj*	polite	
2029	**reciso**-*adj*	flat	
2030	**stravagante**-*adj*	extravagant	
2031	**cinquanta**-*num*	fifty	
2032	**vanga**-*la*	spade	
2033	**piazzare**-*vb*	place, be placed	
2034	**arricciare**-*vb*	curl	
2035	**dubbioso**-*adj*	doubtful	
2036	**testa**-*la*	head	
2037	**commosso**-*adj*	moved, unrest	
2038	**minerale**-*adj; il*	mineral; mineral	
2039	**indirizzo**-*i*	address	
2040	**ostrica**-*la*	oyster	
2041	**comprendonio**-*il*	savvy	
2042	**cantone**-*il*	canton	
2043	**radice**-*la*	root, stem	
2044	**ombra**-*la*	shadow	
2045	**carattere**-*il*	character	
2046	**vignetta**-*la*	cartoon	
2047	**sveltezza**-*la*	speed	
2048	**mare**-*il*	sea, seaside	
2049	**scorgere**-*vb*	notice, make out	
2050	**invertire**-*vb*	reverse, be inverted	
2051	**frontespizio**-*il*	title page	
2052	**serietà**-*la*	seriousness, reliability	
2053	**sculacciare**-*vb*	spank	
2054	**irritabile**-*adj*	irritable, edgy	
2055	**aggirare**-*vb*	bypass	
2056	**indiavolato**-*adj*	furious	
2057	**metro**-*il*	meter	
2058	**aperto**-*adj; i*	open	
2059	**affollare**-*vb*	crowd	
2060	**cortese**-*adj*	courteous, polite	
2061	**gabbia**-*la*	cage	
2062	**sollecitudine**-*la*	concern	
2063	**gabbare**-*vb*	cheat	
2064	**soccorrere**-*vb*	help	
2065	**nodo**-*il*	node, knot	
2066	**nembo**-*il*	stormcloud	
2067	**inchiostro**-*il*	ink	
2068	**noia**-*la*	boredom, bore	
2069	**ventiquattro**-*num*	twentyfour	
2070	**serrato**-*adj*	serried	
2071	**pennello**-*il*	brush	
2072	**congiunto**-*adj; il*	joined; kinsman	
2073	**lampo**-*il*	flash	

2074	**noto**-*adj*	known	
2075	**cavallo**-*il*	horse	
2076	**moderno**-*adj*	modern	
2077	**disposto**-*adj; adv*	willing; ready	
2078	**scagliare**-*vb*	throw	
2079	**brutto**-*adj; il*	ugly, bad; bad, ugliness	
2080	**vuotare**-*vb*	empty, deplete	
2081	**vuoto**-*adj; il*	empty	
2082	**fornello**-*il*	stove	
2083	**ricerca**-*la*	search, research	
2084	**esprimere**-*vb*	express, voice	
2085	**ricco**-*adj; il*	rich	
2086	**prima**-*adv; art*	first, before; before	
2087	**calpestare**-*vb*	trample, trample on	
2088	**sciogliere**-*vb*	dissolve, loosen	
2089	**secchia**-*la*	bucket	
2090	**ingresso**-*lo*	entrance	
2091	**mucchio**-*il*	pile	
2092	**elefante**-*il*	elephant	
2093	**qui**-*adv; con*	here; where	
2094	**dintorno**-*il*	vicinity	
2095	**addormentare**-*vb*	fall asleep	
2096	**salmone**-*il*	salmon	
2097	**incipriare**-*vb*	powder	
2098	**adirata**-*adj*	angry	
2099	**dipendere**-*vb*	depend	
2100	**novello**-*adj*	new, early	
2101	**nervo**-*il*	nerve	
2102	**vestire**-*vb*	dress	
2103	**largo**-*adj*	wide, large, loose	
2104	**sol**-*il*	sol	
2105	**macchina**-*la*	machine	
2106	**sentimento**-*il*	feeling	
2107	**fumare**-*vb*	smoke	
2108	**puntellare**-*vb*	shore	
2109	**secondare**-*vb*	comply	
2110	**riferire**-*vb*	report, refer	
2111	**tenerezza**-*la*	tenderness, sweetness	
2112	**leccare**-*vb*	lick	
2113	**accigliato**-*adj*	frowning	
2114	**sano**-*adj*	healthy, wholesome	
2115	**grondare**-*vb*	drip	
2116	**imbecille**-*adj; il/la*	imbecile	
2117	**accigliata**-*adj*	frowning	
2118	**assaggiare**-*vb*	taste, assay	
2119	**uff**-*int*	Oof!	
2120	**anzi**-*adv; con*	rather	
2121	**nuca**-*la*	nape	
2122	**sventolare**-*vb*	wave	
2123	**tremolante**-*adj*	flickering	
2124	**stridente**-*adj*	strident	
2125	**uva**-*le*	grapes	
2126	**mancare**-*vb*	miss	
2127	**risolino**-*il*	titter	
2128	**lassù**-*adv*	up there, above, yonder	
2129	**considerare**-*vb*	consider	
2130	**storico**-*adj; lo*	historical; historian	
2131	**casualmente**-*adv*	casually	
2132	**doppiamente**-*adv*	doubly	
2133	**rivedere**-*vb*	review, revise	
2134	**accovacciare**-*vb*	squat, crouch	
2135	**colpevole**-*adj; il/la*	guilty	
2136	**mappa**-*la*	map	
2137	**infiammare**-*vb*	inflame	
2138	**dimettere**-*vb*	resign	
2139	**arguire**-*vb*	deduce	
2140	**prova**-*la*	test	
2141	**canarino**-*il*	canary	
2142	**espressione**-*la*	expression	
2143	**margherita**-*la*	daisy	
2144	**piuma**-*la*	feather, down	
2145	**sbuffante**-*adj*	puffing	
2146	**interrogare**-*vb*	query, interrogate	
2147	**infreddatura**-*la*	cold	
2148	**ardire**-*vb; il*	courage; boldness	
2149	**patatrac**-*il*	crash	
2150	**seccato**-*adj*	annoyed	
2151	**infocare**-*vb*	set fire to	
2152	**mancato**-*adj*	failed, unsuccessful	
2153	**pelle**-*la*	skin	
2154	**turchino**-*adj; il*	blue; deep blue	
2155	**provocare**-*vb*	cause, provoke	
2156	**papale**-*adj*	papal	
2157	**ascia**-*la*	ax, adze	
2158	**antico**-*adj*	ancient	
2159	**farfalla**-*la*	butterfly	
2160	**triste**-*adj*	sad	
2161	**bulbo**-*lo*	bulb	
2162	**estate**-*le*	summer	
2163	**vacillare**-*vb*	falter	
2164	**asse**-*il*	axis, axle	
2165	**civiltà**-*la*	civilization	

2166	**assistere**-*vb*	assist, attend
2167	**discussione**-*la*	discussion
2168	**tramutare**-*vb*	convert
2169	**fame**-*la*	hunger
2170	**spiritoso**-*adj*	humorous
2171	**acconsentire**-*vb*	agree, consent
2172	**profondità**-*la*	depth, deep
2173	**cattivo**-*adj*	bad; baddie, bad person
2174	**nanna**-*la*	beddy-bye
2175	**casco**-*il*	helmet
2176	**pentirsi**-*vb*	repent
2177	**magnificamente**-*adv*	beautifully
2178	**arena**-*le*	arena
2179	**sommare**-*vb; adv; phr*	add; all in all; all things considered
2180	**figlia**-*la*	daughter
2181	**sfiorare**-*vb*	touch, brush
2182	**mulinare**-*vb*	whirl
2183	**restaurare**-*vb*	restore
2184	**fradicio**-*adj*	wet, soggy
2185	**incominciare**-*vb*	begin
2186	**trappola**-*la*	trap
2187	**scoperchiare**-*vb*	unroof, untile
2188	**cadente**-*adj*	falling, sagging
2189	**muscolare**-*adj*	muscular
2190	**oramai**-*adv*	by now
2191	**compitare**-*vb*	spell
2192	**acconciare**-*vb*	style
2193	**paperone**-*il*	scrooge
2194	**terrore**-*il*	terror
2195	**zucca**-*la*	pumpkin, gourd
2196	**galleria**-*la*	gallery
2197	**umile**-*adj*	humble, menial
2198	**porcellana**-*la*	porcelain
2199	**comitiva**-*la*	party
2200	**casotto**-*il*	shed, mess (coll)
2201	**solido**-*adj; il*	solid; solid
2202	**ragazzona**-*la*	big girl
2203	**uscita**-*la*	exit
2204	**impallidire**-*vb*	pale
2205	**contorcere**-*vb*	contort
2206	**irritare**-*vb*	irritate, anger
2207	**illuminare**-*vb*	illuminate, enlighten
2208	**grugno**-*il*	snout
2209	**sorridere**-*vb*	smile
2210	**reggere**-*vb*	hold, stand
2211	**sorriso**-*il*	smile
2212	**perso**-*adj*	lost
2213	**bislungo**-*adj*	oblong
2214	**spingere**-*vb*	push
2215	**nessuno**-*adj; prn*	no; nobody, anyone
2216	**amaro**-*adj; il*	bitter; bitter, tonic liqour
2217	**zufolare**-*vb*	play the whistle
2218	**stivaletto**-*lo*	ankle boot
2219	**stormire**-*vb*	rustle
2220	**montare**-*vb*	mount, assemble
2221	**cerimoniale**-*adj; nn*	ceremonial; etiquette
2222	**contrastare**-*vb*	counteract
2223	**querela**-*la*	complaint
2224	**capitombolare**-*vb*	tumble
2225	**busca**-*la*	search
2226	**lungaggine**-*la*	slowness
2227	**rischiare**-*vb*	risk
2228	**frittura**-*la*	frying
2229	**turbamento**-*il*	agitation
2230	**cerchio**-*il*	circle; rim
2231	**natale**-*adj; il*	Christmas
2232	**riunire**-*vb*	gather, reunite
2233	**bizzarro**-*adj*	bizarre, strange
2234	**pulito**-*adj*	clean, clean
2235	**crostino**-*il*	crouton
2236	**esperimento**-*il*	experiment
2237	**semplice**-*adj*	simple
2238	**lagnarsi**-*vb*	complain
2239	**sole**-*il*	sun
2240	**improvviso**-*adj; adv*	sudden
2241	**rivoltato**-*adj*	upturned
2242	**reggia**-*la*	royal palace
2243	**rissa**-*la*	fight, brawl
2244	**cuoco**-*il*	cook
2245	**regio**-*adj*	royal
2246	**sfoggio**-*il*	display
2247	**disperazione**-*la*	despair, desolation
2248	**dilettare**-*vb*	delight
2249	**inoltrare**-*vb*	forward
2250	**caldaia**-*la*	boiler
2251	**accusato**-*i*	defendant
2252	**trenta**-*num*	thirty
2253	**affamato**-*adj*	hungry
2254	**pendere**-*vb*	hang, tip
2255	**familiarmente**-*adv*	familiar

2256	**scottante**-*adj*	pressing	
2257	**odiare**-*vb*	hate	
2258	**incendiare**-*vb*	fire	
2259	**rianimare**-*vb*	revive	
2260	**pensiero**-*il*	thought	
2261	**aiutare**-*vb*	help	
2262	**protesto**-*il*	protest	
2263	**crollare**-*vb*	collapse, crumble	

2264	**aggruppare**-*vb*	clump, group	
2265	**enormemente**-*adv*	enormously	
2266	**respirare**-*vb*	breathe	
2267	**intimorire**-*vb*	intimidate	
2268	**cartone**-*il*	cardboard	
2269	**simpatico**-*adj*	nice, sympathetic	
2270	**bellezza**-*la*	beauty	

Italian-English Dictionary

Italian-*Part of Speech*	Translation	
a*al, allo, all', alla, ai, agli, alla-*prp*	to, in, at	[a]
abbaiare-*vb*	bark	[abbajare]
abbandonare-*vb*	abandon sth, leave sth.	[abbandonare]
abbandonato-*adj*	abandoned, forsaken	[abbandonato]
abbassare-*vb*	lower	[abbassare]
abbastanza-*adv; adj*	enough	[abbastantsa]
abbisognare-*vb*	be in need of	[abbizoɲɲare]
abbrustolire-*vb*	toast	[abbrustolire]
abile-*adj*	skillful, able	[abile]
abitare-*vb*	live	[abitare]
abito-*il*	dress, suit, attire	[abito]
abituare-*vb*	accustom	[abitware]
abituato-*adj*	wont	[abitwato]
accadere-*vb*	happen	[akkadere]
accadere-*vb*	happen	[akkadere]
accanto-*adv*	next	[akkanto]
accentare-*vb*	accent	[attʃentare]
accerchiare-*vb*	encircle	[attʃerkjare]
accettare-*vb*	accept	[attʃettare]
acchiappare-*vb*	catch	[akkjappare]
accigliata-*adj*	frowning	[attʃiʎʎata]
accigliato-*adj*	frowning	[attʃiʎʎato]
accingere-*vb*	wrap	[attʃindʒere]
accoccolarsi-*vb*	curl up	[akkokkolarsi]
accomodare-*vb*	accommodate	[akkomodare]
acconciare-*vb*	style	[akkontʃare]
acconsentire-*vb*	agree, consent	[akkonsentire]
accorgersi-*vb*	notice, realize	[akkˈɔrdʒersi]
accorto-*adj*	shrewd	[akkorto]
accovacciare-*vb*	squat, crouch	[akkovattʃare]
accozzaglia-*la*	jumble	[akkottsaʎʎa]
accrescere-*vb*	increase	[akkreʃʃere]
accusa-*la*	accusation, charge, prosecution	[akkuza]
accusato-*i*	defendant	[akkuzato]
acerba-*adj*	unripe	[atʃerba]
aceto-*il*	vinegar	[atʃeto]

acqua-*le*	water	[akkwa]
acquavite-*la*	brandy	[akkwavite]
acuminato-*adj*	sharp	[akuminato]
acuto-*adj; il*	acute; high note	[akuto]
adagiare-*vb*	lay down	[adadʒare]
adagio-*il; adv*	adage; adagio	[adadʒo]
adatto-*adj*	suitable	[adatto]
addio-*il*	goodbye, farewell	[addˈio]
addolcire-*vb*	sweeten	[addoltʃire]
addormentare-*vb*	fall asleep	[addormentare]
addossare-*vb*	lean	[addossare]
adeguato-*adj*	adequate	[adegwato]
adesso-*adv*	now	[adˈɛsso]
adirata-*adj*	angry	[adirata]
adottare-*vb*	adopt	[adottare]
adunghiare-*vb*	grab with nails	[aduŋgjare]
affacciare-*vb*	show	[affattʃare]
affamato-*adj*	hungry	[affamato]
affannare-*vb*	trouble	[affannare]
affannato-*adj*	breathless	[affannato]
affare-*il*	deal, business, affair	[affare]
affaticare-*vb*	fatigue	[affatikare]
affatto-*adv*	at all, quite	[affatto]
afferrare-*vb*	grab, grasp	[afferrare]
affettuoso-*adj*	affectionate, loving	[affettwozo]
affissare-*vb*	direct, fix	[affissare]
affogare-*vb*	drown	[affogare]
affollare-*vb*	crowd	[affollare]
affondare-*vb*	sink, founder	[affondare]
affrettare-*vb*	hasten, expedite	[affrettare]
aggiornare-*vb*	update	[addʒornare]
aggirare-*vb*	bypass	[addʒirare]
aggiungere-*vb*	add	[addʒundʒere]
aggruppare-*vb*	clump, group	[aggruppare]
agire-*vb*	act	[adʒire]
agitare-*vb*	shake, stir	[adʒitare]
aguzzare-*vb*	sharpen	[aguttsare]
ahi-*int*	ouch	[ai]
ah-*int*	ha	[a]
aiuola-*la*	flowerbed	[ajwola]
aiutare-*vb*	help	[ajutare]
ala-*le*	wing	[ala]

al-art	a	[al]
albero-il	tree	[albero]
alcun-adj	any	[alkun]
alcun-adj	any	[alkun]
alcune-prn	several, some	[alkune]
alcuno-adj	any, some	[alkuno]
alfine-adv	in order	[alfine]
alimentare-adj; vb	alimentary; feed	[alimentare]
allegrezza-la	joyfulness	[allegrettsa]
allettare-vb	lure	[allettare]
allontanare-vb	remove, avert	[allontanare]
allora-adv	then	[allora]
allorchè-con	when	[allork'ɛ]
allungare-vb	stretch, lengthen	[alluŋgare]
almeno-adv	at least	[almeno]
alquanto-adv	somewhat, a few	[alkwanto]
altezza-le	height	[altettsa]
alto-adj; lo	high, tall	[alto]
altresì-adv	moreover	[altrez'i]
altrimenti-adv	otherwise	[altrimenti]
altro-adj; prn; adv; gli	other, more	[altro]
altrove-adv	elsewhere	[altrove]
altrui-adj	others	[altrwi]
alzare-vb	raise	[altsare]
amare-vb	love	[amare]
amaro-adj; il	bitter; bitter, tonic liqour	[amaro]
ambizione-le	ambition	[ambittsjone]
ameno-adj	pleasant	[ameno]
amichevolmente-adv	amicably	[amikevolmente]
amico-lo	friend	[amiko]
ammalato-adj; il	sick; sick person	[ammalato]
ammasso-il	cluster	[ammasso]
ammazzare-vb	kill	[ammattsare]
amo-lo	hook, bait	[amo]
amore-il	(my) love	[amore]
amorino-il	cherub	[amorino]
ampolla-la	ampoule	[ampolla]
anche-adv	also, even; anchor	[aŋke]
ancora-adv; con; le	yet, still, more; more	[aŋkora]
ancorchè-con	although	[aŋkork'ɛ]

andare-vb	go, move, proceed, run	[andare]
andito-lo	corridor	[andito]
anelare-vb	yearn	[anelare]
angolare-adj	angular	[aŋgolare]
angolo-lo	angle, corner	[aŋgolo]
angoscia-le	anguish	[aŋgoʃʃa]
angosciato-adj	distressed	[aŋgoʃʃato]
angusto-adj	narrow	[aŋgusto]
animale-adj; il	animal	[animale]
animare-vb	animate	[animare]
animo-il	mind	[animo]
anitra-la	duck	[anitra]
anno-gli	year	[anno]
annoiare-vb	bore, get bored	[annojare]
annoiato-adj	bored	[annojato]
ansietà-la	anxiety	[ansjet'a]
antico-adj	ancient	[antiko]
antipatia-la	dislike	[antipatja]
anzi-adv; con	rather	[antsi]
apertamente-adv	openly	[apertamente]
aperto-adj; i	open	[aperto]
apice-il	apex, peak	[apitʃe]
apparecchiare-vb	lay	[apparekkjare]
apparenza-le	appearance, guise	[apparentsa]
apparire-vb	appear, show	[apparire]
apparizione-le	appearance	[apparittsjone]
appartenere-vb	belong	[appartenere]
appassire-vb	wither	[appassire]
appellare-vb	appeal	[appellare]
appena-adv; adj	just, (as) soon (as)	[appena]
appetito-il	appetite, hunger	[appetito]
appianare-vb	smooth	[appjanare]
appiccicare-vb	stick	[appittʃikare]
applaudire-vb	applaud, cheer	[applaudire]
applauso-il	applause	[applauzo]
appoggiare-vb	support, rest	[appoddʒare]
appresso-prp; adv	near; lateral	[appresso]
approdare-vb	land	[approdare]
approvazione-la	approval, endorsement	[approvattsjone]
appunto-adv; i	just	[appunto]
aprire-vb	open	[aprire]

aquilotto-*il*	eaglet	[akwilotto]
arancia-*la*	orange	[arantʃa]
arcigno-*adj*	surly	[artʃiɲɲo]
arco-*lo*	bow	[arko]
ardire-*vb; il*	courage; boldness	[ardire]
ardito-*adj*	bold	[ardito]
arena-*le*	arena	[arena]
argomento-*gli*	topic, subject, argument	[argomento]
arguire-*vb*	deduce	[argwire]
aria-*la*	air, song	[arja]
aritmetica-*la*	arithmetic	[aritmetika]
armare-*vb*	arm	[armare]
armento-*il*	herd	[armento]
arrabbiato-*adj*	angry	[arrabbjato]
arrampicare-*vb*	climb	[arrampikare]
arricciare-*vb*	curl	[arrittʃare]
arrivare-*vb*	arrive	[arrivare]
arrosto-*adj; il*	roast; roast meet	[arrosto]
arruffare-*vb*	ruffle	[arruffare]
arruffato-*adj*	ruffled	[arruffato]
ascella-*le*	armpit, lath	[aʃʃella]
ascia-*la*	ax, adze	[aʃʃa]
asciugare-*vb*	dry, wipe	[aʃʃugare]
ascoltare-*vb*	listen	[askoltare]
aspettare-*vb*	wait	[aspettare]
aspetto-*lo*	appearance, look, aspect	[aspˈɛtto]
aspro-*adj*	sour, harsh	[aspro]
assaggiare-*vb*	taste, assay	[assaddʒare]
assai-*adv*	very	[assai]
assaporare-*vb*	savor	[assaporare]
assassinare-*vb*	assassinate	[assassinare]
assassinio-*il*	murder, assasination	[assassinjo]
asse-*il*	axis, axle	[asse]
assemblea-*le*	assembly, meeting	[assemblea]
assenza-*le*	absence	[assentsa]
assistere-*vb*	assist, attend	[assistere]
assomigliare-*vb*	look like, resemble	[assomiʎʎare]
assopimento-*il*	drowsiness	[assopimento]
assottigliare-*vb*	thin	[assottiʎʎare]
assumere-*vb*	take, assume	[assumere]
astro-*gli*	star	[astro]
attaccare-*vb*	attack	[attakkare]
attaccato-*adj*	attached	[attakkato]
attacco-*lo*	attack	[attakko]
attendere-*vb*	wait for	[attendere]
attenzione-*le*	caution	[attentsjone]
attimo-*lo*	moment, instant	[ˈattimo]
atto-*gli; adj*	act	[atto]
attorno-*adv*	about; around	[attorno]
attraente-*adj*	attractive	[attraente]
audace-*adj*	bold, daring	[audatʃe]
austero-*adj*	austere	[austero]
autorevole-*adj*	authoritative	[autorevole]
autorità-*le*	authority	[autoritˈa]
avanti-*adv*	forward, ahead, on	[avanti]
avanzare-*vb*	advance, put forward	[avantsare]
avere-*vb*	have	[avere]
avvedersi-*vb*	notice	[avvedersi]
avvedutezza-*la*	foresight	[avvedutettsa]
avvenire-*adj; il; vb*	future; future; occur	[avvenire]
avventare-*vb*	fling, hurl	[avventare]
avventura-*le*	adventure	[avventura]
avventurare-*vb*	venture	[avventurare]
avvertimento-*il*	warning, caution	[avvertimento]
avvicinare-*vb*	approach	[avvitʃinare]
avviluppare-*vb*	envelop	[avviluppare]

B

babbo-*il*	dad, father	[babbo]
baciare-*vb*	kiss	[batʃare]
badare-*vb*	look after	[badare]
baffo-*il*	whiskers	[baffo]
bagnare-*vb*	wet, soak	[baɲɲare]
bagno-*il*	bathroom	[baɲɲo]
balbettare-*vb*	stutter, babble	[balbettare]
ballare-*vb*	dance	[ballare]
ballo-*il*	dance, ball	[ballo]
bambina-*la*	child	[bambina]
bambino-*il*	child, baby, boy/girl	[bambino]
basso-*adj; il*	low, bottom, lower; bass	[basso]
bastare-*vb*	suffice	[bastare]
bastonare-*vb*	beat, club	[bastonare]
battere-*vb*	beat	[battere]
beati-*adj*	blessed	[beati]

beccare-*vb*	peck, catch	[bekkare]
bellezza-*la*	beauty	[bellettsa]
bellino-*adj*	pretty	[bellino]
bello-*adj*	beautiful	[b'ɛllo]
benchè-*con*	although	[beŋk'ɛ]
bene-*adv; il; adj*	very; well, good; good, asset	[b'ɛne]
benissimo-*adv*	very well, fine	[benissimo]
bere-*vb; il*	drinking	[bere]
bestia-*la*	beast	[bestja]
bestiolina-*f*	peewee	[bestjolina]
bianco-*adj; il*	white	[bjaŋko]
bianco-*adj; il*	white	[bjaŋko]
bimba-*la*	infant	[bimba]
bimbo-*il*	baby, child	[bimbo]
birba-*la*	brat	[birba]
bisbigliare-*vb*	whisper	[bizbiʎʎare]
bisbiglio-*il*	whisper	[bizbiʎʎo]
bislungo-*adj*	oblong	[bizluŋgo]
bisognare-*vb*	must	[bizoɲɲare]
bisogno-*il*	need	[bizoɲɲo]
bisticciare-*vb*	quarrel	[bistittʃare]
bisticcio-*il*	quarrel	[bistittʃo]
bizzarro-*adj*	bizarre, strange	[biddzarro]
bocca-*la*	mouth	[bokka]
bocconcino-*il*	morsel	[bokkontʃino]
bontà-*la*	goodness	[bont'a]
borbottare-*vb*	mutter	[borbottare]
bottiglia-*la*	bottle	[bottiʎʎa]
botto-*il*	blow, hit; explosion	[botto]
braccetto-*il*	arm	[brattʃetto]
braccio-*il*	arm	[brattʃo]
bramare-*vb*	long	[bramare]
breve-*adj; la*	short	[breve]
bricco-*il*	jug	[brikko]
briciolo-*lo*	bit	[britʃolo]
briga-*la*	bother, trouble	[briga]
brillare-*vb*	shine, glitter	[brillare]
brivido-*il*	thrill, prickle	[brivido]
brodoso-*adj*	watery	[brodozo]
broncio-*il*	pout, sulk	[brontʃo]
brontolare-*vb*	grumble	[brontolare]
bruco-*il*	caterpillar	[bruko]
brutto-*adj; il*	ugly, bad; bad, ugliness	[brutto]

brutto-*adj; il*	ugly, bad; bad, ugliness	[brutto]
buca-*la*	hole, pit	[buka]
bucare-*vb*	puncture	[bukare]
buco-*il*	hole	[buko]
bulbo-*lo*	bulb	[bulbo]
buon-*adj*	delicious	[bw'ɔn]
buono-*adj; il*	good; voucher, coupon	[bw'ɔno]
burbero-*adj; il*	gruff; curmudgeon	[burbero]
burro-*il*	butter	[burro]
busca-*la*	search	[buska]
buttare-*vb*	throw	[buttare]

C

caccia-*la*	hunting	[kattʃa]
cacciare-*vb*	hunt, throw out	[kattʃare]
cacciata-*la*	dislodgement	[kattʃata]
cadente-*adj*	falling, sagging	[kadente]
cadere-*vb*	fall	[kadere]
caduto-*adj*	fallen	[kaduto]
cagnolino-*il*	puppy, doggie	[kaɲɲolino]
cala-*la*	cove	[kala]
calcio-*il*	football, soccer	[kaltʃo]
caldaia-*la*	boiler	[kaldaja]
calderone-*il*	cauldron	[kalderone]
calpestare-*vb*	trample, trample on	[kalpestare]
calza-*la*	stocking	[kaltsa]
cameretta-*la*	little room	[kameretta]
cameriera-*la*	waitress	[kamerjera]
caminetto-*il*	fireplace	[kaminetto]
camino-*il*	fireplace	[kamino]
camminare-*vb*	walk	[kamminare]
camomilla-*la*	chamomile	[kamomilla]
campanello-*il*	bell	[kampanello]
campo-*il*	field	[kampo]
canarino-*il*	canary	[kanarino]
candela-*la*	candle, spark plug	[kandela]
candido-*adj; il*	white; white	[kandido]
cane-*il*	dog	[kane]
canna-*la*	cane, barrel, rod	[kanna]
cannocchiale-*il*	telescope	[kannokkjale]
cantante-*il/la; adj*	singer; singing	[kantante]

cantare-*vb*	sing	[kantare]		cavare-*vb*	get, dig	[kavare]
cantata-*la*	cantata	[kantata]		ceffo-*il*	mug	[tʃeffo]
cantonata-*la*	corner	[kantonata]		cenere-*la*	ash	[tʃenere]
cantone-*il*	canton	[kantone]		cenno-*il*	sign	[tʃenno]
canzonare-*vb*	tease	[kantsonare]		centesimo-*il*	hundredth; cent	[tʃentezimo]
capello-*il*	hair	[kapello]		centro-*il*	center	[tʃˈɛntro]
capire-*vb*	understand	[kapire]		ce-*prn*	us	[tʃe]
capitale-*adj; la*	capital	[kapitale]		cerca-*la*	search	[tʃerka]
capitare-*vb*	happen, occur	[kapitare]		cercare-*vb*	search	[tʃerkare]
capitolo-*il*	chapter	[kapitolo]		cerchio-*il*	circle; rim	[tʃerkjo]
capitombolare-*vb*	tumble	[kapitombolare]		cerimoniale-*adj; nn*	ceremonial; etiquette	[tʃerimonjale]
capitombolo-*il*	tumble	[kapitombolo]		certamente-*adv*	of course	[tʃertamente]
capo-*il*	boss	[kapo]		certo-*adj; adv*	certain; of course	[tʃˈɛrto]
capovolgere-*vb*	invert, reverse	[kapovoldʒere]		cervello-*il*	brain	[tʃervˈɛllo]
cappellaio-*il*	hatter	[kappellajo]		cessare-*vb*	cease	[tʃessare]
cappello-*il*	hat	[kappello]		cetriolo-*il*	cucumber	[tʃetrjolo]
capriola-*la*	somersault	[kaprjola]		che-*con; prn; adj*	that; which, who; what	[ke]
carattere-*il*	character	[karattere]		chiamare-*vb*	call	[kjamare]
cardo-*il*	thistle	[kardo]		chiamata-*la*	(telephone) call	[kjamata]
carezza-*la*	caress	[karettsa]		chiaramente-*adv*	clearly	[kjaramente]
carezzevole-*adj*	caressing	[karettsevole]				
carico-*il; adj*	load, freight	[kariko]		chiaro-*adj; adv*	clear; light	[kjaro]
carino-*adj*	cute, nice, pretty	[karino]		chiave-*la*	key	[kjave]
caro-*adj*	dear, expensive; dear	[karo]		chiedere-*vb*	ask (for), enquire	[kjˈɛdere]
carrettata-*la*	cartful	[karrettata]		chiedere-*vb*	ask (for), enquire	[kjˈɛdere]
carro-*il*	wagon	[karro]		chiodo-*il*	nail	[kjodo]
carta-*la*	paper, card, map	[karta]		chi-*prn*	who	[ki]
cartello-*il*	cartel, sign	[kartello]		chiunque-*prn*	anyone	[kjuŋkwe]
cartone-*il*	cardboard	[kartone]		chiusa-*le*	close, lock, sluice	[kjuza]
casa-*la*	house, home	[kaza]		chiuso-*adj; lo*	closed	[kjuzo]
cascare-*vb*	fall	[kaskare]		ci-*adv; prn*	ourselves, us	[tʃi]
casco-*il*	helmet	[kasko]		ciarlare-*vb*	chatter	[tʃarlare]
caso-*il*	case	[kazo]		ciascuna-*prn*	each	[tʃaskuna]
casotto-*il*	shed, mess (coll)	[kazotto]		cielo-*il*	sky	[tʃˈɛlo]
casseruola-*le*	casserole	[kasserwola]		cielo-*il*	sky	[tʃˈɛlo]
casualmente-*adv*	casually	[kazwalmente]		cifra-*la*	figure, number	[tʃifra]
				ciliegia-*la*	cherry	[tʃiljedʒa]
catino-*il*	basin	[katino]		cima-*la*	top	[tʃima]
cattivo-*adj*	bad; baddie, bad person	[kattivo]		cingere-*vb*	encircle	[tʃindʒere]
causa-*la*	cause	[kˈauza]		cinguettare-*vb*	chirp	[tʃiŋgwettare]
cavaliere-*il*	knight	[kavaljere]		cinquanta-*num*	fifty	[tʃiŋkwanta]
cavallo-*il*	horse	[kavallo]		cinque-*num*	five	[tʃiŋkwe]
				ciocca-*la*	lock	[tʃokka]

cioè-adv; abr	i.e., that is, namely	[tʃoˈɛ]	**comparire**-vb	appear	[komparire]
ciò-prn	that, it	[tʃˈɔ]	**compassione**-la	compassion, sympathy	[kompassjone]
cipiglio-il	frown	[tʃipiʎʎo]	**compitare**-vb	spell	[kompitare]
cipolla-la	onion	[tʃipolla]	**comporre**-vb	compose, dial	[komporre]
circa-adv; prp	about	[tʃirka]	**composto**-adj; il	composed; compound	[komposto]
circolare-adj; la; vb	circular; circular; circulate	[tʃirkolare]	**comprare**-vb	buy	[komprare]
circondare-vb	surround, encircle	[tʃirkondare]	**comprendere**-vb	understand	[komprendere]
citare-vb	quote, mention	[tʃitare]	**comprendonio**-il	savvy	[komprendonjo]
civettare-vb	flirt, jilt	[tʃivettare]	**comune**-adj; il	common; community, town	[komune]
civile-adj; lo	civil; civilian	[tʃivile]	**comunicare**-vb	communicate	[komunikare]
civiltà-la	civilization	[tʃiviltˈa]	**comunque**-adv; con	anyway; though	[komuŋkwe]
classico-adj; il	classic	[klassiko]	**concavo**-adj; il	concave; concave	[koŋkavo]
coccodrillo-il	crocodile	[kokkodrillo]	**concedere**-vb	grant	[kontʃedere]
coda-la	queue, tail	[koda]	**concertare**-vb	concert	[kontʃertare]
codesto-adj	that, this	[kodesto]	**condannare**-vb	convict	[kondannare]
cogliere-vb	take, catch	[koʎʎere]	**condurre**-vb	lead, carry out	[kondurre]
cognizione-la	cognition, acquaintance	[koɲɲittsjone]	**confetto**-il	candy	[konfetto]
colà-adv	there	[kolˈa]	**conficcare**-vb	stick, drive	[konfikkare]
colare-vb	strain, drip	[kolare]	**confidare**-vb	trust, rely	[konfidare]
collare-il; vb	collar; size	[kollare]	**confondere**-vb	confound	[konfondere]
colle-il	hill	[kolle]	**conformare**-vb	conform	[konformare]
collera-la	anger, rage	[kollera]	**confusione**-la	confusion	[konfuzjone]
colombo-il	pigeon	[kolombo]	**confuso**-adj	confused, fuzzy	[konfuzo]
colorare-vb	color	[kolorare]	**congiunto**-adj; il	joined; kinsman	[kondʒunto]
colorire-vb	color	[kolorire]	**conigliera**-la	rabbit hutch	[koniʎʎera]
colpevole-adj; il/la	guilty	[kolpevole]	**coniglio**-il	rabbit	[koniʎʎo]
colpire-vb	hit	[kolpire]	**conoscere**-vb	know	[konoʃʃere]
colpo-il	hit	[kolpo]	**con**-prp; con	with, by	[kon]
coltello-il	knife	[koltello]	**consegnare**-vb	deliver	[konseɲɲare]
comandare-vb	command	[komandare]	**conserto**-adj	crossed	[konserto]
comandata-la	squad	[komandata]	**conservare**-vb	keep, preserve	[konservare]
comare-la	godmother	[komare]	**considerare**-vb	consider	[konsiderare]
combattimento-il	combat	[kombattimento]	**consigliere**-il	advisor, councilor	[konsiʎʎere]
come-adv; prn; prp; con	as, how	[kome]	**consiglio**-il	advice, council, board	[konsiʎʎo]
cominciare-vb; lo	begin	[komintʃare]	**consistere**-vb	consist	[konsistere]
comitiva-la	party	[komitiva]	**consultare**-vb	consult, examine	[konsultare]
commedia-la	comedy	[kommedja]	**contare**-vb	count	[kontare]
commosso-adj	moved, unrest	[kommosso]	**contegno**-il	behavior, manner	[konteɲɲo]
comodo-adj; il	comfortable	[komodo]	**contenere**-vb	contain	[kontenere]
compare-gli	gaffer	[kompare]			

contentare-*vb*	satisfy	[kontentare]		credere-*vb*	believe	[kr'edere]
contento-*adj*	happy	[kontento]		credo-*lo*	creed, credo	[kredo]
continuare-*vb*	continue	[kontinware]		cremare-*vb*	cremate	[kremare]
continuo-*adj*	continuous	[kontinwo]		crescere-*vb*	grow	[kreʃʃere]
contorcere-*vb*	contort	[kontortʃere]		crisalide-*la*	chrysalis	[krizalide]
contraddanza-*la*	contredanse	[kontraddantsa]		cristallo-*il*	crystal	[kristallo]
contraddire-*vb*	contradict	[kontraddire]		crollare-*vb*	collapse, crumble	[krollare]
contrastare-*vb*	counteract	[kontrastare]		croquet-*il*	croquet	[krokwet]
contro-*adv; prp; il*	against, counter; against, versus	[kontro]		crostino-*il*	crouton	[krostino]
convenire-*vb*	agree	[konvenire]		crudo-*adj*	raw, piping	[krudo]
conversazione-*la*	conversation	[konversattsjone]		cucchiaino-*il*	teaspoon	[kukkjaino]
				cucciolo-*il*	puppy	[kuttʃolo]
convertire-*vb*	convert	[konvertire]		cucina-*la*	kitchen	[kutʃina]
coperto-*adj; lo*	covered	[koperto]		cui-*prn; con*	which	[k'ui]
coppia-*la*	couple	[koppja]		cullare-*vb*	rock	[kullare]
coprire-*vb*	cover	[koprire]		cuoco-*il*	cook	[kwoko]
coraggio-*il*	courage	[koraddʒo]		cuoco-*il*	cook	[kwoko]
coraggioso-*adj*	courageous	[koraddʒozo]		cuore-*il*	heart, core	[kw'ore]
coro-*il*	choir	[koro]		curiosità-*la*	curiosity	[kurjozit'a]
corona-*la*	crown, wreath	[korona]		curioso-*adj*	curious	[kurjozo]
corpo-*il*	body	[k'ɔrpo]		curvare-*vb*	bend	[kurvare]
correre-*vb*	run	[korrere]		curvatura-*la*	curvature, bending	[kurvatura]
correttamente-*adv*	correctly	[korrettamente]		cuscino-*il*	pillow	[kuʃʃino]
corridoio-*il*	aisle, hallway	[korridojo]		**D**		
corrucciata-*adj*	frowning, annoyed	[korruttʃata]				
corso-*il*	course	[korso]		da*dal, dallo, dall', dalla, dai, dagli, dalle-*prp*	from	[da]
cortese-*adj*	courteous, polite	[korteze]				
cortigiano-*il*	courtier	[kortidʒano]		danzare-*vb*	dance	[dantsare]
cortina-*la*	curtain	[kortina]		dare-*vb*	give	[dare]
corto-*adj*	short	[korto]		dato-*adj; il*	given; fact, datum	[dato]
corvo-*il*	crow, rook	[korvo]		davanti-*adj; adv; prp; gli*	front; in front	[davanti]
cosa-*prn; la*	what; thing	[k'ɔza]				
così-*adv; con*	so, thus; that	[koz'i]		davvero-*adv*	really	[davvero]
costa-*la*	coast, coastline	[kosta]		debole-*adj; il/la*	weak	[debole]
costo-*il*	cost	[kosto]		decapitare-*vb*	decapitate	[dekapitare]
costoro-*prn*	them	[kostoro]		decapitato-*adj*	beheaded	[dekapitato]
cotanto-*adj*	so	[kotanto]		decollare-*vb*	take off, decollate	[dekollare]
covare-*vb*	hatch, sit	[kovare]		deferenza-*la*	deference	[deferentsa]
cranio-*il*	skull	[kranjo]		delicatezza-*la*	delicacy, gentleness	[delikatettsa]
creanza-*la*	civility	[kreantsa]		delicato-*adj*	delicate, gentle	[delikato]
creatura-*la*	creature	[kreatura]		delitto-*il*	crime	[delitto]
creaturina-*la*	bundle, heap	[kreaturina]		deliziare-*vb*	delight	[delittsjare]
credenza-*la*	belief, sideboard	[kredentsa]		delizioso-*adj*	delicious	[delittsjozo]

della-*adj*	any	[della]	**diritto**-*il; adj; adv*	right, law; straight; straight	[diritto]
deludere-*vb*	disappoint	[deludere]	**discendere**-*vb*	descend, drop	[diʃʃendere]
dente-*il*	tooth	[dˈɛnte]	**discernere**-*vb*	discern, descry	[diʃʃernere]
dentro-*adv; prp*	in, inside	[dentro]	**discesa**-*la*	descent	[diʃʃeza]
deporre-*vb*	lay, testify	[deporre]	**discorrere**-*vb*	talk	[diskorrere]
derelitto-*adj*	derelict	[derelitto]	**discorso**-*il*	speech	[diskorso]
derisione-*la*	derision	[derizjone]	**discussione**-*la*	discussion	[diskussjone]
desiderare-*vb*	wish	[deziderare]	**disdegnare**-*vb*	disdain	[dizdeɲɲare]
desinare-*lo; vb*	dinner; dine	[dezinare]	**disdegnoso**-*adj*	disdainful	[dizdeɲɲozo]
desolante-*adj*	distressing	[dezolante]	**disegnare**-*vb*	draw, sketch	[dizeɲɲare]
destrezza-*la*	dexterity	[destrettsa]	**disfare**-*vb*	undo, unpack	[disfare]
destro-*adj; il*	right	[destro]	**disperatamente**-*adv*	desperately	[disperatamente]
detestare-*vb*	loathe	[detestare]	**disperato**-*adj*	desperate	[disperato]
dettare-*vb*	dictate	[dettare]	**disperazione**-*la*	despair, desolation	[disperattsjone]
di*del, dello, dell', della, dei, degli, delle-*prp*	of, to; than, and	[di]	**dispetto**-*lo*	spite, annoyance	[dispetto]
			dispettoso-*adj*	spiteful	[dispettozo]
dialogo-*il*	dialogue, conversation	[djalogo]	**dispiacere**-*il; vb*	dislike, be sorry	[dispjatʃere]
diamante-*il*	diamond	[djamante]	**disposto**-*adj; adv*	willing; ready	[disposto]
diamine-*int*	heck	[djamine]	**disprezzo**-*il*	contempt	[disprettso]
dianzi-*adv*	just now	[djantsi]	**distaccare**-*vb*	detach, second	[distakkare]
dieci-*num*	ten	[djˈetʃi]	**distanza**-*la*	distance	[distantsa]
dietro-*prp; il; adj; adv*	behind; back, rear; after; after	[djˈɛtro]	**distinguere**-*vb*	distinguish, differentiate	[distiŋgwere]
difetto-*il*	defect, default	[difetto]	**distrazione**-*la*	distraction	[distrattsjone]
difficile-*adj*	difficult	[diffˈitʃile]	**distribuire**-*vb*	distribute, deliver	[distribwire]
difficoltà-*le*	difficulties, difficulty, trouble	[diffikoltˈa]	**disturbo**-*il*	disorder	[disturbo]
			disubbidire-*vb*	disobey	[dizubbidire]
dilatare-*vb*	dilate	[dilatare]	**ditale**-*il*	thimble	[ditale]
dileguare-*vb*	vanish	[dilegware]	**dito**-*il*	finger	[dito]
dilettare-*vb*	delight	[dilettare]	**divenire**-*vb*	become	[divenire]
dilungato-*adj*	pulled out	[diluŋgato]	**diventare**-*vb*	become	[diventare]
dimenare-*vb*	wiggle	[dimenare]	**diverso**-*adj*	different	[divˈɛrso]
dimenticare-*vb*	forget	[dimentikare]	**divertire**-*vb*	entertain	[divertire]
dimenticato-*adj*	forgotten	[dimentikato]	**dividere**-*vb*	divide, share	[dividere]
dimettere-*vb*	resign	[dimettere]	**divorare**-*vb*	devour	[divorare]
diminuire-*vb*	decrease, reduce	[diminwire]	**documentare**-*vb*	document	[dokumentare]
dimorare-*vb*	dwell, reside	[dimorare]			
dintorno-*il*	vicinity	[dintorno]	**dodici**-*num*	twelve	[dˈɔditʃi]
dipendere-*vb*	depend	[dipendere]	**dolere**-*vb*	ache, be sorry	[dolere]
dire-*vb*	say	[dire]	**dolore**-*il*	ache, pain	[dolore]
dire-*vb*	say	[dire]	**domanda**-*la*	demand, question	[domanda]
direzione-*la*	direction, management	[direttsjone]	**domandare**-*vb*	ask, request	[domandare]
dirigere-*vb*	direct	[diridʒere]			

domani-*adv; gli*	tomorrow	[domani]
donna-*la*	woman	[dɔnna]
donnola-*la*	weasel	[donnola]
dopo-*adv; prp*	after	[dopo]
doppiamente-*adv*	doubly	[doppjamente]
dorato-*adj*	golden, gold-plated	[dorato]
dormire-*vb*	sleep	[dormire]
dove-*adv; con*	where; where	[dove]
dovere-*il; vb; av*	have to, must; duty	[dovere]
dovunque-*adv; con*	anywhere	[dovuŋkwe]
dritto-*adj; adv*	straight, upright; right	[dritto]
dubbio-*il; adj*	doubtful; doubt	[dubbjo]
dubbioso-*adj*	doubtful	[dubbjozo]
dubitare-*vb*	doubt	[dubitare]
duchessa-*la*	duchess	[dukessa]
due-*l; num*	two	[dʼue]
dunque-*adv*	therefore	[duŋkwe]
duodecimo-*num*	twelfth	[dwodetʃimo]
durante-*prp*	during, in, over; while	[durante]
duro-*adj; il*	hard	[duro]

E

ebbene-*adv*	so, well	[ebbene]
eccellente-*adj*	excellent	[ettʃellente]
eccettuare-*vb*	except	[ettʃettware]
eccitare-*vb*	excite, energize	[ettʃitare]
ecco-*adv*	here	[ˈɛkko]
eccomi-*int*	coming!	[ekkomi]
eccoti-*int*	here you are	[ekkoti]
eco-*gli*	echo	[eko]
educare-*vb*	educate, bring up	[edukare]
effetto-*il*	effect	[effetto]
egli-*prn*	he	[eʎʎi]
eh-*int*	huh	[ˈɛ]
elce-*il*	ilex	[eltʃe]
elefante-*il*	elephant	[elefante]
elegante-*adj*	elegant	[elegante]
elevare-*vb*	raise, rise	[elevare]
ella-*prn*	she	[ella]
empio-*adj*	impious	[empjo]

energico-*adj*	energetic	[enerdʒiko]
enfasi-*le*	emphasis	[enfazi]
enorme-*adj*	huge	[enorme]
enormemente-*adv*	enormously	[enormemente]
entrambi-*adj*	both, either	[entrambi]
entrare-*vb*	enter	[entrare]
entrata-*la*	entrance	[entrata]
eppure-*con*	and yet	[eppure]
equilibrio-*lo*	equilibrium	[ekwilibrjo]
erba-*le*	grass, pot, herb	[erba]
erudizione-*le*	erudition	[erudittsjone]
esaminare-*vb*	examine, study	[ezaminare]
eseguire-*vb*	perform, execute	[ezegwire]
esempio-*gli*	example	[ezempjo]
esistere-*vb*	exist	[ezistere]
esperimento-*il*	experiment	[esperimento]
espressione-*la*	expression	[espressjone]
esprimere-*vb*	express, voice	[esprimere]
essa-*prn*	it	[essa]
esse-*prn*	they	[esse]
essere-*vb; gli*	be; being	[ˈɛssere]
essi-*prn*	they, them	[essi]
esso-*prn*	it, he	[esso]
estate-*le*	summer	[estate]
est-*lo*	East	[est]
estrarre-*vb*	extract, pull out	[estrarre]
estremità-*le*	end, butt	[estremitˈa]
età-*le*	age	[etˈa]
evitare-*vb; il*	avoid	[evitare]
extra-*adj*	extra	[ekstra]

F

fa-*adv*	ago	[fa]
faccenda-*la*	affair	[fattʃenda]
facile-*adj; adv*	easy	[fˈatʃile]
facilmente-*adv*	easily	[fatʃilmente]
falso-*adj; il*	false	[falso]
fame-*la*	hunger	[fame]
famiglia-*la*	family	[famiʎʎa]
familiarmente-*adv*	familiar	[familjarmente]
fanciulla-*la*	girl	[fantʃulla]

fanciullezza-*la*	childhood	[fantʃullettsa]	**focolare**-*il; il*	hearth; astronomer	[fokolare]
fanciullo-*il*	child	[fantʃullo]	**foglia**-*la*	leaf	[foʎʎa]
fantasticare-*vb*	daydream	[fantastikare]	**foglio**-*il*	sheet, leaf	[foʎʎo]
fante-*il*	knave, infantryman	[fante]	**folla**-*la*	crowd	[folla]
fare-*vb*	do	[fare]	**follemente**-*adv*	madly, wildly	[follemente]
farfalla-*la*	butterfly	[farfalla]	**fondamento**-*il*	foundation, grounding	[fondamento]
fattore-*il*	factor, consideration	[fattore]	**fondo**-*il; adj*	background, bottom, fund; deep	[fondo]
fattoria-*la*	farm	[fattorja]			
favore-*il*	favor	[favore]	**fontana**-*la*	fountain	[fontana]
fendere-*vb*	cleave, slit	[fendere]	**forbire**-*vb*	furbish	[forbire]
fermare-*vb*	stop	[fermare]	**foresta**-*la*	forest	[foresta]
fermezza-*la*	firmness	[fermettsa]	**forma**-*la*	form	[forma]
feroce-*adj*	fierce, savage	[ferotʃe]	**formare**-*vb*	form, train	[formare]
ferrovia-*la*	railway, rail	[ferrovja]	**fornello**-*il*	stove	[fornello]
fetta-*la*	slice, cut	[fetta]	**forse**-*adv*	perhaps	[forse]
fiacco-*adj*	weak	[fjakko]	**forte**-*adj; il; adv*	strong; forte; loudly	[fˈɔrte]
fiamma-*la*	flame	[fjamma]	**forzare**-*vb*	force, compel	[fortsare]
fianco-*il*	side	[fjaŋko]	**fracasso**-*il*	din, crash	[frakasso]
fianco-*il*	side	[fjaŋko]	**fradicio**-*adj*	wet, soggy	[fraditʃo]
fiatare-*vb*	breathe	[fjatare]	**francese**-*adj; il*	French	[frantʃeze]
fiato-*il*	breath	[fjato]	**franco**-*il; adj*	frank, free; franc	[fraŋko]
ficcare-*vb*	poke, stick	[fikkare]	**fra**-*prp; adv*	between, among	[fra]
fidanzare-*vb*	affiance	[fidantsare]	**frase**-*la*	phrase, sentence	[fraze]
fiero-*adj*	proud	[fjero]	**fratello**-*il*	brother	[fratˈɛllo]
figlia-*la*	daughter	[fiʎʎa]	**fresco**-*adj; il*	fresh, cool	[fresko]
figliare-*vb*	calve	[fiʎʎare]	**fretta**-*la*	hurry	[fretta]
figliuolo-*il*	son	[fiʎʎwolo]	**frettoloso**-*adj*	hasty	[frettolozo]
figurare-*vb*	appear, figure	[figurare]	**friggere**-*vb*	fry	[friddʒere]
figuro-*il*	character	[figuro]	**frittura**-*la*	frying	[frittura]
filastrocca-*la*	doggerel	[filastrokka]	**fronte**-*la*	front, forehead	[fronte]
filo-*il*	wire	[filo]	**frontespizio**-*il*	title page	[frontespittsjo]
finalmente-*adv*	finally	[finalmente]	**frullare**-*vb*	whisk, flutter	[frullare]
fine-*la; adj*	purpose; end; fine	[fine]	**fuggevole**-*adj*	fleeting	[fuddʒevole]
finestra-*la*	window	[finestra]	**fuggire**-*vb*	flee	[fuddʒire]
fingere-*vb*	pretend	[findʒere]	**fumare**-*vb*	smoke	[fumare]
finire-*vb*	end, finish	[finire]	**fumo**-*il*	smoke	[fumo]
fioco-*adj*	dim	[fjoko]	**fune**-*la*	cable, wire; rope, linen	[fune]
fiore-*il*	flower	[fjore]			
firma-*la*	signature	[firma]	**fungo**-*il*	mushroom	[fuŋgo]
firmare-*vb*	sign	[firmare]	**fuoco**-*il*	fire	[fwˈɔko]
fissare-*vb*	fix, secure	[fissare]	**fuori**-*adv*	out, outside	[fwˈɔri]
fisso-*adj; adv*	fixed; fixedly	[fisso]	**furia**-*la*	fury, rampage	[furja]
fiume-*il*	river	[fjume]	**furiosamente**-*adv*	furiously	[furjozamente]
foca-*la*	seal	[foka]			

furioso-*adj*	furious, mad	[furjozo]
fuso-*adj; il*	melted; spindle	[fuzo]

G

gabbare-*vb*	cheat	[gabbare]
gabbia-*la*	cage	[gabbja]
galantuomo-*il*	gentleman	[galantwomo]
galleria-*la*	gallery	[gallerja]
gamba-*la*	leg	[gamba]
gambero-*il*	crayfish	[gambero]
ganascia-*la*	jaw	[ganaʃʃa]
garbato-*adj*	polite	[garbato]
garbo-*il*	politeness	[garbo]
gatta-*la*	cat	[gatta]
gatto-*il*	cat	[gatto]
gazza-*la*	magpie	[gattsa]
gemito-*il*	groan, whine	[dʒemito]
generale-*adj; il*	general	[dʒenerale]
generalmente-*adv*	generally, as a rule	[dʒeneralmente]
genere-*il*	gender, kind, genre	[dʒ'ɛnere]
gente-*la*	people	[dʒ'ɛnte]
gentile-*adj*	kind, gentle	[dʒentile]
geografia-*la*	geography	[dʒografja]
ghignare-*vb*	sneer	[giɲɲare]
ghigno-*il*	fleer	[giɲɲo]
ghirlanda-*la*	garland	[girlanda]
ghiro-*il*	dormouse	[giro]
già-*adv*	already	[dʒ'a]
giacere-*vb*	lie	[dʒatʃere]
giammai-*adv*	never	[dʒammai]
giardiniere-*il*	gardener	[dʒardinjere]
giardino-*il*	garden	[dʒardino]
ginocchio-*il*	knee	[dʒinokkjo]
giocondo-*adj*	jocund	[dʒokondo]
giornale-*il*	newspaper, journal	[dʒornale]
giornata-*la*	day	[dʒornata]
giorno-*il*	day	[dʒorno]
giovanetto-*il*	lad	[dʒovanetto]
giovare-*vb*	profit	[dʒovare]
giovinezza-*la*	youth, girlhood	[dʒovinettsa]
girare-*vb*	turn	[dʒirare]
giro-*il*	tour	[dʒiro]

giro-*il*	tour	[dʒiro]
giù-*adv*	down	[dʒu]
giudicare-*vb*	judge	[dʒudikare]
giudice-*il*	judge	[dʒuditʃe]
giungere-*vb*	reach	[dʒundʒere]
giurare-*vb*	swear	[dʒurare]
giurare-*vb*	swear	[dʒurare]
giusto-*adj; adv*	right, just, fair; correctly	[dʒusto]
giusto-*adj; adv*	right, just, fair; correctly	[dʒusto]
globo-*il*	globe, orb	[globo]
gocciolare-*vb*	drip	[gottʃolare]
gola-*la*	throat	[gola]
gomito-*il*	elbow	[gomito]
gonnellino-*il*	kilt	[gonnellino]
gonzo-*il*	dupe	[gontso]
gota-*la*	cheek	[gota]
governare-*vb*	govern, steer	[governare]
gradire-*vb*	like	[gradire]
grado-*il*	degree	[grado]
grammatico-*il*	grammarian	[grammatiko]
gran-*adj*	great	[gran]
granchio-*il*	crab	[graŋkjo]
grande-*adj*	great, great	[grande]
grandine-*la*	hailstorm	[grandine]
granduca-*il*	Grand Duke	[granduka]
grasso-*adj; il*	fat	[grasso]
grattare-*vb*	scratch, scrape	[grattare]
grave-*adj*	serious, severe	[grave]
gravemente-*adv*	seriously, sorely	[gravemente]
gravità-*la; abr*	severity; G	[gravit'a]
grazia-*la*	grace, pardon	[grattsja]
grazie-*int*	thank you	[grattsje]
grazioso-*adj; adv*	pretty; pretty	[grattsjozo]
gretto-*adj*	narrow	[gretto]
gridare-*vb*	shout	[gridare]
grido-*il*	cry	[grido]
grifone-*il*	griffin	[grifone]
grondare-*vb*	drip	[grondare]
grongo-*il*	conger	[groŋgo]
grossezza-*la*	thickness	[grossettsa]
grosso-*adj*	big, thick	[gr'ɔsso]

grugnire-*vb*	grunt	[gruɲɲire]	
grugno-*il*	snout	[gruɲɲo]	
guadagnare-*vb*	earn, gain	[gwadaɲɲare]	
guaio-*il*	trouble	[gwajo]	
guaire-*vb*	yelp	[gwaire]	
guanciale-*nn*	pillow	[gwantʃale]	
guanto-*il*	glove, gauntlet	[gwanto]	
guardare-*vb*	look, watch	[gwardare]	
guardare-*vb*	look, watch	[gwardare]	
guardata-*la*	slant	[gwardata]	
guardia-*la*	guard	[gwardja]	
guizzare-*vb*	flicker	[gwiddzare]	
gustare-*vb*	enjoy, taste	[gustare]	
gusto-*il*	taste	[gusto]	

I

idea-*la*	idea	[idˈɛa]
ideare-*vb*	design	[ideare]
idiota-*adj; il, la*	idiotic, stupid; idiot	[idjˈɔta]
ieri-*adv; lo*	yesterday	[jˈɛri]
il* lo, l', la, i, gli, le-*art*	the	[il]
illuminare-*vb*	illuminate, enlighten	[illuminare]
illustrazione-*la*	illustration	[illustrattsjone]
illustre-*adj*	illustrious, distinguished	[illustre]
imbarazzante-*adj*	embarrassing	[imbarattsante]
imbarazzare-*vb*	embarrass, perplex	[imbarattsare]
imbarazzo-*il*	embarrassment	[imbarattso]
imbecille-*adj; il/la*	imbecile	[imbetʃille]
imbroglio-*il*	cheat, imbroglio	[imbroʎʎo]
imitare-*vb*	imitate, mimic	[imitare]
immaginare-*vb*	imagine	[immadʒinare]
immediatamente-*adv*	immediately	[immedjatamente]
immenso-*adj*	immense	[immenso]
impacciare-*vb*	hinder	[impattʃare]
impallidire-*vb*	pale	[impallidire]
imparare-*vb*	learn	[imparare]
impaurire-*vb*	frighten, get frightened	[impaurire]
impaziente-*adj*	impatient	[impattsjente]
impazienza-*le*	impatience	[impattsjentsa]

impazzare-*vb*	go crazy	[impattsare]
impazzata-*la*	madness	[impattsata]
impedire-*vb*	prevent, impede	[impedire]
impensierire-*vb*	worry	[impensjerire]
impertinente-*adj*	impertinent, naughty	[impertinente]
imperturbabilità-*la*	equability	[imperturbabilitˈa]
impeto-*il*	impetus, fit	[impeto]
impiccare-*vb*	hang	[impikkare]
impiegare-*vb*	use, take	[impjegare]
importante-*adj*	important	[importante]
importare-*vb*	import	[importare]
importo-*il*	amount	[importo]
impossibile-*adj*	impossible	[impossibile]
impressione-*le*	impression	[impressjone]
imprimere-*vb*	give, impress	[imprimere]
improvviso-*adj; adv*	sudden	[improvvizo]
in*nel, nello, nell', nella, nei, negli, nelle-*prp*	in, into	[in]
inanellato-*adj*	annulate	[inanellato]
incastrare-*vb*	fit	[iŋkastrare]
incatenare-*vb*	enchain	[iŋkatenare]
incendiare-*vb*	fire	[intʃendjare]
inchiodare-*vb*	nail, rivet	[iŋkjodare]
inchiostro-*il*	ink	[iŋkjostro]
incipriare-*vb*	powder	[intʃiprjare]
inciso-*adj*	incidentally	[intʃizo]
incollare-*vb*	paste, stick	[iŋkollare]
incolpare-*vb*	blame, accuse	[iŋkolpare]
incominciare-*vb*	begin	[iŋkomintʃare]
incomodo-*adj*	uncomfortable	[iŋkomodo]
incontrare-*vb*	meet	[iŋkontrare]
incoraggiare-*vb*	encourage, foster	[iŋkoraddʒare]
increspare-*vb*	ruffle	[iŋkrespare]
incrociare-*vb*	cross, meet	[iŋkrotʃare]
indi-*adv*	therefrom	[indi]
India-*la*	India	[indja]
indiavolato-*adj*	furious	[indjavolato]
indicare-*vb*	indicate, show	[indikare]
indicare-*vb*	indicate, show	[indikare]
indietro-*adv*	back	[indjˈɛtro]
indirizzare-*vb*	address	[indiriddzare]

indirizzo-*i*	address	[indiriddzo]
indovinare-*vb*	guess	[indovinare]
indovinare-*vb*	guess	[indovinare]
indovinello-*il*	riddle, quiz	[indovinello]
infiammare-*vb*	inflame	[infjammare]
infilare-*vb*	insert, thread	[infilare]
infocare-*vb*	set fire to	[infokare]
inforcare-*vb*	get on	[inforkare]
infreddatura-*la*	cold	[infreddatura]
ingannare-*vb*	deceive, fool	[ingannare]
inghiottire-*vb*	swallow, gulp	[ingjottire]
inginocchiarsi-*vb*	kneel	[indʒinokkjarsi]
ingiusto-*adj*	unfair, wrongful	[indʒusto]
ingoiare-*vb*	gobble	[ingojare]
ingollare-*vb*	gobble	[ingollare]
ingresso-*lo*	entrance	[ingresso]
innamorato-*adj; il*	in love; lover	[innamorato]
innanzi-*prp; adv*	before; forward	[innantsi]
innocente-*adj*	innocent	[innotʃente]
innumerevole-*adj*	countless, numerous	[innumerevole]
inoltrare-*vb*	forward	[inoltrare]
inopinato-*adj*	unexpected	[inopinato]
inquieto-*adj*	restless, worried	[inkwjeto]
insegnare-*vb*	teach	[insennare]
insieme-*adv; il/la*	together; set, whole	[insjɛme]
intanto-*adv*	in the meantime	[intanto]
intendere-*vb*	hear, mean, intend	[intendere]
intento-*adj; il*	intent; aim	[intento]
intenzione-*le*	intention	[intentsjone]
interessante-*adj*	interesting	[interessante]
interesse-*lo*	interest	[interesse]
internare-*vb*	intern	[internare]
intero-*adj; i*	entire, full, whole; whole	[intero]
interrogare-*vb*	query, interrogate	[interrogare]
interrompere-*vb*	stop, interrupt	[interrompere]
inteso-*adj*	understood	[intezo]
intiero-*adj*	entire	[intjero]
intimorire-*vb*	intimidate	[intimorire]
intorno-*adv*	around, round	[intorno]
inutile-*adj*	useless, unnecessary	[inutile]
inutilmente-*adv*	uselessly	[inutilmente]
invano-*adv; adj*	in vain; no purpose	[invano]
invece-*adv*	instead	[invetʃe]
inventare-*vb*	invent	[inventare]
inverno-*il*	winter	[inverno]
invertire-*vb*	reverse, be inverted	[invertire]
invitare-*vb*	invite	[invitare]
invitato-*il*	guest	[invitato]
invito-*lo*	invitation	[invito]
involti-*gli*	bundle	[involti]
inzuppare-*vb*	soak	[intsuppare]
io-*prn; gli*	I	['io]
ippopotamo-*il*	hippopotamus	[ippopotamo]
ira-*le*	anger, rage	[ira]
irato-*adj*	angry	[irato]
irritabile-*adj*	irritable, edgy	[irritabile]
irritare-*vb*	irritate, anger	[irritare]
iscrizione-*le*	entry, registration	[iskrittsjone]
istante-*il*	instant	[istante]
italiano-*adj; lo*	Italian	[italjano]
ivi-*adv*	therein	[ivi]

L

là-*adv*	there	[l'a]
labbro-*il*	lip	[labbro]
lacrima-*la*	tear	[lakrima]
lagnarsi-*vb*	complain	[lannarsi]
lagnarsi-*vb*	complain	[lannarsi]
lamina-*la*	foil	[lamina]
lampada-*la*	lamp	[lampada]
lampo-*il*	flash	[lampo]
lancetta-*la*	hand	[lantʃetta]
languido-*adj*	languid	[langwido]
largo-*adj*	wide, large, loose	[largo]
l'-*art*	the	[l']
lasciare-*vb*	leave	[laʃʃare]
lasciata-*adj*	left, dropped	[laʃʃata]
lassù-*adv*	up there, above, yonder	[lassu]
latina-*adj; la*	latina; latina	[latina]
latitudine-*la*	latitude	[latitudine]
lato-*il; adj*	side	[lato]
latrare-*vb*	bark	[latrare]

latte-*nm*	milk	[latte]
lavagna-*la*	blackboard	[lavaɲɲa]
lavare-*vb*	wash	[lavare]
lealmente-*adv*	loyally	[lealmente]
leccare-*vb*	lick	[lekkare]
legaccio-*il*	string	[legattʃo]
legare-*vb*	tie	[legare]
leggere-*vb*	read	[leddʒere]
legno-*il*	wood	[leɲɲo]
lei-*prn*	she, her	[lˈɛi]
lentamente-*adv*	slowly	[lentamente]
lepre-*la*	hare	[lepre]
lesione-*la*	lesion, injury	[lezjone]
lesso-*adj; il*	boiled; boiled meat	[lesso]
lestezza-*la*	deftness	[lestettsa]
lesto-*adj*	quick	[lesto]
letizia-*la*	joy	[letittsja]
lettera-*la*	letter	[lˈettera]
letto-*il*	bed	[lˈɛtto]
levare-*vb; il*	upbeat	[levare]
lezione-*la*	lesson	[lettsjone]
lì-*adv*	there	[lˈi]
liberare-*vb*	release	[liberare]
libero-*adj*	free	[lˈibero]
liberò-*adj*	free	[liberˈɔ]
librare-*vb*	weight	[librare]
libriccino-*il*	booklet	[librittʃino]
libro-*il*	book	[libro]
lieto-*adj*	happy	[ljeto]
linea-*la*	line, figure	[lˈinea]
lingua-*la*	tongue, language	[liŋgwa]
li-*prn*	them	[li]
liquore-*il*	liquor, liqueur	[likwore]
lira-*la*	lira	[lira]
lista-*la*	list	[lista]
litigare-*vb*	quarrel	[litigare]
livrea-*la*	livery	[livrea]
loggione-*il*	gallery	[loddʒone]
longitudine-*la*	longitude	[londʒitudine]
lontananza-*la*	distance	[lontanantsa]
lontano-*adv; adj; prp*	far	[lontano]
loro-*prn*	their	[loro]
luccicante-*adj*	shimmering	[luttʃikante]
luccicone-*il*	large tear	[luttʃikone]
lucente-*adj*	shiny, lucent	[lutʃente]
lucertola-*la*	lizard	[lutʃertola]
lui-*prn*	him, he	[lˈui]
lumaca-*la*	snail	[lumaka]
luminoso-*adj*	bright, light	[luminozo]
lungaggine-*la*	slowness	[luŋgaddʒine]
lungi-*adv*	far	[lundʒi]
lungo-*adj; prp; il*	long; along; length	[luŋgo]
luogo-*il*	place	[lwogo]
lussureggiante-*adj*	lush	[lussureddʒante]
lustro-*il; adj*	shine; shiny	[lustro]

M

macchina-*la*	machine	[makkina]
ma-*con*	but	[ma]
maestà-*la*	majesty	[maestˈa]
maestro-*il; adj*	master, teacher, meastro	[maˈɛstro]
magari-*adv*	maybe, perhaps, even	[magari]
maggio-*gli*	May	[maddʒo]
magico-*adj*	magical	[madʒiko]
magnificamente-*adv*	beautifully	[maɲɲifikamente]
magnifico-*adj*	magnificent	[maɲɲifiko]
mai-*adv*	never	[mai]
malandrino-*il*	rogue	[malandrino]
malcontento-*adj; il*	discontent; dissatisfaction	[malkontento]
male-*adv; il*	bad, evil	[male]
malinconico-*adj*	melancholy, pensive	[maliŋkoniko]
malinconico-*adj*	melancholy, pensive	[maliŋkoniko]
mancare-*vb*	miss	[maŋkare]
mancato-*adj*	failed, unsuccessful	[maŋkato]
mandare-*vb*	send	[mandare]
maneggiare-*vb*	handle, use	[maneddʒare]
mangiare-*vb; il*	eat	[mandʒare]
mangiata-*la*	feed	[mandʒata]
maniera-*la*	way, manner	[manjera]
mano-*la*	hand	[mano]
mano-*la*	hand	[mano]
mantenere-*vb*	keep, maintain	[mantenere]
mappa-*la*	map	[mappa]

mare-*il*	sea, seaside	[mare]
mare-*il*	sea, seaside	[mare]
margherita-*la*	daisy	[margerita]
marino-*adj*	marine, sea; marina, marine, navy	[marino]
marzo-*gli*	March	[martso]
mascella-*la*	jaw, maxilla	[maʃʃella]
matita-*la*	pencil	[matita]
matrona-*la*	matron	[matrona]
mattina-*la*	morning	[mattina]
matto-*adj; il*	crazy; madman	[matto]
maturo-*adj*	mature, adult	[maturo]
mazzo-*il*	deck, bunch	[mattso]
medesimo-*adj*	same	[medezimo]
meditabondo-*adj*	musing	[meditabondo]
meglio-*adv*	better, best	[mˈɛʎʎo]
memoria-*la*	storage	[memorja]
menare-*vb*	lead	[menare]
meno-*adj; adv; prp; lo; con*	less; less; unless; no so (much as)	[meno]
mente-*la*	mind	[mente]
mentire-*vb*	lie	[mentire]
mento-*il*	chin	[mento]
mentre-*con; adv; gli*	while, as, whereas	[mentre]
me-*prn*	me	[me]
meraviglia-*la*	wonder	[meraviʎʎa]
meravigliare-*vb*	wonder, surprise	[meraviʎʎare]
meraviglioso-*adj*	wonderful	[meraviʎʎozo]
meritare-*vb*	deserve	[meritare]
meschino-*adj*	petty, mean	[meskino]
mese-*il*	month	[meze]
mestare-*vb*	stir	[mestare]
mestizia-*la*	mournfulness	[mestittsja]
mesto-*adj*	sad	[mesto]
metà-*la*	half	[metˈa]
metodo-*il*	method	[metodo]
metro-*il*	meter	[metro]
mettere-*vb*	put	[mˈettere]
mezzo-*il; adj*	half, middle, means; half, middle	[mˈɛddzo]
mezz'ora-*la*	half an hour	[mettsora]
micio-*il*	pussy, tomcat	[mitʃo]
miglio-*il*	mile	[miʎʎo]

miglior-*adj*	best	[miʎʎor]
migliore-*adj; il*	best	[miʎʎore]
mille-*i; adj*	one thousand	[mille]
minacciare-*vb*	threaten, impend	[minattʃare]
minerale-*adj; il*	mineral; mineral	[minerale]
minestra-*la*	soup	[minestra]
miniera-*la*	mine	[minjera]
minimo-*adj; il*	minimum	[minimo]
minuto-*adj; il*	minute	[minuto]
mio-*prn*	my	[mˈio]
mi-*prn*	me	[mi]
miserabile-*adj; il*	miserable; wretch	[mizerabile]
mistero-*il*	mystery	[mistero]
misto-*adj; il*	mixed; mixture	[misto]
misura-*la*	measure	[mizura]
misurare-*vb*	measure, gauge	[mizurare]
mo'-*adv*	now	[moˈ]
mobiliare-*adj; vb*	movable; furnish	[mobiljare]
moderazione-*la*	moderation	[moderattsjone]
moderno-*adj*	modern	[moderno]
modo-*il*	way, manner	[mˈɔdo]
moglie-*la*	wife	[moʎʎe]
mollo-*adj*	soaked, flabby	[mollo]
molto-*adj; adv; gli*	very, much	[molto]
momento-*il*	moment	[momento]
mondo-*il; adj*	world	[mondo]
montare-*vb*	mount, assemble	[montare]
morale-*adj; la*	moral	[morale]
mordere-*vb*	bite	[mordere]
morire-*vb; phr*	die	[morire]
mormorare-*vb*	murmur, whisper	[mormorare]
morsicare-*vb*	bite	[morsikare]
mortale-*adj; adv*	mortal; deadly, fatal; deathly	[mortale]
mortalmente-*adv*	mortally	[mortalmente]
morto-*adj; il*	dead, died	[mˈɔrto]
moscone-*il*	bluebottle	[moskone]
mostra-*la*	show	[mostra]
mostrare-*vb*	show	[mostrare]
mostruosità-*le*	monstrosity	[mostrwozitˈa]
motivare-*vb*	motivate	[motivare]

moto-*il*	motion, motorbike	[moto]	
motto-*il*	motto	[motto]	
movimento-*il*	movement	[movimento]	
mozzare-*vb*	cut off	[mottsare]	
mucchio-*il*	pile	[mukkjo]	
muggito-*adj; il*	lowing; roar	[muddʒito]	
mulinare-*vb*	whirl	[mulinare]	
muovere-*vb*	move	[mwovere]	
muscolare-*adj*	muscular	[muskolare]	
musica-*la*	music	[muzika]	
muta-*la*	pack	[muta]	
mutamento-*il*	change	[mutamento]	
mutare-*vb*	change, slough	[mutare]	
muto-*adj; il*	silent; mute	[muto]	

N

nanna-*la*	beddy-bye	[nanna]
narrare-*vb*	tell, relate	[narrare]
nascondere-*vb*	hide	[naskondere]
nasello-*il*	hake	[nazello]
naso-*il*	nose	[nazo]
natale-*adj; il*	Christmas	[natale]
naturale-*adj*	natural	[naturale]
naturalmente-*adv*	naturally	[naturalmente]
ne-*adj; prn*	any; of it, of them	[ne]
negare-*vb*	deny, negate	[negare]
nembo-*il*	stormcloud	[nembo]
nemmeno-*adv; con*	not even, neither	[nemmeno]
neppure-*adv; con*	not even, neither	[neppure]
nervo-*il*	nerve	[nervo]
nervoso-*adj*	nervous	[nervozo]
nessun-*adj*	no	[nessun]
nessuno-*adj; prn*	no; nobody, anyone	[nessuno]
nessuno-*adj; prn*	no; nobody, anyone	[nessuno]
nettare-*il; vb*	nectar; clean	[nettare]
nido-*il*	nest	[nido]
niente-*lo; prn*	nothing, anything; any, none	[njˈɛnte]
ninnare-*vb*	lullaby	[ninnare]
nitido-*adj*	clear	[nitido]

no-*adv; il*	no, not; no	[nˈɔ]
nocca-*la*	knuckle	[nokka]
nodo-*il*	node, knot	[nodo]
noia-*la*	boredom, bore	[noja]
noi-*prn*	we	[noi]
nome-*il*	name	[nome]
nominare-*vb*	appoint, name	[nominare]
non-*adv*	not, non	[non]
nostro-*prn*	our	[nˈɔstro]
notare-*vb*	note	[notare]
noto-*adj*	known	[noto]
notte-*la*	night	[nˈɔtte]
nottola-*la*	noctule	[nottola]
novelletta-*la*	novelette	[novelletta]
novello-*adj*	new, early	[novello]
nove-*num*	nine	[nˈɔve]
nuca-*la*	nape	[nuka]
nulla-*il; prn*	nothing; nothing, anything	[nulla]
nuotare-*vb*	swim	[nwotare]
nuovamente-*adv*	again	[nwovamente]
nuovo-*adj*	new	[nwˈɔvo]

O

oca-*le*	goose	[oka]
occasione-*le*	opportunity	[okkazjone]
occhiali-*gli*	glasses	[okkjali]
occhio-*il*	eye	[ˈɔkkjo]
occhio-*il*	eye	[ˈɔkkjo]
occhione-*il*	stone curlew	[okkjone]
occulto-*adj*	occult, hidden	[okkulto]
occupare-*vb*	occupy	[okkupare]
occupato-*adj*	busy	[okkupato]
o-*con*	or	[ˈɔ]
od-*con*	or	[od]
odiare-*vb*	hate	[odjare]
offendere-*vb*	offend	[offendere]
offeso-*adj*	offended	[offezo]
offrire-*vb*	offer	[offrire]
oggi-*adv; il*	today	[ˈɔddʒi]
ogni-*adj*	every	[oɲni]
ognuno-*adj; prn*	each	[oɲnuno]
oh-*int*	oh	[o]

oltre-*adv; prp*	over; over, more than, beyond	[oltre]
oltremodo-*adv*	exceedingly	[oltremodo]
ombra-*la*	shadow	[ombra]
omero-*il*	humerus	[omero]
onde-*adv; conj; prn*	hence, whence; so that, so as; of which, whose	[onde]
opera-*le*	opera	[ˈɔpera]
operazione-*le*	operation	[operattsjone]
opportunità-*le*	opportunity	[opportunitˈa]
opposto-*adj; il*	opposite; opposite	[opposto]
oppure-*con*	or, or else	[oppure]
ora-*adv; con; la*	now; now; now, time, hour	[ora]
oramai-*adv*	by now	[oramai]
ordinare-*vb*	order	[ordinare]
ordine-*gli*	order	[ˈordine]
orecchio-*il*	ear	[orekkjo]
orecchio-*il*	ear	[orekkjo]
originale-*adj; il*	original	[oridʒinale]
origliare-*vb*	eavesdrop	[oriʎʎare]
orlo-*ill*	hem	[orlo]
ormai-*adv*	by now, almost, by then	[ormai]
ornato-*adj; il*	adorned; embellishment	[ornato]
oro-*il*	gold	[oro]
orribile-*adj*	horrible	[orribile]
osare-*vb*	dare	[ozare]
osservare-*vb*	observe, see	[osservare]
osservazione-*le*	observation, remark	[osservattsjone]
osso-*il*	bone	[osso]
ostacolo-*il*	obstacle, hurdle	[ostakolo]
ostrica-*la*	oyster	[ostrika]
ottone-*il*	brass	[ottone]

P

pace-*la*	peace	[patʃe]
padella-*la*	pan	[padella]
padrone-*il, la*	boss, master, owner, host/mistress, hostess	[padrone]
paese-*il*	country, village	[paeze]
pagare-*vb*	pay	[pagare]
paio-*il*	pair	[pajo]

paladino-*il*	paladin	[paladino]
palchetto-*il*	shelf	[palketto]
paletta-*la*	scoop	[paletta]
palla-*la*	ball	[palla]
pallido-*adj*	pale, faint	[pallido]
panciotto-*il*	waistcoat	[pantʃotto]
pane-*il*	bread	[pane]
panno-*il*	cloth	[panno]
papa-*il*	Pope	[papa]
papale-*adj*	papal	[papale]
paperone-*il*	scrooge	[paperone]
parere-*vb*	think, seem; opinion	[parere]
parete-*la*	wall	[parete]
pari-*adj; il*	equal	[pari]
parlamento-*il*	parliament	[parlamento]
parlare-*vb*	speak, talk	[parlare]
parola-*la*	word	[parˈɔla]
parolina-*la*	a quick word	[parolina]
parolone-*il*	long word	[parolone]
parrucca-*la*	wig	[parrukka]
parruccone-*adj; il*	blimpish; mossback	[parrukkone]
partecipare-*vb*	take part	[partetʃipare]
parte-*la*	part	[parte]
partire-*vb*	leave	[partire]
Pasqua-*la*	Easter	[paskwa]
passaggio-*il*	passage	[passaddʒo]
passare-*vb*	pass, spend, switch	[passare]
passato-*adj; il*	past	[passato]
passo-*il*	passage, step, pace, stride	[passo]
pasticciare-*vb*	mess up, mull	[pastittʃare]
pasticcino-*il*	pastry	[pastittʃino]
pasticcio-*il*	mess, pie	[pastittʃo]
pasto-*il*	meal	[pasto]
pastorello-*lo*	swain	[pastorello]
patata-*la*	potato, pussy (coll)	[patata]
patatrac-*il*	crash	[patatrak]
patibolo-*il*	scaffold	[patibolo]
paura-*la*	fear	[paura]
pavimento-*il*	floor	[pavimento]
pazienza-*la*	patience	[pattsjentsa]
pazzerello-*il*	daft	[pattserello]
pazzo-*adj; il; phr*	crazy	[pattso]

peccare-*vb*	sin	[pekkare]	
pecora-*la*	sheep	[pekora]	
peggio-*adj; il; adv*	worse	[p'ɛddʒo]	
pellegrino-*il*	pilgrim	[pellegrino]	
pelle-*la*	skin	[pelle]	
pelo-*il*	hair, fur, coat	[pelo]	
pena-*la*	penalty	[pena]	
pendere-*vb*	hang, tip	[pendere]	
penetrare-*vb*	penetrate, enter	[penetrare]	
pennellate-*le*	brushstrokes	[pennellate]	
pennello-*il*	brush	[pennello]	
pensare-*vb*	think	[pensare]	
pensiero-*il*	thought	[pensjero]	
pensieroso-*adj*	thoughtful	[pensjerozo]	
pentirsi-*vb*	repent	[pentirsi]	
pentirsi-*vb*	repent	[pentirsi]	
penzoloni-*il; adv*	hanging; dingle-dangle	[pentsoloni]	
pepaiola-*la*	pepperpot	[pepajola]	
pepe-*il*	pepper	[pepe]	
perché-*con; adv; prp*	because, why; why	[perk'e]	
perciò-*con; adv*	therefore; accordingly	[pertʃ'ɔ]	
percorrere-*vb*	travel, walk	[perkorrere]	
perdere-*vb*	lose	[p'ɛrdere]	
perdono-*il*	pardon, forgiveness	[perdono]	
perduto-*adj*	lost	[perduto]	
perenne-*adj*	perennial, perpetual	[perenne]	
pergamena-*la*	parchment	[pergamena]	
pericoloso-*adj*	dangerous	[perikolozo]	
permettere-*vb*	allow	[permettere]	
però-*con; adv*	but, yet; however	[per'ɔ]	
per-*prp; adv*	for, to, by, in	[per]	
perso-*adj*	lost	[p'ɛrso]	
persona-*la*	person	[persona]	
personale-*il; adj*	staff	[personale]	
personalità-*la*	personality	[personalit'a]	
persuadere-*vb*	persuade, convince	[perswadere]	
pesce-*il*	fish	[peʃʃe]	
pesciolino-*il*	minnow	[peʃʃolino]	
pestare-*vb*	pound, beat	[pestare]	
petto-*il*	chest	[petto]	
pezzettino-*il*	snippet	[pettsettino]	
pezzo-*il*	piece	[p'ɛttso]	
piacere-*vb*	pleasure; like	[pjatʃere]	
piagnucolare-*vb*	whine, whimper	[pjaɲɲukolare]	
piangere-*vb*	cry	[pjandʒere]	
piano-*il; adj; adv*	plan, floor, piano; plane, flat	[pjano]	
piantato-*adj*	planted	[pjantato]	
pianto-*il; adj*	tears; lamented	[pjanto]	
piattino-*il*	saucer	[pjattino]	
piatto-*adj; il*	dish, plate	[pjatto]	
piazzare-*vb*	place, be placed	[pjattsare]	
picchiare-*vb*	beat	[pikkjare]	
piccina-*la*	kiddie	[pittʃina]	
piccino-*adj; il*	little; child	[pittʃino]	
piccolo-*adj; il*	little, small	[pikkolo]	
piede-*il*	foot	[pj'ɛde]	
piedino-*il*	toothsie	[pjedino]	
piegare-*vb*	fold	[pjegare]	
piemontese-*adj*	piedmontese	[pjemonteze]	
pieno-*adj; il*	full	[pj'ɛno]	
pigiare-*vb*	press	[pidʒare]	
pigliare-*vb*	grab, take	[piʎʎare]	
pigro-*adj; il*	lazy; idler	[pigro]	
piovere-*vb*	rain	[pjovere]	
pipa-*la*	pipe	[pipa]	
pitoccare-*vb*	beg	[pitokkare]	
più-*adj; i; adv; con*	more, most	[pju]	
piuma-*la*	feather, down	[pjuma]	
piuttosto-*adv*	rather, quite, pretty	[pjutt'ɔsto]	
pizzicare-*vb*	pinch, pluck	[piddzikare]	
pizzicotto-*il*	nip	[piddzikotto]	
poco-*adj; adv; gli*	little; a litte, not much; bit	[p'ɔko]	
poesia-*la*	poetry	[poezja]	
poggio-*il*	hillock	[podd3o]	
poi-*adv; con*	then	[p'ɔi]	
polipo-*il*	octopus	[polipo]	
pollice-*il*	inch	[pollitʃe]	
polvere-*la*	dust	[polvere]	
pompare-*vb*	pump	[pompare]	
ponderare-*vb*	ponder	[ponderare]	
popolare-*adj; vb; abr*	populair; to populate	[popolare]	
porcellana-*la*	porcelain	[portʃellana]	

porcellino-*il*	piggy, little pig	[portʃellino]
porco-*il*	pig	[porko]
porgere-*vb*	extend	[pordʒere]
porporino-*adj*	purplish	[porporino]
porre-*vb*	put, place	[porre]
porta-*nn*	door, port	[pˈɔrta]
portare-*vb*	bring	[portare]
posa-*la*	pose, laying	[poza]
posizione-*la*	position	[pozittsjone]
possibile-*adj*	possible	[possibile]
posto-*il*	place, spot, location	[posto]
potere-*vb; il*	be able; power	[potere]
poveretto-*adj; il*	poor; poor thing	[poveretto]
poverino-*il*	poor darling	[poverino]
povero-*adj; il*	poor; the poor	[povero]
pozzo-*il*	well	[pottso]
prato-*il*	meadow	[prato]
precipizio-*il*	precipice	[pretʃipittsjo]
prediligere-*vb*	prefer	[predilidʒere]
preferire-*vb*	prefer	[preferire]
pregare-*vb*	pray	[pregare]
prego-*int*	please, you're welcome	[prˈɛgo]
premere-*vb*	press, depress	[premere]
premiare-*vb*	reward	[premjare]
premiato-*adj; il*	prize; prizewinner	[premjato]
premio-*il*	prize	[prˈɛmjo]
premura-*la*	care	[premura]
prendere-*vb*	take	[prˈɛndere]
preparare-*vb*	prepare	[preparare]
presa-*la*	outlet	[preza]
presentare-*vb*	present, submit	[prezentare]
pressochè-*adv*	almost	[pressokˈɛ]
presso-*prp; adv; adj*	at, in; near; close	[presso]
prestare-*vb*	loan, give	[prestare]
presto-*adv*	soon, early	[prˈɛsto]
preterito-*il*	pretext, excuse	[pretesto]
prigione-*la*	prison	[pridʒone]
prigioniero-*il; adj*	prisoner	[pridʒonjero]
prima-*adv; art*	first, before; before	[prima]
prima-*adv; art*	first, before; before	[prima]
primo-*num; adj*	first	[primo]
principale-*adj; il*	main	[printʃipale]

principino-*il*	prince	[printʃipino]
principio-*il*	principle	[printʃipjo]
probabilmente-*adv*	probably	[probabilmente]
procacciare-*vb*	procure	[prokattʃare]
processare-*vb*	try	[protʃessare]
processione-*la*	procession	[protʃessjone]
processo-*il*	process	[protʃesso]
produrre-*vb*	produce	[produrre]
profferire-*vb*	proffer	[profferire]
profittare-*vb*	profit	[profittare]
profondamente-*adv*	deeply	[profondamente]
profondità-*la*	depth, deep	[profonditˈa]
profondo-*adj*	deep	[profondo]
programma-*il*	program	[programma]
progredire-*vb*	progress	[progredire]
promettere-*vb*	promise	[promettere]
prontamente-*adv*	readily	[prontamente]
pronto-*adj; adv*	ready	[pronto]
pronunziare-*vb*	speak	[pronuntsjare]
propizio-*adj*	favorable	[propittsjo]
proporre-*vb*	propose, put forward	[proporre]
proposito-*il*	purpose, intention	[propozito]
proprio-*adj; il; prn; adv*	one's own; own; its; just, exactly	[prˈɔprjo]
prorompere-*vb*	burst	[prorompere]
protesto-*il*	protest	[protesto]
protetto-*adj*	safe	[protetto]
prova-*la*	test	[prˈɔva]
provare-*vb*	try	[provare]
proverbio-*il*	proverb, saying	[proverbjo]
provocare-*vb*	cause, provoke	[provokare]
prudente-*adj*	prudent	[prudente]
prudentemente-*adv*	prudently	[prudentemente]
prudenza-*la*	prudence, caution	[prudentsa]
pulcino-*il*	chick	[pultʃino]
pulito-*adj*	clean, clean	[pulito]
punire-*vb*	punish	[punire]
puntare-*vb*	point, aim	[puntare]
puntellare-*vb*	shore	[puntellare]
punto-*il*	point	[punto]
punzecchiare-*vb*	prick	[puntsekkjare]

pur-*adv*	while	[pur]
purchè-*con*	provided	[purkˈɛ]
pure-*adv*	also	[pure]

Q

qua-*adv*	here	[kwa]
quadro-*il*	painting, picture, panel, square	[kwadro]
quaggiù-*adv*	hither	[kwaddʒu]
qual-*adv; prn*	everytime, whenever; what, which	[kwal]
qualche-*adj; prn*	some, few, any; a few	[kwalke]
qualcheduno-*il*	someone	[kwalkeduno]
quale-*adj; prn; con*	what, which; which; as	[kwale]
quando-*adv; con*	when	[kwando]
quanto-*adv; con; il*	as, how much; than	[kwanto]
quaranta-*num*	forty	[kwaranta]
quartina-*la*	quatrain	[kwartina]
quasi-*adv; pfx*	almost, nearly	[kwazi]
quattordici-*num*	fourteen	[kwattorditʃi]
quattrocento-*num*	four hundred	[kwattrotʃento]
quattro-*num*	four	[kwattro]
quello-*adj; prn*	one	[kwello]
querela-*la*	complaint	[kwerela]
querelare-*vb*	sue	[kwerelare]
questione-*la*	question	[kwestjone]
questo-*adj; prn*	this; such, this one	[kwesto]
qui-*adv; con*	here; where	[kwi]
quieto-*adj*	quiet	[kwjeto]
quindi-*adv*	then	[kwindi]
quindici-*num*	fifteen	[kwinditʃi]
quinto-*adj*	fifth	[kwinto]

R

rabbia-*la*	anger	[rabbja]
rabbioso-*adj*	angry, rabid	[rabbjozo]
raccattare-*vb*	pick up	[rakkattare]
raccogliere-*vb*	gather	[rakkoʎʎere]
raccontare-*vb*	tell	[rakkontare]

racconto-*il*	(short) story	[rakkonto]
radice-*la*	root, stem	[raditʃe]
ragazza-*la*	girl	[ragattsa]
ragazzina-*la*	little girl	[ragattsina]
ragazzo-*il*	boy(friend)/girl(friend)	[ragattso]
ragazzona-*la*	big girl	[ragattsona]
raggiro-*il*	swindle	[raddʒiro]
raggiungere-*vb*	reach	[raddʒundʒere]
ragione-*la; adj*	reason	[radʒone]
rallegrare-*vb*	cheer, brighten	[rallegrare]
rammentare-*vb*	remind	[rammentare]
ramo-*il*	branch, bough	[ramo]
ranocchio-*il*	frog	[ranokkjo]
ranuncolo-*il*	buttercup	[ranuŋkolo]
rapidamente-*adv*	quickly	[rapidamente]
rapire-*vb*	kidnap	[rapire]
rappresentare-*vb*	represent	[rapprezentare]
raramente-*adv*	rarely	[raramente]
raschiare-*vb*	scrape	[raskjare]
rassegnare-*vb*	resign oneself	[rasseɲɲare]
rasserenare-*vb*	cheer up	[rasserenare]
rassomigliare-*vb*	resemble	[rassomiʎʎare]
razza-*la*	race, breed, stingray	[rattsa]
razzo-*il*	rocket, squib	[rattso]
reale-*adj*	real, actual	[reale]
realtà-*la*	reality	[realtˈa]
recare-*vb*	cause	[rekare]
reciso-*adj*	flat	[retʃizo]
recitare-*vb*	recite	[retʃitare]
regale-*adj*	kingly	[regale]
regalo-*il*	gift, present	[regalo]
reggere-*vb*	hold, stand	[reddʒere]
reggia-*la*	royal palace	[reddʒa]
regina-*la*	queen	[redʒina]
regio-*adj*	royal	[redʒo]
regola-*la*	rule	[regola]
regolare-*adj; vb*	regular; adjust	[regolare]
re-*il*	king	[re]
rendere-*vb*	make	[rendere]
replicare-*vb*	replicate, reply	[replikare]
resa-*la*	yield	[reza]

respingere-*vb*	reject, dismiss	[respindʒere]	
respirare-*vb*	breathe	[respirare]	
respiro-*il*	breath	[respiro]	
restare-*vb*	stay, remain, maintain	[restare]	
restaurare-*vb*	restore	[restaurare]	
resto-*il*	rest	[rˈɛsto]	
riandare-*vb*	go again	[rjandare]	
rianimare-*vb*	revive	[rjanimare]	
riapparire-*vb*	reappear	[rjapparire]	
riavere-*vb*	get back	[rjavere]	
riccio-*adj; il*	curly; hedgehog	[rittʃo]	
ricco-*adj; il*	rich	[rikko]	
ricerca-*la*	search, research	[ritʃerka]	
ricercare-*vb*	search, search for	[ritʃerkare]	
richiamare-*vb*	call, recall	[rikjamare]	
ricominciare-*vb*	recommence	[rikomintʃare]	
ricomparire-*vb*	reappear	[rikomparire]	
ricondurre-*vb*	bring back	[rikondurre]	
riconoscere-*vb*	recognize	[rikonoʃʃere]	
ricoprire-*vb*	cover, hold	[rikoprire]	
ricordare-*vb*	remember	[rikordare]	
ricordo-*lo*	memory	[rikˈɔrdo]	
ricoverare-*vb*	shelter	[rikoverare]	
ricrescere-*vb*	grow back	[rikreʃʃere]	
ridere-*vb*	laugh	[ridere]	
ridicolo-*adj; il*	ridiculous	[ridikolo]	
ridiventare-*vb*	come again	[ridiventare]	
ridurre-*vb*	reduce	[ridurre]	
riempire-*vb*	fill	[rjempire]	
riempire-*vb*	fill	[rjempire]	
rifare-*vb*	redo, rebuild	[rifare]	
riferire-*vb*	report, refer	[riferire]	
rifiutare-*vb*	refuse	[rifjutare]	
riflettere-*vb*	reflect	[riflettere]	
rigettare-*vb*	reject	[ridʒettare]	
rigoglioso-*adj*	luxuriant	[rigoʎʎozo]	
riguardare-*vb*	concern	[rigwardare]	
rilucente-*adj*	shining	[rilutʃente]	
rimanere-*vb*	stay	[rimanere]	
rimettere-*vb*	replace, return	[rimettere]	
rimpiccolire-*vb*	make smaller	[rimpikkolire]	
rimproverare-*vb*	reproach, blame	[rimproverare]	
rincominciare-*vb*	start again	[riŋkomintʃare]	
rinfrescare-*vb*	refresh, cool	[rinfreskare]	
riparare-*vb*	repair	[riparare]	
ripassare-*vb*	revise	[ripassare]	
ripensare-*vb*	think back	[ripensare]	
ripetere-*vb*	repeat	[ripetere]	
ripetizione-*la*	repetition, private lesson	[ripetittsjone]	
ripieno-*il; adj*	filling; stuffed	[ripjeno]	
riporre-*vb*	put	[riporre]	
riposare-*vb*	rest	[ripozare]	
riprendere-*vb*	resume	[riprendere]	
risata-*la*	laugh	[rizata]	
rischiare-*vb*	risk	[riskjare]	
riso-*il*	rice	[rizo]	
risolino-*il*	titter	[rizolino]	
risoluto-*adj*	resolute	[rizoluto]	
risolvere-*vb*	solve	[rizolvere]	
rispettivo-*adj*	respective	[rispettivo]	
rispetto-*il*	respect	[rispˈɛtto]	
rispettoso-*adj*	respectful	[rispettozo]	
risplendente-*adj*	resplendent	[risplendente]	
rispondere-*vb*	answer	[rispondere]	
risposare-*vb*	remarry	[rispozare]	
rissa-*la*	fight, brawl	[rissa]	
ristabilire-*vb*	restore, re-establish	[ristabilire]	
ristoro-*il*	refreshment	[ristoro]	
ristringere-*vb*	shrink again	[ristrindʒere]	
risvegliare-*vb*	awaken, revive	[rizveʎʎare]	
ritardare-*vb*	delay, defer	[ritardare]	
ritirare-*vb; adv*	withdraw; throw again	[ritirare]	
ritornare-*vb*	return	[ritornare]	
ritorno-*il*	return	[ritorno]	
ritratto-*il*	portrait	[ritratto]	
ritrovare-*vb*	find	[ritrovare]	
riunire-*vb*	gather, reunite	[rjunire]	
riuscire-*vb*	succeed, able	[rjuʃʃire]	
rivedere-*vb*	review, revise	[rivedere]	
riverenza-*la*	reverence	[riverentsa]	
rivolgere-*vb*	turn, direct	[rivoldʒere]	
rivoltare-*vb*	turn over	[rivoltare]	
rivoltato-*adj*	upturned	[rivoltato]	

rizzare-*vb*	raise	[riddzare]	sbalzare-*vb*	throw	[zbaltsare]
romano-*adj; il*	Roman; Roman	[romano]	sbattere-*vb*	slam, beat	[zbattere]
romanzo-*il*	novel, romance	[romandzo]	sbirciare-*vb*	peek	[zbirtʃare]
rompere-*vb*	break	[rompere]	sbranare-*vb*	savage	[zbranare]
rondella-*la*	washer	[rondella]	sbrogliare-*vb*	unravel	[zbroʎʎare]
rose-*adj*	rose	[roze]	sbuffante-*adj*	puffing	[zbuffante]
rosso-*adj; il*	red	[rˈɔsso]	scaffale-*lo*	shelf	[skaffale]
rotoloni (cadere ..)-*exp*	tumble down	[rotoloni]	scagliare-*vb*	throw	[skaʎʎare]
rotondo-*adj*	round	[rotondo]	scala-*la*	ladder, scale, stairs	[skala]
rovesciare-*vb*	overthrow, topple	[roveʃʃare]	scambiare-*vb*	exchange, swap	[skambjare]
rovescio-*adj; il*	reverse; back	[roveʃʃo]	scampare-*vb*	escape	[skampare]
rubare-*vb*	steal	[rubare]	scappare-*vb*	escape	[skappare]
ruminare-*vb*	ruminate	[ruminare]	scarabocchiare-*vb*	doodle, scribble	[skarabokkjare]
rumore-*il*	noise	[rumore]	scarabocchio-*lo*	scribble	[skarabokkjo]
ruota-*la*	wheel	[rwota]	scaraventare-*vb*	hurl	[skaraventare]
rupe-*la*	cliff	[rupe]	scarpa-*la*	shoe	[skarpa]
ruzzo-*il*	romp	[ruttso]	scatola-*la*	box	[skatola]
ruzzolare-*vb*	tumble	[ruttsolare]	scavare-*vb*	dig	[skavare]
ruzzolone-*il*	tumble	[ruttsolone]	scegliere-*vb*	choose	[ʃeʎʎere]
ruzzoloni-*il*	tumble	[ruttsoloni]	scempiaggini-*la*	foolery	[ʃempjaddʒini]
			scendere-*vb*	get off	[ʃendere]

S

			scherzare-*vb*	joke	[skertsare]
			schiaffeggiare-*vb*	slap	[skjaffeddʒare]
sacco-*il; adv*	bag, sack; a lot	[sakko]	schiena-*la*	back	[skjena]
saettare-*vb*	dart	[saettare]	schifoso-*adj*	lousy (fa schifo= it sucks)	[skifozo]
saggio-*adj; il*	wise; test	[saddʒo]			
saio-*il*	habit	[sajo]	schizzare-*vb*	splash, squirt	[skiddzare]
sala-*la*	room	[sala]	scioccare-*vb*	shock	[ʃokkare]
salmone-*il*	salmon	[salmone]	sciocchezza-*la*	foolishness	[ʃokkettsa]
salone-*il*	lounge	[salone]	sciocco-*adj; lo*	silly	[ʃokko]
salsa-*la*	sauce	[salsa]	sciogliere-*vb*	dissolve, loosen	[ʃoʎʎere]
saltare-*vb*	skip, jump	[saltare]	scivolare-*vb*	slip, slide	[ʃivolare]
saltellare-*vb*	hop	[saltellare]	scodella-*le*	bowl	[skodella]
salto-*il*	leap, jump	[salto]	scommettere-*vb*	bet	[skommettere]
salutare-*adj; vb*	healthy; greet, say goodbye to	[salutare]	scomporre-*vb*	decompose	[skomporre]
salvo-*prp; adj*	save, but; safe	[salvo]	sconsolare-*vb*	discourage	[skonsolare]
sangue-*il*	blood	[saŋgwe]	scoperchiare-*vb*	unroof, untile	[skoperkjare]
sano-*adj*	healthy, wholesome	[sano]	scoppiare-*vb*	burst, break out	[skoppjare]
sapere-*vb*	know	[sapere]	scoppiettare-*vb*	crackle	[skoppjettare]
sapore-*il*	flavor, taste	[sapore]	scoprire-*vb*	discover	[skoprire]
sassolino-*il*	pebble	[sassolino]	scordare-*vb*	forget	[skordare]
sbadigliare-*vb*	yawn	[zbadiʎʎare]	scorgere-*vb*	notice, make out	[skordʒere]
sbagliare-*vb*	make a mistake	[zbaʎʎare]			

scorrere-*vb*	slide, flow	[skorrere]
scorso-*adj*	last	[skorso]
scortese-*adj*	rude, impolite	[skorteze]
scossa-*la*	shock	[skossa]
scosso-*il; adj*	shaken; upset	[skosso]
scottante-*adj*	pressing	[skottante]
scottare-*vb*	burn, scald	[skottare]
scricchiolare-*vb*	creak	[skrikkjolare]
scritto-*adj; lo*	written	[skritto]
scritturare-*vb*	engage	[skritturare]
scrivere-*vb*	write	[skrivere]
sculacciare-*vb*	spank	[skulattʃare]
scuola-*la*	school	[skwˈɔla]
scuotere-*vb*	shake, shook	[skwotere]
scusa-*la*	sorry	[skuza]
scusare-*vb*	excuse	[skuzare]
sdegnare-*vb*	disdain	[zdeɲɲare]
sdegnoso-*adj*	disdainful	[zdeɲɲozo]
sdraiare-*vb*	lie down	[zdrajare]
sdrucciolare-*vb*	slip	[zdruttʃolare]
sdrucciolevole-*adj*	slippery	[zdruttʃolevole]
seccare-*vb*	dry, bother	[sekkare]
seccato-*adj*	annoyed	[sekkato]
secchia-*la*	bucket	[sekkja]
secco-*adj*	dry	[sekko]
secernere-*vb*	secrete	[setʃernere]
secolo-*il*	century	[sekolo]
se-*con*	if	[se]
secondare-*vb*	comply	[sekondare]
secondo-*adj; adv; num; prp; con*	according to; second	[sekondo]
sedere-*vb*	sit down	[sedere]
sedici-*num*	sixteen	[seditʃi]
seggio-*il*	seat	[seddʒo]
seggiolone-*il*	high chair	[seddʒolone]
segnale-*il*	signal, sign	[seɲɲale]
segnare-*vb*	score, sign	[seɲɲare]
segno-*il*	sign	[seɲɲo]
seguente-*adj*	following, next	[segwente]
seguire-*vb*	follow	[segwire]
seguitare-*vb*	continue	[segwitare]
sei-*num*	six	[sˈɛi]
selvaggio-*adj; il*	wild	[selvaddʒo]

sembrare-*vb*	seem, look, sound	[sembrare]
semichiusi-*adj*	half-closed	[semikjuzi]
semplice-*adj*	simple	[sˈemplitʃe]
semplicemente-*adv*	simply	[semplitʃemente]
sempre-*adv*	always	[sˈɛmpre]
senape-*la*	mustard	[senape]
sensazione-*la*	sensation	[sensattsjone]
sensibilità-*la*	feeling, sensibility	[sensibilitˈa]
senso-*il*	direction, sense, meaning	[sˈɛnso]
sentenza-*la*	judgment, sentence	[sententsa]
sentenziare-*vb*	moralize	[sententsjare]
sentimento-*il*	feeling	[sentimento]
sentire-*vb*	feel, hear	[sentire]
senza-*prp*	without	[sˈentsa]
sepolcrale-*adj*	sepulchral	[sepolkrale]
sera-*la*	evening	[sera]
seriamente-*adv*	seriously	[serjamente]
serie-*la*	series, set	[serje]
serietà-*la*	seriousness, reliability	[serjetˈa]
serpente-*il*	snake, serpent	[serpente]
serrato-*adj*	serried	[serrato]
servire-*vb*	serve	[servire]
servitore-*il*	servant	[servitore]
servizievole-*adj*	helpful	[servittsjevole]
servizio-*il*	service, report	[servittsjo]
sette-*i*	seven	[sˈɛtte]
settimana-*la*	week	[settimana]
severamente-*adv*	severely	[severamente]
severo-*adj; il*	severe; martinet	[severo]
sfilare-*vb*	parade	[sfilare]
sfiorare-*vb*	touch, brush	[sfjorare]
sfoggio-*il*	display	[sfoddʒo]
sfolgorante-*adj*	blazing	[sfolgorante]
sfolgorare-*vb*	blaze	[sfolgorare]
sfondare-*vb*	break through, stave	[sfondare]
sforzare-*vb*	strain, force	[sfortsare]
sforzo-*lo*	effort	[sfortso]
sfracellare-*vb*	smash	[sfratʃellare]
sgabello-*lo*	stool	[zgabello]
sgarbatezza-*la*	rudeness	[zgarbatettsa]
sghignazzare-*vb*	sneer	[zgiɲɲattsare]

sguardo-*lo*	look	[zgwardo]	
sguazzare-*vb*	wallow	[zgwattsare]	
sibilante-*adj; la*	sibilant; sibilant	[sibilante]	
siccome-*con*	since	[sikkome]	
sicuramente-*adv*	certainly	[sikuramente]	
sicuro-*adj; lo*	sure, safe, secure	[sikuro]	
siepe-*la*	hedge	[sjepe]	
significare-*vb*	mean	[siɲɲifikare]	
signora-*la; abr*	lady, Mrs.	[siɲɲora]	
signore-*il/la; abr*	Mr. / Mrs.	[siɲɲore]	
signore-*il/la; abr*	Mr. / Mrs.	[siɲɲore]	
signorina-*la; abr*	young lady	[siɲɲorina]	
sì-*int*	yes, yeah	[sˈi]	
silenziare-*vb*	mute	[silentsjare]	
silenzioso-*adj*	silent	[silentsjozo]	
sillabare-*vb*	syllabify	[sillabare]	
simile-*adj*	similar, alike	[simile]	
simpatico-*adj*	nice, sympathetic	[simpatiko]	
sin-*con*	since	[sin]	
singhiozzare-*vb*	sob	[siŋgjottsare]	
singhiozzo-*il*	sob	[siŋgjottso]	
sinistra-*la*	left	[sinistra]	
sinistro-*adj*	left	[sinistro]	
si-*prn*	one-, its-, thems-, him-, her-, yourself	[si]	
slanciare-*vb*	hurl, fling	[zlantʃare]	
slargare-*vb*	broaden, widen	[zlargare]	
smarrire-*vb*	lose, get lost	[smarrire]	
smarrito-*adj*	lost	[smarrito]	
smettere-*vb*	stop	[smettere]	
smorzare-*vb*	dampen	[smortsare]	
soave-*adj*	sweet	[soave]	
soccorrere-*vb*	help	[sokkorrere]	
società-*la*	society	[sotʃetˈa]	
soffice-*adj*	soft	[soffitʃe]	
soffitto-*il*	ceiling	[soffitto]	
soffocare-*vb*	choke, smother	[soffokare]	
soffrire-*vb*	suffer	[soffrire]	
soggetto-*adj; il*	subject	[soddʒetto]	
soggiungere-*vb*	add	[soddʒundʒere]	
sognare-*vb*	dream	[soɲɲare]	
sogno-*il*	dream	[soɲɲo]	
solco-*il*	groove	[solko]	
soldato-*il*	soldier	[soldato]	
sole-*il*	sun	[sole]	
solenne-*adj*	solemn, impressive	[solenne]	
soletta-*la*	insole	[soletta]	
solido-*adj; il*	solid; solid	[solido]	
sol-*il*	sol	[sol]	
solito-*adj; il*	usual	[sˈɔlito]	
sollecitamente-*adv*	solicitously	[solletʃitamente]	
sollecitare-*vb*	urge	[solletʃitare]	
sollecitudine-*la*	concern	[solletʃitudine]	
sollevare-*vb*	lift, raise	[sollevare]	
sollievo-*il*	relief, solace	[solljevo]	
solo-*adj; adv*	only	[solo]	
soltanto-*adv*	only, solely	[soltanto]	
sommare-*vb; adv; phr*	add; all in all; all things considered	[sommare]	
sommesso-*adj*	low	[sommesso]	
sommo-*adj*	highest	[sommo]	
sonnacchioso-*adv*	sleepily	[sonnakkjozo]	
sonnecchiare-*vb*	doze	[sonnekkjare]	
sonnellino-*il*	nap, doze	[sonnellino]	
sonno-*il*	sleep	[sonno]	
sonnolento-*adj*	sleepy	[sonnolento]	
sopportare-*vb*	bear	[sopportare]	
soppressata-*la*	headcheese	[soppressata]	
soppressione-*la*	abolition	[soppressjone]	
sopprimere-*vb*	abolish	[sopprimere]	
sopra-*adv; prp; le*	above, on	[sopra]	
sorcio-*il*	mouse	[sortʃo]	
sorella-*la*	sister	[sorˈɛlla]	
sorellina-*la*	litte sister, younger sister, baby sister	[sorellina]	
sorprendere-*vb*	surprise	[sorprendere]	
sorreggere-*vb*	support	[sorreddʒere]	
sorridente-*adj*	smiling	[sorridente]	
sorridere-*vb*	smile	[sorridere]	
sorriso-*il*	smile	[sorrizo]	
sorta-*la*	kind	[sorta]	
sorte-*la*	fate	[sorte]	
sospirare-*vb*	sigh	[sospirare]	
sospiro-*il*	sigh	[sospiro]	

sostenere-*vb*	support, bear	[sostenere]
sostenuto-*adj*	fast	[sostenuto]
sotterra-*adv*	underground	[sotterra]
sottile-*adj*	thin, slim	[sottile]
sotto-*adv; prp; adj*	under, below; under	[sotto]
sottomissione-*la*	submission, subjection	[sottomissjone]
spaccato-*adj; lo*	split; cutaway	[spakkato]
spalancare-*vb*	open wide	[spalaŋkare]
spalla-*la*	shoulder	[spalla]
sparire-*vb*	disappear	[sparire]
spaventare-*vb*	scare, frighten	[spaventare]
spaventato-*adj*	afraid	[spaventato]
spaventevole-*adj*	frightful	[spaventevole]
spazio-*lo*	space	[spattsjo]
spazioso-*adj*	spacious	[spattsjozo]
spazzolare-*vb*	brush	[spattsolare]
specchio-*il*	mirror	[spekkjo]
specie-*le*	species, kind	[spˈɛtʃe]
spegnere-*vb*	switch off, turn off	[speɲɲere]
speranza-*la*	hope	[sperantsa]
sperare-*vb*	hope	[sperare]
spesso-*adv; adj*	often; thick	[spesso]
spettare-*vb*	belong	[spettare]
spezzare-*vb*	break	[spettsare]
spiaggia-*la*	beach	[spjaddʒa]
spicciolo-*lo*	change	[spittʃolo]
spiegare-*vb*	explain	[spjegare]
spiegazione-*la*	explanation	[spjegattsjone]
spingere-*vb*	push	[spindʒere]
spiritoso-*adj*	humorous	[spiritozo]
sponda-*la*	bank	[sponda]
sposare-*vb*	marry	[spozare]
sprofondare-*vb*	collapse	[sprofondare]
squadrare-*vb*	square	[skwadrare]
squarciagola-*adv*	lustily	[skwartʃagola]
squillo-*lo*	ring	[skwillo]
staccare-*vb*	remove, separate	[stakkare]
stagno-*il; adj*	pond; watertight	[staɲɲo]
stamane-*adv*	this morning	[stamane]
stanco-*adj*	tired	[staŋko]
stanotte-*adv*	tonight	[stanotte]

stare-*vb*	stay	[stare]
stare-*vb*	stay	[stare]
starnutare-*vb*	sneeze	[starnutare]
starnutire-*vb*	sneeze	[starnutire]
starnuto-*lo*	sneeze	[starnuto]
stato-*il*	state	[stato]
statura-*la*	stature	[statura]
stazione-*la*	station	[stattsjone]
steccato-*i*	steccato	[stekkato]
stellare-*adj*	stellar	[stellare]
stelo-*lo*	stem	[stelo]
stesso-*adj; prn; lo*	same; itself	[stesso]
stima-*la*	estimate, esteem	[stima]
stiracchiare-*vb*	stretch	[stirakkjare]
stivaletto-*lo*	ankle boot	[stivaletto]
stomaco-*lo*	stomach	[stomako]
storia-*la*	history, story	[stˈɔrja]
storico-*adj; lo*	historical; historian	[storiko]
storiella-*la*	joke	[storjella]
stormire-*vb*	rustle	[stormire]
strada-*la*	(large) street, road	[strada]
stralunare-*vb*	roll	[stralunare]
stranezza-*la*	strangeness	[stranettsa]
strano-*adj*	strange	[strano]
straordinario-*adj; lo*	extraordinary; overtime	[straordinarjo]
strappare-*vb*	rip, tear	[strappare]
stravagante-*adj*	extravagant	[stravagante]
strepito-*il*	barking	[strepito]
stretto-*adj; lo*	strict, strait; narrow	[stretto]
stridente-*adj*	strident	[stridente]
stridere-*vb*	screech, squeal	[stridere]
stridulo-*adj*	shrill	[stridulo]
strillare-*vb*	scream, shriek	[strillare]
strillo-*lo*	scream, squeal	[strillo]
stringere-*vb*	tighten	[strindʒere]
strisciare-*vb*	crawl, slither	[striʃʃare]
strofa-*la*	stanza	[strofa]
stropicciare-*vb*	rub	[stropittʃare]
stroppia (il troppo ...)-*exp*	to much of a good thing	[stroppja]
strozzato-*adj*	choking	[strottsato]
studiare-*vb*	study	[studjare]
stupefare-*vb*	stupefy, stun	[stupefare]

stupido-*adj; lo*	stupid	[st'upido]	**tavolino**-*il*	table	[tavolino]
stupire-*vb*	amaze, astonish	[stupire]	**tazza**-*la*	cup	[tattsa]
stupore-*lo*	amazement, wonder	[stupore]	**teco**-*prn*	with you	[teko]
sturare-*vb*	unblock	[sturare]	**tegola**-*la*	tile	[tegola]
subitaneo-*adj*	sudden	[subitaneo]	**tè**-*il*	tea	[t'ɛ]
subito-*adv*	immediately, at once	[subito]	**telescopio**-*il*	telescope	[teleskopjo]
succedere-*vb*	happen, occur, succeed	[suttʃedere]	**temere**-*vb*	fear, be afraid	[temere]
sufficiente-*adj*	enough, sufficient	[suffitʃente]	**tempo**-*il*	time, weather	[t'ɛmpo]
suo-*adj; prn*	your; its	[s'uo]	**tenere**-*vb*	hold, keep	[tenere]
suolo-*il*	soil	[swolo]	**tenerezza**-*la*	tenderness, sweetness	[tenerettsa]
suonare-*vb*	play (music or instrument), sound, ring	[swonare]	**tentare**-*vb*	attempt, try, tempt	[tentare]
			tentativo-*il*	attempt	[tentativo]
			tentennare-*vb*	waver	[tentennare]
suono-*il*	sound	[swono]	**teoria**-*la*	theory	[teorja]
superare-*vb*	exceed	[superare]	**te**-*prn*	you	[te]
supplicare-*vb*	beg, plead	[supplikare]	**terminare**-*vb*	end, conclude	[terminare]
supporre-*vb*	suppose	[supporre]	**termine**-*il*	term	[termine]
surrogato-*il; adj*	surrogate; ersatz	[surrogato]	**terra**-*la*	land, earth	[t'ɛrra]
svanire-*vb*	fade, vanish	[zvanire]	**terrazzino**-*il*	balcony	[terrattsino]
sveltezza-*la*	speed	[zveltettsa]	**terreno**-*il; adj*	ground, soil; earthly	[terreno]
sventolare-*vb*	wave	[zventolare]	**terribile**-*adj*	terrible	[terribile]
sventurato-*adj*	unfortunate	[zventurato]	**terrore**-*il*	terror	[terrore]
sviare-*vb*	divert	[zvjare]	**testa**-*la*	head	[t'ɛsta]
svoltare-*vb*	turn	[zvoltare]	**testare**-*vb*	test	[testare]
			teste-*il, la*	witness	[teste]
T			**testimone**-*il/la*	witness	[testimone]
			testimonianza-*la*	testimony	[testimonjantsa]
tacchino-*il*	turkey	[takkino]	**testimoniare**-*vb*	witness, testify	[testimonjare]
taccuino-*il*	notebook	[takkwino]	**testolina**-*la*	small head	[testolina]
tacere-*vb*	be silent	[tatʃere]	**tetto**-*il*	roof	[tetto]
tagliare-*vb*	cut	[taʎʎare]	**timidamente**-*adv*	shyly	[timidamente]
tagliare-*vb*	cut	[taʎʎare]			
taglio-*il*	cut, cutting	[taʎʎo]	**timidezza**-*la*	shyness	[timidettsa]
tale-*adj; prn; art; phr*	such; such; a, an	[tale]	**timido**-*adj; il*	shy; milksop	[timido]
talmente-*adv*	so	[talmente]	**timore**-*il*	fear, awe	[timore]
talvolta-*adv*	at times	[talvolta]	**timoroso**-*adj*	afraid	[timorozo]
tanto-*adv; adj*	much, so	[tanto]	**tirare**-*vb*	pull	[tirare]
tardi-*adv*	late	[tardi]	**tirchio**-*adj; il*	stingy; miser	[tirkjo]
tartagliare-*vb*	stutter	[tartaʎʎare]	**titolo**-*il*	title	[titolo]
tartaruga-*la*	tortoise	[tartaruga]	**toccare**-*vb*	touch	[tokkare]
tasca-*la*	pocket	[taska]	**tocco**-*il; adj*	touch	[tokko]
taschino-*il*	pocket	[taskino]	**togliere**-*vb*	remove, take off	[toʎʎere]
tavola-*la*	table	[tavola]	**tondo**-*adj; il*	round; round	[tondo]

topo-*il*	mouse	[topo]	**tuo**-*adj*	your	[t'uo]
toppa-*la*	patch	[toppa]	**tuonare**-*vb*	thunder	[twonare]
torcere-*vb*	twist	[tortʃere]	**tuono**-*il*	thunder	[twono]
tornare-*vb*	return	[tornare]	**tu**-*prn*	you	[tu]
torre-*la*	tower	[torre]	**turbamento**-*il*	agitation	[turbamento]
torrone-*gli*	nougat	[torrone]	**turchino**-*adj; il*	blue; deep blue	[turkino]
toscano-*adj; il*	Tuscan; Tuscan	[toskano]	**turco**-*adj; il*	Turkish; Turk	[turko]
tosto-*il; adj*	toast; bad-ass	[tosto]	**tuttavia**-*adv; con*	however, nevertheless; but, yet	[tuttavja]
totalmente-*adv*	totally	[totalmente]	**tutto**-*adj; il*	all	[tutto]
tracciare-*vb*	draw	[trattʃare]			
tramutare-*vb*	convert	[tramutare]	**U**		
tranquillamente-*adv*	quietly	[traŋkwillamente]			
trappola-*la*	trap	[trappola]	**ubbidire**-*vb*	obey	[ubbidire]
trarre-*vb*	draw, get	[trarre]	**uccellino**-*il*	birdie	[uttʃellino]
trasalire-*vb*	wince	[trazalire]	**uccello**-*il*	bird	[uttʃello]
trasformare-*vb*	transform, turn	[trasformare]	**uccello**-*il*	bird	[uttʃello]
trasformazione-*la*	transformation	[trasformattsjone]	**uccidere**-*vb*	kill	[uttʃidere]
trattare-*vb*	treat	[trattare]	**udire**-*vb*	hear	[udire]
tratto-*il*	stretch	[tratto]	**uditorio**-*il; adj*	audience; auditory	[uditorjo]
traversare-*vb*	navigate	[traversare]	**ufficiale**-*adj; il*	official	[uffitʃale]
traverso-*adj*	cross, oblique	[traverso]	**uff**-*int*	Oof!	[uff]
tredici-*num*	thirteen	[treditʃi]	**ultimamente**-*adv*	lately	[ultimamente]
tre-*l; num*	three	[tre]			
tremante-*adj*	trembling, shaking	[tremante]	**ultimo**-*adj*	last, latest	['ultimo]
tremarella-*la*	shivers	[tremarella]	**umile**-*adj*	humble, menial	[umile]
tremare-*vb*	tremble, shake	[tremare]	**umore**-*il*	mood, humor	[umore]
tremolante-*adj*	flickering	[tremolante]	**un, uno, una**-*art; prn*	a, an; one	[un]
tremulo-*adj*	trembling	[tremulo]	**un'**-*art*	a	[un']
trenta-*num*	thirty	[trenta]	**undecimo**-*num*	eleventh	[undetʃimo]
tribunale-*il*	court	[tribunale]	**unghia**-*le*	nail	[uŋgja]
trionfare-*vb*	triumph	[trjonfare]	**unguento**-*il*	ointment	[uŋgwento]
triste-*adj*	sad	[triste]	**unire**-*vb*	unite	[unire]
triste-*adj*	sad	[triste]	**uno**-*art; adj; prn; nn*	a; one; any; a man	[uno]
tromba-*la*	trumpet, bugle	[tromba]	**uovo**-*lo*	egg	[wovo]
trono-*il*	throne	[trono]	**uragano**-*il*	hurricane	[uragano]
troppo-*adv; con; adj*	too much	[tr'ɔppo]	**urlare**-*vb*	scream	[urlare]
trottare-*vb*	trot	[trottare]	**urlo**-*gli*	yell, cry, shout	[urlo]
trovare-*vb*	find	[trovare]	**urtare**-*vb*	bump, strike	[urtare]
truffare-*vb*	cheat, defraud	[truffare]	**usare**-*vb*	use	[uzare]
truppa-*la*	troop	[truppa]	**usciere**-*il*	usher	[uʃʃere]
tuffare-*vb*	dive, dip	[tuffare]	**uscio**-*il*	door	[uʃʃo]
tulipano-*il*	tulip	[tulipano]			

uscire-*vb*	go out, leave	[uʃʃire]
uscita-*la*	exit	[uʃʃita]
uso-*lo*	use, usage	[uzo]
utile-*adj; il*	helpful, useful; profit	[utile]
uva-*le*	grapes	[uva]

V

vacanza-*la*	holiday, vacation	[vakantsa]
vacillare-*vb*	falter	[vatʃillare]
vagare-*vb*	wander, roam	[vagare]
valere-*vb*	be worth	[valere]
vanga-*la*	spade	[vaŋga]
vantaggio-*il*	advantage	[vantaddʒo]
vantare-*vb*	claim	[vantare]
vapore-*il*	steam, vapor	[vapore]
variante-*la*	variant	[varjante]
vasetto-*il*	jar	[vazetto]
vaso-*il*	vase	[vazo]
vecchio-*adj; il*	old; old (wo)man	[vˈɛkkjo]
vecchio-*adj; il*	old; old (wo)man	[vˈɛkkjo]
vedere-*vb*	see	[vedere]
veduta-*la*	view	[veduta]
vegetale-*adj*	vegetable	[vedʒetale]
veglia-*la*	vigil	[veʎʎa]
vegliare-*vb*	watch over	[veʎʎare]
velare-*vb; adj*	veil; velar	[velare]
veleno-*il*	poison	[veleno]
velluto-*il*	velvet	[velluto]
velocemente-*adv*	quickly	[velotʃemente]
vendere-*vb*	sell	[vendere]
vendetta-*la*	vengeance	[vendetta]
venire-*vb*	come	[venire]
ventaglio-*il*	fan	[ventaʎʎo]
ventesimo-*adj*	twentieth, twentieth	[ventezimo]
venti-*i*	twenty	[venti]
ventiquattro-*num*	twentyfour	[ventikwattro]
vento-*il*	wind	[vento]
ve-*prn*	you	[ve]
veramente-*adv*	really	[veramente]
verde-*adj; il*	green	[verde]

verdeggiante-*adj*	verdant	[verdeddʒante]
verdetto-*il*	verdict, judgment	[verdetto]
verga-*la*	rod	[verga]
vergognarsi-*vb*	be ashamed	[vergoɲɲarsi]
veridico-*adj*	truthful	[veridiko]
verità-*la*	truth	[veritˈa]
verme-*il*	worm, maggot	[verme]
vero-*adj*	true	[vero]
versare-*vb*	pour, spill	[versare]
verso-*prp; il*	to, towards; direction, way	[vˈɛrso]
vestire-*vb*	dress	[vestire]
vetrina-*la*	showcase	[vetrina]
vetrino-*il*	slide	[vetrino]
vetro-*il*	glass	[vetro]
via-*prp; adv; la*	via, by; away; street	[vˈia]
vicenda-*la*	event	[vitʃenda]
vicino-*adj; adv; il*	close, near	[vitʃino]
vignetta-*la*	cartoon	[viɲɲetta]
vile-*adj; il*	vile; dastard	[vile]
vincere-*vb*	win	[vintʃere]
vino-*il*	wine	[vino]
vinto-*il; adj*	loser; defeated	[vinto]
violento-*adj*	violent	[vjolento]
violenza-*la*	violence	[vjolentsa]
vi-*prn; adv*	you; there	[vi]
virtù-*le*	virtue	[virtu]
viscoso-*adj*	viscous	[viskozo]
visione-*la*	vision	[vizjone]
visita-*la*	visit	[vizita]
visitare-*vb*	visit, see	[vizitare]
viso-*il*	face	[vizo]
viso-*il*	face	[vizo]
vita-*la*	life, waist	[vita]
vivamente-*adv*	vividly	[vivamente]
vivente-*adj*	living, living being	[vivente]
vivere-*vb*	live	[vivere]
vivo-*adj; lo*	alive, live	[vivo]
voce-*la*	entry, voice, item	[votʃe]
vociare-*vb*	shout	[votʃare]
vocina-*la*	small voice	[votʃina]
voi-*prn*	you	[voi]
volare-*vb*	fly	[volare]

volere-*vb*	want	[volere]	**zampino**-*il*	claw	[tsampino]
volgare-*adj*	vulgar, gross	[volgare]	**zanzara**-*la*	mosquito	[dzantsara]
volgere-*vb*	turn	[voldʒere]	**zappare**-*vb*	hoe	[tsappare]
volo-*il*	flight	[volo]	**zittire**-*vb*	silence	[tsittire]
volta-*la*	time, turn	[vˈɔlta]	**zitto**-*adj*	silent, quiet	[dzitto]
voltare-*vb*	turn	[voltare]	**zolla**-*la*	plate	[dzolla]
vostro-*adj*	your (pl)	[vˈɔstro]	**zucca**-*la*	pumpkin, gourd	[tsukka]
vuotare-*vb*	empty, deplete	[vwotare]	**zufolare**-*vb*	play the whistle	[tsufolare]
vuoto-*adj; il*	empty	[vwoto]	**zuppiera**-*la*	tureen	[tsuppjera]
			zuppo-*adj*	soaked	[tsuppo]

Z

zampa-*la*	paw	[tsampa]

Contact, Further Reading & Resources

For more tools, tips & tricks visit our site www.mostusedwords.com. We publish various language learning resources.

We hope that you will find this bilingual book a truly handy tool. If you like it, please let others know about it, so they can enjoy it too. Or leave a review/comment online, e.g. on social media, blogs or on forums.

Frequency Dictionaries

The most common 2.500 words in any language account for roughly 90% of all spoken language and 80% of all written texts.

We listed all these essential words and more for you in our Frequency Dictionaries. The books range from the most common 2.500 words to the most common 10.000 words.

In addition, we give you word usage through dual language example sentences and phonetic spelling of foreign words by the help of the International Phonetic Alphabet (IPA).

We are always working hard to add more languages to our selection. Currently we have frequency dictionaries available for the following languages: Italian, French, Swedish, Spanish, German, Dutch, Romanian, Finnish, Russian, Portuguese and more. Please visit https://store.mostusedwords.com/frequency-dictionaries for more information

Bilingual books

We're creating a selection of dual language books. Our selection is ever expanding.

Current and future bilingual books are available in English, Spanish, Portuguese, Italian, French, and German.

For more information, check https://store.mostusedwords.com/bilingual-books. Check back regularly for new books and languages.

Other language learning methods

You'll find reviews of other 3rd party language learning applications, software, audio courses, and apps. There are so many available, and some are (much) better than others.

Check out our reviews at www.mostusedwords.com/reviews.

Contact

If you have any questions, you can contact us through e-mail info@mostusedwords.com.

Made in the USA
Monee, IL
09 October 2024